For my mother

Contents

Author's Note

The Quiet Damage is a work of nonfiction; the narratives it contains are based to a large extent on hundreds of hours of interviews conducted over the phone, in person, and via Zoom with the characters as well as with their relatives, friends, colleagues, and other pertinent individuals. While working to verify their accounts, I also reviewed text messages, emails, phone records, Facebook chat logs, academic and employment documents, medical files, personal essays, letters, and journal entries, along with public records and open-source information, including housing records, live and archived social media posts, police reports, and court documents.

Some details, such as elements of a character's childhood memory, could not be concretely corroborated; when possible, I consulted with people who were privy to the information in question to confirm its accuracy. Nonetheless, in writing this book, I relied in part on characters' recollections and interpretations of events that shaped their lives. Their stories are *their stories*—bravely shared here with you at personal risk.

To protect their privacy, they are all identified by pseudonyms. (This excludes public figures and experts quoted in their professional capacities.) Certain familial details and personal identifying characteristics, like a character's physical attributes, for one example, have also been changed for this reason.

To help me narratively reconstruct scenes I did not witness—in as much detail as possible—characters shared images and other supporting materials with me, such as videos of a specific booth at a restaurant where an important conversation had previously occurred, or they brought me to places in person to observe for myself. They also answered many, many questions about details major and minute—down to the texture of a couch cushion or the precise length of a phone call. I am immensely, endlessly grateful to each of them.

Prologue: Shed My DNA

—Emily—

Adam used to view his life in two parts: life before losing his dad, and life after.

It happened a month shy of his ninth birthday and a month after Super Bowl XXXIV, when the Tennessee Titans faced off against the St. Louis Rams. Despite his protests, Adam had stayed home to watch on TV while his dad drove out to be there in person. The next morning was a school day, after all. It was the only Titans game they'd been apart all season—and a nail-biter to the very end: With six seconds left on the clock, the Titans tried for a score-tying touchdown. They fell one yard short. It was the team's first Super Bowl appearance in franchise history, and the last game Adam's dad would ever see. Just after dark in their quiet Tennessee town on March 1, 2000, he slipped into the barn outside their family home, pointed a .357 Magnum revolver at his chest, and turned Adam's world upside down.

The first part of Adam's life was damn near perfect. He was the baby of the family, a skinny, bright-eyed, and incessantly curious kid whose only worries were finishing his homework and quarreling with his twin sisters. They lived on a sprawling country estate with a long gravel driveway snaking back from the road to their own sequestered oasis. It was a grand yet charming property—the kind of upscale Tudor-style home with a butter-yellow and red-brick exterior covered in flowering vines that one might expect to find in a luxury cottage magazine. To a fourth-grade boy, it was also a giant playground: There was a cornfield, a pond with white water lilies that was large enough to swim and fish in, a dense forest, an apple orchard, a basketball court, the barn, and, inside, a big TV room with a pinball machine where Adam and his dad, Dan, watched sports together.

The two would hide out in there for hours, leaping from the couch to high-five at each touchdown or home run. Game Day was Adam's favorite day. It didn't matter who or what was playing. Any time he got to spend alone with his dad was special. Dan was an important man; Adam understood this from a young age. He was known to most as Dr. Porter, the oncologist, but to Adam, he was a hero.

Dan was an unfailingly endearing man with disarming blue eyes, deep-set dimples that perked up when he laughed, and a mop of salt-and-pepper hair that he'd comb behind his ears on workdays. He was the tallest guy in every room. He was also immensely successful and indulged in his wealth, smoking the finest Cuban cigars, driving high-end luxury cars, and attending the kind of prestigious, exclusive sporting events that most people only dream of: the World Series, the Masters, the Olympics, the Super Bowl. Wickedly smart and deadly funny, he could turn his children's grumpiest days into giggle-fests with silly pranks and goofy voices. He liked to take his son out for rides in the passenger seat of his convertible, shuttling him to soccer games or tae kwon do lessons with the top down. With the wind in his hair and his daddy by his side, Adam felt invincible.

He was his father's son and his mother's baby. Emily Porter loved each of her children endlessly; she told them so daily and showered them with hugs and kisses, even in public as they'd try to wriggle free from her embrace. At the same time, she was the disciplinarian of the household, quick to scold but also quick to forgive—especially Adam. As her youngest, he could do no real wrong in her eyes.

When she wasn't caring for her kids, Emily was out in the barn. It was her private bliss. She had grown up on a small cattle ranch and now ran her own one-woman farm with a couple cows and goats, a few hens, a rooster, two rescued pigs, and an alpaca. It was purely a labor of love, producing only enough eggs and milk for their family breakfast table. But to watch her work was to witness an artist at her craft. She had a way of making the most grueling tasks look effortless, with a sleek golden blond braid down her back and such a petite frame it was remarkable to see her hauling around bales of straw and slop buckets on her own.

Emily didn't have many friends. She had always seemed to have found it easier to connect with animals, and she preferred solo hobbies. The few people who truly knew her knew that she would do anything for them—

and that she expected the same in return. They knew that behind the cool, reserved exterior the rest of the world saw was an intensely caring, vulnerable woman who was in fact prone to oversharing, overreacting, and overextending herself for those she loved.

Emily was working as an interior designer in the early '80s when she met a dashing medical intern named Dan who laughed like a sailor and dressed like a Kennedy. It was a whirlwind romance. Within a year, she had left everything behind to follow him around the country for his residency and fellowship, marrying him along the way. They eventually settled down outside of Nashville, trading a fast-paced life for one of opulent small-town charm with bucolic pastures nestled amid forests of white oaks, sweetgums, and pines. As ruralites, Dan could commute into the city and Emily could be a stay-at-home mom with lots of land and fresh air. It was a happy marriage in its early years. Only toward the end did eight-year-old Adam notice that something might be wrong.

Things were different in the days following the Super Bowl. His parents barely spoke to each other. When they did, his mom would yell and cry. His dad even started sleeping away from the house; Adam didn't know where. On February 29, Dan picked Adam up and took him out for lunch, just the two of them. They talked. They laughed. They had wings. Everything felt normal again, like it would all be okay.

After arriving back at the house, Dan handed his son a card. It was white with two cartoon bears on the front and a thick red border filled with little candy-cane striped hearts. Inside was a short message scrawled in black ink.

> *I love you very much—I miss you—*
> Love Daddy

It was the last time Adam ever saw him.

The next day was a blur, one that each sibling would remember slightly differently. Adam recalls sitting at the top of the stairs with his sisters, listening in silent distress to the muffled sounds of their parents shouting in a room below, out of sight. Things went quiet for a while, until, suddenly, a lineup of patrol cars blasted down the driveway. Emily appeared and rushed the children out onto the front porch, where they sat alone on the swing in flashes of red and blue until an officer put them into the back of his car and drove away without explaining anything. As small as he was, Adam felt cramped. He tucked his knees into his chest and tried to calm himself down. The mother of one of his soccer teammates was waiting for them at the end of the driveway. She took them to the mall, bought them ice cream cones, and told them everything would be all right.

Adam, Leah, and Jessica returned home the following afternoon to find their mother, red-faced and puffy-eyed, sitting next to their paternal grandparents. Adam was surprised to see them; visits were usually up at their house on Easter or Thanksgiving. Only then did he notice something that would define the second part of his life: the absence of his father.

As a newly single mother to three heartbroken children, Emily had no time to mourn. She immediately enrolled them in bereavement classes to work through their grief—never seeking any professional support herself—and did her best to restore a semblance of normalcy to their lives by going through the motions of old routines. The kids still had sports games, piano lessons, and chores; Emily still had the farm.

While the twins had pieced together much of what had happened, she tried to shield her young son from the details. Adam didn't need to know the secrets that had driven his father to suicide, or the lengths he'd gone to trying to hide them from his family. For now, he could remember his dad as the man he'd always known him to be, untarnished by issues too complex for a child to fully understand.

Mornings were the hardest. Adam was trapped in his own personal Groundhog Day hell. He would wake up hoping, desperately, that it had all been a nightmare, only to relive over, and over, and over again the anguish of realizing that his daddy wasn't coming back. Dan's death touched every part of his existence. It was a gnawing pain that was with him always, spiraling him through a cycle of misery, confusion, and anger. Nowhere felt safe anymore. At home, the agony was palpable, like a biting chill in the air upon walking through the door, harshened at night by the stifled cries coming from his mother's bedroom. At school, his beloved father had become a point of ridicule, his suicide reduced to ammo in locker rooms and hallways. Adam had never felt so alone. Emily started getting calls from the school about him misbehaving, and she would catch him stealing money from her more than once.

Finances were of new concern for the family. It had been nearly two decades since Emily had last worked, but she knew she could no longer afford to be a stay-at-home parent indefinitely. Before having children, she had contemplated pivoting into a career in law. Becoming a lawyer seemed like a way she could find justice for the powerless, she told her kids. It was a chance to start over. So for the next three years, after bringing them home from school, she made her way into the city for her own classes, where she took an interest in guardian ad litem work and the field of crimes against children.

Adam tagged along on some evenings, sitting quietly by his mother's side at the back of the lecture room. It was exhilarating to walk across the vibrant, bustling campus, especially for a boy growing up in the country. But most of all, Adam loved to watch Emily raise her hand and answer her professors' questions. He had never realized how smart she was. She had always just been *Mom*. But here she was, brilliant and fearless, dazzling her law instructors right in front of him. Each time she spoke, Adam glanced around the room to see if her peers were as impressed as he was. He hoped they all knew that she was *his* mom. Even though he didn't understand what torts or civil procedures were, Adam knew that she was going to be a lawyer, that she was doing this for her children, and that she was going to make the world a better place. Slowly, things were beginning to feel a little less heavy.

By the time Adam started high school, Leah and Jessica had gone off to college. It was just him and Emily alone in the house. She had finished law school with top honors and was working at a large firm while preparing to launch a solo practice. Adam was overjoyed to have her all to himself. While other boys his age were playing video games or trying to impress girls and generally loathed spending time with their parents, he was basking in his mother's attention. Once a month, the two of them would go out for extravagant dinners at fancy restaurants with tasting menus, giddy with the excitement of not knowing what crazy or exotic dish would be served next. It was a ritual they'd call their "little food journeys." At home they'd watch *Jeopardy!* and *Lost,* never caring much for the news or politics, though Emily's disdain for Republicans was hardly a secret. Even living in the Bible Belt, she had raised her children to be socially progressive, instilling in them the values that she and Dan had shared.

As college loomed, Adam became something of a farmhand, despite hating manual labor and longing to live in a big city. Helping out around the barn gave him more time to bond with his mom before he left. So they'd scoop manure and urine-soaked shavings together with pitchforks, the pungent ammonia masking the stench of the feces. Then Emily would plant flowers while Adam spread pine straw around the property until his hands blistered and bled and calloused over. Over time, they were growing close enough to tell each other anything. When Adam finally learned the full story of what had happened to his dad, it broke his heart all over again—this time, for his mom.

Super Bowl XXXIV had marked the beginning of the end of Dan's life. Already drowning in debt from a gambling problem, he had wagered a pile of money he didn't have on a Titans victory. Days later, Emily would catch him on the phone with another woman. His world was falling apart all around him and he was powerless to stop it. So on that tragic March evening, he grabbed a gun from his desk, vanished into the barn, and ended it all.

Secretly, Adam feared he might one day meet the same fate. He was like his father in ways good and dark. Both smart as whips, they shared an uncanny ability to ace their exams after barely studying, befuddling their teachers. They also had the same addictive personality. Dan, Adam learned, had made it through med school while doing hard drugs, keeping his habit under control without falling too far behind to catch up.

Adam fell into drugs and gambling too. In high school, he got into trouble for smoking pot and stealing scratch-off lottery tickets. By college, he was deep into sports betting. Getting stoned and immersing himself in a college basketball game with money on the line was a way to hit the pause button: For a few wonderfully numb hours at a time, the gnawing pain went away. It got bad, sometimes—even scary—to the point where he'd have to borrow money he knew he couldn't repay just to climb out from under his debt. Other times, when life was going particularly well, he'd go several weeks or longer without the impulse to place a wager. But he could never truly quit. Just like his dad in med school, he still managed to keep himself in check, graduating with distinction from his undergraduate program while hiding his private torment from the world.

Adam's single greatest inspiration was his mom. Following in her footsteps, he applied to law school. His admission essay was about her.

"For the first time since my father's suicide, I opened up and allowed myself to truly bond with my mother," he wrote of his nights spent sitting in on her lectures. "And though, as an elementary school student, I rarely ever understood the material being taught in her classes, I harbored no doubt in my dream to attend law school, just like my newfound hero."

Emily was the first person he called when he was accepted. She was so happy she cried. It was, for Adam, the best feeling in the world.

By the time Adam was thirty, he was living in San Francisco. He stood a slouching six-foot-three with flecks of gray in his dark blond hair, Dan's dimples, and kind blue eyes that looked at once tired but focused. And he was, professionally, extremely successful. As an attorney at a major international law firm, he earned a salary well into the six-figure range. He was right where he'd wanted to be: working as a lawyer, just like his mom.

But he hadn't spoken to her in months. The last words they'd exchanged were in a pair of jaw-dropping emails Emily had sent just before Christmas of 2020, seven weeks after Adam had voted to elect Joe Biden as president of the United States.

Over forty-four seething lines, she broke her son's heart and spit in his face.

"PAIN IS COMING FOR YOU," she promised, "AND YOUR BELOVED CHINA JOE, FRAUD OBAMA AND HIS MAN WIFE MICHAEL."

She called Adam a "monster," a "huge disappointment," and an "utter embarrassment." He was no child of hers, she declared, just a "spoiled evil brat" who deserved to suffer for his choices. She claimed that he wouldn't survive the bombshells that would soon shatter his faux reality—that he'd end up like Dan.

"Shed my DNA," Emily wrote, twisting the dagger. "I am DONE WITH YOU."

Adam used to view his life in two parts: life before losing his dad, and life after. Until one day, he found himself navigating a third part that felt, in a way, painfully familiar yet uniquely traumatizing: life after losing his mom.

It wasn't a bullet that had taken her away, but an intangible poison infecting many millions of minds—one that was bottled and sold by conspiracy theory–mongers operating from down in the online fever swamps up to the chambers of Congress, then passed around by the poisoned, like wine.

Adam wasn't ready to say goodbye. *Not again.* This time, he was going to save his parent. He was going to find the antidote.

On February 11, 2021, my inbox erupted with a cascade of emails from strangers across the country sharing chilling, hauntingly similar stories. *Hundreds* of them.

There was a navy veteran in California who was thinking of leaving his wife, unable to endure one more rant about Tom Hanks torturing children for pleasure. A college senior in Washington, D.C., who'd spent the pandemic hiding in her bedroom from her conspiracy theory–obsessed mother. A Rhode Island man whose brother, consumed by online doomsday projections, had started stockpiling assault weapons to prepare for a civil war. An elderly woman in Arizona whose daughter was restricting her from seeing her beloved grandson as decades-belated revenge for having her vaccinated as a child. A new divorcée in Utah whose husband of thirty years had disappeared into a vortex of YouTube videos about baby-eating Democrats and had never returned. And there was Adam, still reeling from his mother's words.

They were all reaching out in response to an article I'd written about families splintered by QAnon—and they all had the same question.

What happened to the person I love?

The havoc that QAnon and similar conspiracy theories have wrought on American democracy and public health is well documented. Less acknowledged is the crippling devastation that they unleash inside the home, behind closed doors and out of public view. Dinner tables become battlegrounds, holiday visits become dreaded obligations, loved ones become strangers, and cherished relationships become painful memories.

Under QAnon's expansive umbrella are two camps of people; combined, they double the population of California. In the first are the true believers, who think Donald Trump and a mysterious government insider known as "Q" are (perpetually) in the final stages of a treacherous, unseen battle to liberate humanity from "the Deep State," a satanic cabal of globalist elites who rule the world from the shadows while buying and selling children to rape, mutilate, and eat. (One such believer was elected—and reelected—as House representative of Georgia's Fourteenth Congressional District; several have proven violent, even murderous.) And in the second, much larger camp, which emerged over the pandemic as QAnon ideology blended insidiously into mainstream discourse, are those who embrace some or all of the core conspiracy theories but don't identify with the movement.

The distinction doesn't matter much, frankly. In 2021, a staggering 15 percent of Americans agreed that the government, media, and financial worlds were "controlled by Satan-worshipping pedophiles," polling found. By late 2023, that number had rocketed to 25 percent. This is not a passing chapter of the culture wars, and Emily is no anomaly: There are plenty of intelligent, seemingly *normal* individuals who have come to see the world through this lens. Broadly speaking, QAnon is now a collective of Baby Boomers, young people, ruralites, urbanites, white supremacists, people of color, right-wing extremists—even progressives. For many, the allure is less about what it makes them think than how it makes them *feel*.

The Quiet Damage tells the story of five ordinary families from very different walks of life, all torn apart at the seams—real people consumed by fake news trying to find a way back to each other, and to themselves. Their intensely honest and harrowing accounts lay bare an American crisis that's much bigger than any singular movement. They'll be familiar to anybody who's had a loved one transformed by fanatical belief, from radical politics to religious fundamentalism and other forms of extremism. Braided together across three parts, these narratives are enriched by injections of historical context, psychological and sociological insights, and original reporting. They also offer a rare window into the minds of individuals who were sucked deep into the conspiracy theory quagmire and managed to make it back out, at a cost.

Over the chapters ahead, I hope to give you a nuanced understanding of belief in the unbelievable; to show you why so many people latch onto, and feverishly cling to, outlandish falsehoods, even in the face of cold, hard facts, and even as their lives fall apart as a result; and to help you see how that conviction could compel a parent to tell her child to shed her DNA. I aim to recover some of these people from the realm of *the other*. To try—in spite of their horrifying, often unacceptable beliefs—to return some sense of personhood and dignity to them, so that we might see them not as lunatics and lost causes, but as people we know: friends, family, colleagues, whose circumstances and choices have led them down a dark path. Without this baseline recognition of their fundamental humanness, despite the humanity their beliefs sometimes deny to others, it's impossible to truly consider what real solutions could look like.

It's my hope, as well, to open your mind to a different way of thinking about this crisis altogether and how we might move forward. After talking and listening to hundreds of conspiracy theory–shattered families over three years, what's clear to me is this: Worthy interventions like fact-checking labels and tech regulations and media literacy trainings will never be enough. This goes deeper than true versus false, and information itself. We need to confront the roots of our collective vulnerability. Because none of us are as immune as we'd like to think.

PART I

BREAKING
POINT

1

THE PLAN TO SAVE THE WORLD

—Matt—

Matt gazed out the window at the trees and tried to calm his racing mind. It was autumn of 2019 in eastern Missouri, and the leaves had started to fall from their branches, blanketing the grass in crimson and amber. In the distance, people walked down the street in the late afternoon sun, going about their business as they pleased. Matt envied them.

He glanced back inside at the clock on the wall and sighed, his foot tapping anxiously against the leg of his chair. Half an hour left to go.

"Matt?"

His wife's voice pierced his daze. Seated a few feet over, across from their marriage counselor, she was staring right at him with dark mascara tears streaming down her cheeks.

"Matt," echoed Dr. Fellows, looking up from the notepad he'd been scribbling away in behind his desk. "Andrea just told you she feels like a single mother."

His words hung in the air between them as Matt tried to refocus. From the moment they'd sat down, Andrea had been divulging through sobs how he had devolved from a loving, supportive partner into a distracted, inattentive roommate who rarely emerged from the basement. Now Dr. Fellows was studying him like an animal in a lab, trying to figure out what was going on with him. Matt looked at Andrea. Even if he told them, he knew they wouldn't believe it.

A thirty-eight-year-old God-fearing Republican, Matt had a pointy brown beard and chin-length hair tucked under a baseball cap to complete his daily jeans-and-tee ensemble. He was a pensive, soft-spoken man of relatively few words, especially in counseling. But his eyes, a few shades of blue lighter than his wife's, told a story of their own. They were crinkled with laugh lines from years of silly moments goofing around with Andrea and their two young kids and framed with dark circles from months of late-night doomscrolling marathons. He didn't laugh much anymore.

"Is there anything you want to say?" Dr. Fellows nudged.

Matt leaned back in his chair with his hands on his knees and exhaled deeply through his nose. There were lots of things he wanted to say. Things so earth-shattering, so unbelievably surreal and crazy, that they would think he was, well, *crazy*.

"I'm sorry, Andrea," he offered instead. "You're right."

Matt loved his wife. He and Andrea were college sweethearts; they had met through a student ministry group back when he was a shy, dorky senior who looked like Shaggy from *Scooby-Doo* and she was a bubbly brunette in her freshman year far out of his league. It was she who had pursued him, though, striking up flirty, late-night conversations on AOL Instant Messenger. They had a lot in common. Both had been raised with Christian conservative values in rural Missouri households where saying grace before meals was mandatory and the radio was set to Rush Limbaugh.

Their marriage wasn't perfect, Matt knew that. It didn't help that they'd spent most of it trapped in an unwinnable *Tetris* game of debt. No matter how many times they tried to reconfigure their life to make payments, the debts just kept stacking back up. Between Matt's job at a small Christian radio station and Andrea's as a middle-school librarian, their combined annual income was a little over $50,000. That didn't leave much for week-end getaways, dinners at Olive Garden, or the other relative luxuries they'd imagined while building a family together. Maxed-out credit cards and past-due bills piled on the kitchen counter had never been part of that vision. To Matt, it felt like even though they'd lived by the book—going to college, finding jobs, getting married, having kids, following Christ—the promise of financial security remained ever out of reach.

But money troubles weren't the reason Andrea had insisted on counseling. Matt knew that too. Everything she'd told Dr. Fellows over the preceding thirty minutes was true: He *had* been mentally and emotionally checked out of their family life for the past year. It wasn't because he didn't care, though. . . . He was just preoccupied with far more important things than date nights and bedtime routines—things he desperately wanted to get back to, instead of sitting here being judged by a man with a notepad. Andrea would understand soon enough. One day—*any* day now—everything would be revealed. Her anger toward him would melt into gratitude and she would feel foolish for having wasted his time with the relative trivialities they discussed in counseling once she knew what he'd been up to.

He was on a mission to save the fucking world.

The Plan

Life as Matt knew it had begun to unravel one year earlier, on September 24, 2018. It was a typical Monday and he was down in his home office in the basement. He'd been a remote employee for the past five of his sixteen years with the radio station, since Andrea's parents had sold them their hillside home in a quiet city nestled along the riverbanks of the Illinois border. The "dungeon," as Matt called his workspace, was a cramped, windowless room that he'd never gotten around to properly decorating, beyond hanging up a few St. Louis Cardinals posters and a Beatles 8-track tape to adorn the unfinished drywall.

That afternoon, Matt had just finished producing a concert promo that would air during commercial breaks over the next several weeks. It was a task he completed so frequently he could practically do it in his sleep. Still on the clock, but with little left on his plate for the day, he decided to peruse Facebook. Nothing of interest really caught his eye, just the usual dumb memes and inspirational quotes, until he came across a YouTube video that Andrea's aunt Carol had posted a couple days earlier. It was called "The Plan to Save the World."

"If you haven't watched this video you better!" she'd written. "Get informed! It's about to get real!! God bless America!!"

This oughta be good, Matt thought. Aunt Carol was known to dabble in some pretty wacky conspiracy theories. So, partly out of curiosity, and partly out of boredom, he clicked.

A flaming blue "Q" flashed onto his screen over foreboding music, like the opening scene of a horror film. Then, a voice.

"Have you ever wondered why we go to war, or why you never seem to be able to get out of debt? Why there is poverty, division, and crime?"

Visceral, slickly edited footage of homeless encampments, crime scenes, emaciated children, and armed conflict played as the narrator continued: "We have always accepted these things as just human nature and simply the way the world works. Something inevitable, and due to the weaknesses of human nature that drive us to these actions. This is where we were all tragically wrong. . . . What if it wasn't human nature at all, and as a result of something more deliberate?"

The video's emerging thesis was grim. In just the first few minutes, it asserted that the most powerful people on the planet—national leaders, banking magnates, billionaire business tycoons, Hollywood stars, media moguls, the royal family, and other elites—were all part of a clandestine cabal known as "the Deep State" that had been controlling the world for centuries. Their crimes were boundless. They siphoned money from the public, they ran international sex- and drug-trafficking operations, they poisoned global food supplies, they orchestrated false-flag terror attacks, they ignited wars and genocide, and they did it all in the name of expanding their own power and fortune. They were even responsible for the assassination of John F. Kennedy and the attempted assassination of Ronald Reagan, two of the very few politicians who had fought, in secret and in vain, to bring the Deep State down. To divert attention from these and other atrocities they committed, "the Cabal" used their complete control of the mainstream media to pit "the good guys"—ordinary folks who "just wanna get married, have kids, make a living, and enjoy their liberty"—against each other.

"They convinced us we were the problem so that we would fight and destroy ourselves," the narrator exclaimed, laying out how the media spun the news to turn woman against man, Black against white, Muslim against Christian, and Left against Right.

Matt paused to consider what he'd seen so far. What had struck him immediately was the quality of the video itself. He'd been half-expecting some over-the-top, voiced-over slideshow with dizzyingly excessive zooms and pans, like the slapdash class presentations he'd sat through in high school. Though it was dramatic, this video was so far relatively well produced and compelling. Even the narrator sounded like a professional, not at all like the rantings and ravings of Alex Jones or other tinfoil-hat conspiracy theorists summoned to mind by a title like "The Plan to Save the World." And its core message—that the people in power were corrupt—didn't sound like a conspiracy theory to Matt.

Matt's politics were filtered through his faith. At church and at the radio station, a highly religious, family-run workplace, he'd been taught that Democrats like Barack Obama and Bill and Hillary Clinton, all featured in the video, were anti-Christian wolves in sheep's clothing and inveterate liars. Monica Lewinsky had been invoked in more than one sermon over the years. Matt didn't trust Big Pharma executives either, another contingent of this "Deep State." Too many drug companies had been caught exponentially hiking the prices of lifesaving medications. When his father was dying of prostate cancer, he couldn't help but wonder if there was any truth to the rumors that a cure for cancer existed but had been kept under wraps because the drugs for treatment and palliative care were so wildly profitable. Only God had Matt's full trust.

Parts of the video seemed to confirm things that he already suspected on some level. It certainly made sense to him that greedy elites were rigging the system for their own gain while locking families like his in a state of financial hardship. As President Trump had recently pointed out, Amazon, owned by hectobillionaire Jeff Bezos, hadn't paid a dime in federal taxes the year prior; the tech behemoth had actually received a nine-figure tax refund. Matt and Andrea, meanwhile, waited anxiously each year for the few thousand they got in their returns just to keep their heads above water. As the rich got richer, it had always felt to Matt like *something* was holding him back.

He also saw truth in the video's claim that the mainstream media was intentionally exacerbating social divisions. In his eyes, cable news networks' modus operandi involved riling people up by scapegoating white Republican men for all the world's woes. He'd heard the term *toxic masculinity* too many times to count in the past couple years, and *Trump supporter* was spoken like an insult on just about every channel other than Fox. Trump had been in America's ear griping about the "lamestream" media from the early days of his campaign, and Matt could see why: Ever since voting for him, his distant second choice after retired neurosurgeon and Seventh-Day Adventist Ben Carson, he'd felt typecast in the news as a racist, a misogynist, and a fascist all rolled into one deplorable sack of shit.

"The Plan to Save the World" portrayed people like Matt not as villains but as victims—targets of manufactured outrage intended to distract and divide. On his screen flashed a crowd of protesters, several of them wearing the pink, anti-Trump "pussyhats" from the Women's March that had drawn more than a million Americans into the streets months earlier. If polarizing the nation truly was a media scheme to keep people from noticing something evil going on behind the scenes, it would be a hell of a way to do it.

Matt found himself silently nodding along as the video progressed. It argued that traditional American values were under siege. In side-by-side images, it showed Miley Cyrus in her "wholesome" Disney phase from her *Hannah Montana* days, and on stage in nude-colored panties twerking against Robin Thicke's crotch with her tongue hanging out of her mouth. Matt cringed as he thought about his nine-year-old daughter, Abby, and the shrinking pool of female role models she could look up to. Glorifying moral decay was apparently part of the Deep State's plan to break down American families.

"I could talk all day about how else they deliberately weakened us and it would turn your stomach," the narrator said, his voice dripping with disgust. "We were just trying to get on with living."

Behind his words was a rapid-fire sequence of stills and short clips snapshotting depravity in different forms: footage of 9/11, marching ISIS militants, serial rapist Harvey Weinstein. Each evoked an emotional response before Matt could even process the significance of what he was seeing, or its connection to the Deep State. He could feel himself becoming agitated.

But partway through the thirteen-minute video, the tone abruptly changed. The eerie, somber music became triumphant and upbeat, and the imagery depicting misery and corruption was replaced with an American flag waving in the wind against a cloudless blue sky. After painting a picture of extreme despair, the video was giving viewers a reason for hope: Donald J. Trump had come to the rescue. Picking up where JFK and Reagan left off, Trump and a small team of high-ranking government officials from around the world, as well as allies inside the National Security Agency and the U.S. military, had devised a plan to bring the Deep State to its knees.

The Plan, as it was called, was already under way. The heroes were winning: ISIS, created by the Deep State, was all but defeated; North Korea's nuclear-armed regime, previously loyal to the Deep State, had accepted peace, as shown by a clip of Trump and Kim Jong-un's historic handshake. The dominoes were falling. But the Deep State had yet to face justice, and it was deploying everything in its mighty arsenal to cling to power. The public had witnessed evidence of this retaliation without realizing it, starting with the endless media attacks on Trump.

"The world is currently experiencing a dramatic, covert war of biblical proportions—literally the fight for earth between the forces for good and evil," the narrator boomed as the music reached a crescendo. "May God bless America!"

Matt sat at his desk, trying to process everything he'd just watched. There was a lot to digest that was outside his wheelhouse. But something about it seemed different from other conspiracy theory proselytizing he'd seen. It felt special—exciting, somehow, like he was in on a secret. He couldn't think of any reason why the video's creator would lie. What could they stand to gain from making all of this up? There was no sales pitch, no catch; it just seemed like an earnest message for anyone open-minded enough to listen. Weighing its claims felt a bit like contemplating a lottery ticket purchase: Rationally, you know you're not going to win, yet a tiny voice at the back of your head can't help wondering, *But what if you do?* and out comes your wallet.

Matt knew it wasn't true that an all-powerful crime syndicate of the rich and the famous ruled the world from the shadows.

But what if it were?

Game On

"The Plan to Save the World" didn't turn Matt into a QAnon believer on the spot. He still had a lot of questions—and a lot of doubts. It did, however, plant in his mind a seed of suspicion, just as it had done for many others before him, and as it would continue to do for far more. The creator was a mysterious online figure calling himself "Joe M" who would also co-author an Amazon-bestselling book about QAnon. But the film was his magnum opus, racking up millions of views during its time on YouTube and serving as a prime on-ramp to QAnon for early recruits. Its power was in its populist allure and its relative digestibility. Belying the sheer absurdity of QAnon as a whole, it swept viewers into a gripping tale of conspiracy theories built around nuggets of truth, while saying nothing of baby-eating, faked deaths, or clones. Those elements, for Matt, would come later.

On that September afternoon in his basement, another QAnon video lit up his screen moments after Joe M's ended. Then came another, and yet another—each one launched by YouTube's autoplay function, like a conveyor belt of disinformation algorithmically compiled just for him. Matt learned that QAnon was an online collective of everyday people from all over the country and beyond known as "anons." They gathered on 8chan, a barely moderated message board website, to communicate with "Q," their enigmatic leader.

Q was believed to be a government official with Q-level security clearance who was helping Trump execute the Plan. Or, perhaps, Trump himself was Q; as with Oz behind the curtain, no one knew for sure. But what seemed certain to anons was that Q was at least close to the president: Earlier in the year, one of them had requested that Q get Trump to use the phrase *tip top* as a secret shout-out to the community. Sure enough, during an Easter event two months later, Trump stood between his peacoated wife and a fuzzy white bunny mascot and thanked staffers for keeping the White House—"this incredible house, or building, or whatever you want to call it, because there really is no name for it; it is special"—in "tip top shape."

Matt was captivated. This wasn't just some fringe theory bouncing around the internet; it was a *movement*. Anons, he discovered, were highly organized: Tapping into their unique skill sets, they had launched alternative news networks on YouTube, composed recruitment songs and jingles, designed merchandise, hosted video meet-ups, and drafted their own legal proposals for state referendum votes to unveil when the timing was right. They even had a slogan, "Where We Go One, We Go All" (a phrase they misattributed to JFK that in fact came from the 1996 action-adventure movie *White Squall*).

As YouTube continued lining up videos, Matt kept on watching, unaware from down in the basement that the workday was ending and the daylight was fading. By dinner, he was neck-deep in a sinkhole of Far Right hysteria, his YouTube homepage brimming with QAnon videos and little else.

8chan had a special message board just for Q Drops, the morsels of intel Q leaked to the site. They were typically cryptic and riddle-like, so as not to undermine the Plan or compromise national security. Many professed to report the *real* news that the mainstream media refused to cover, including secret military tribunals and indictments of Deep State criminals. Others forecast the Plan's long-awaited culmination in the Storm, or the Great Awakening, a day of reckoning when Cabal members would be arrested en masse and the rest of the world would finally wake up to the sinister truth about their trusted leaders and idols. Many Q Drops quoted Christian scripture. But most were just vague and eerie.

We are at the PRECIPICE.

[SWAMP] FIGHTING BACK

Remain CALM.

We are here for a reason.

Patriots are in control.

Q

There were nearly three hundred Q Drops posted on 8chan at the time. They were catalogued along with anons' commentary in a chaotic mess of haiku-looking text blocks, memes, video links, heavily annotated photos, and intricate charts resembling TV detective boards without the string or push pins. It was overwhelming. But the videos Matt was watching broke down the Q Drops one by one, like school lessons for anons. The effective teachers—influencer types known as "decoders"—shared their interpretations of Q's messages via their Twitter accounts and YouTube channels, often extrapolating with their own theories. They also reimagined breaking news in real time. Mass shootings became false flags, celebrity deaths turned into secret assassinations, Trump's Twitter tantrums were actually brilliant political chess moves—in the world of QAnon, nothing was what it seemed. Some decoders showed their faces, while others, like Joe M, kept their identities hidden. Matt followed them all, taking an immediate liking to a bald man known as "Praying Medic" who spoke with a preacher's cadence and blended religious teachings into his analyses.

Unlike the cable news anchors and pundits on TV, who sometimes struck Matt as arrogant and patronizing, decoders presented as peers sharing information to be discussed and explored. They spoke often of "we" and "us"—and an ominous "them." And they weren't afraid to ask taboo questions.

The next morning, September 25, 2018, those questions focused on Christine Blasey Ford. The fifty-one-year-old college professor had recently come out against Brett Kavanaugh, Trump's Supreme Court nominee, with a harrowing allegation of sexual assault. At a social gathering when they both were teenagers, she had recalled in detail, a "stumbling drunk" Kavanaugh pinned her down on a bed, covered her mouth, and groped her while his friend watched.

Anons were hungry for answers: *Why come forward now? Did she have an ulterior motive? Was someone pressuring her to thwart Kavanaugh's confirmation?*

Decoders had their theories. One dogged anon even appeared to have found a clue. He or she uploaded to 8chan two images: one from a CBS interview of Blasey Ford's lawyer, Debra Katz, a slim woman with short brown hair; and one grainier picture of Hillary Clinton walking in front of a slim woman with short brown hair.

"The plot thickens . . . ," the anon wrote. Within hours, the second image was ripping across Twitter.

"Friends, if you were looking for undeniable truth who is behind [Blasey Ford's] false allegations, take a hard look at this picture," the QAnon account @Trump45awesome urged in a post retweeted thousands of times. "This will make your blood boil."

People outside the movement began amplifying the photo as well, including a conservative radio host with more than two hundred thousand followers. By Wednesday morning, it had gone so viral that the tabloid website TMZ picked it up, turning an online rumor that Blasey Ford was connected to Clinton into a news story stated as fact. It was an early sign of the QAnon community's remarkable ability to come together as a hive and propel false information from the online fringes into the mainstream discourse.

In a corrective update, TMZ later acknowledged that the woman pictured with Clinton had "mistakenly been identified as Katz." The anon-surfaced photo, which had been taken in 2016, actually showed Clinton with her official campaign photographer, who bore a passing resemblance to Katz. But that didn't slow its spread or quell the ensuing speculation about Blasey Ford. Q shared the photo too, in a Drop:

Are you AWAKE?

The TRUTH is right in front of you.

Think for yourself.

Trust yourself.

Logical thinking.

FAKE NEWS/HWOOD PUPPETS LOST CONTROL.

Q

QAnon wasn't a spectator sport to behold from the sidelines, that much was clear to Matt. It felt like an invitation to be part of something bigger than himself. Integral to its mission was this grassroots network of patriots who worked together to solve mysteries and help Q bring hidden truths to light. Over the next several days and nights, as he scrolled wide-eyed through post after post in which anons and decoders jointly scrutinized typos in Trump's tweets (*coded messages?*) and unexplained letters and numbers in Q Drops (*hints about the date of the Storm?*), Matt was reminded of collaborative, quest-driven video games he'd played with strangers online. Only here, the objective wasn't hunting down monsters or fictitious beasts—it was saving humanity. Whether it was fantasy or reality had yet to be seen.

If QAnon was a game, Matt was ready to play. In his mind, he was embarking on a journey that could change the course of history. In truth, his budding radicalization had set in motion a chain of events that would cost him his marriage, his job, his savings, and very nearly, his life.

2

WE THE PLEBES

—Emily—

When the last of her three children departed for college, Emily was left behind on what was, in effect, her own private island.

Her eight-bedroom country estate-for-one was tucked away out of sight deep on an expansive property enveloped by forest. At the end of the winding driveway, greeting visitors to the residence, were meticulously manicured gardens, a flagstone terrace, and an ornate cedar gazebo perfect for sharing a pitcher of cold sweet tea on a hot Tennessee day, though Emily seldom had company.

She had mostly kept to herself in the years since her husband's suicide. With her kids now off forging their own paths in life—Adam working toward becoming a lawyer, like her; Jessica pursuing a career in politics; and Leah training to be a doctor—Emily had only her farm animals to come home to. She kept the house picture-ready anyway, like a perpetually unbooked B&B begging for guests. Cottage-style decor pieces, muted watercolor paintings, and grinning photos of her children were thoughtfully placed throughout.

Living all alone inside this vast empty nest day after day, night after night, and year after year took its toll. Over time, Emily's children believed, something fundamentally changed in her.

Leah was the first to notice. She looked the most like their mother: small in stature with thick blond hair and green almond eyes. She also lived closest to home and visited Emily the most. The two shared a unique bond. Unlike her twin sister, Leah had been born with a disability that made it difficult for her to walk. Her earliest memories, like much of her childhood, took place by Emily's side in hospital clinics and doctors' offices, waiting for whatever her next test or procedure was—and there was always something.

Emily took her to every appointment, giving her a hand to hold when she was scared or to squeeze when she was in pain. It was Leah's experience as a patient that inspired her to become a doctor. Realizing this dream, she knew, would be a far greater challenge for her than for most other aspiring physicians. Even doing clinical rotations as a medical student—shadowing doctors and residents tending to patients around the hospital—could be overwhelming when her team chose to rush up the stairs rather than wait for the elevator.

People weren't shy about telling Leah what she was incapable of. Deans of admissions at various med schools had suggested diplomatically but matter-of-factly that she wasn't physically cut out for their programs. She enjoyed proving her doubters wrong. But when it all felt like too much, she'd call home, and Emily would remind her, in typical motherly fashion, that her only limitations were those she imposed on herself. Emily was never more than a call away. She helped move Leah into and out of different apartments for college, grad school, med school, residency, and a fellowship, jumping in the car with boxes and duct tape and setting off to wherever her daughter needed her.

It was toward the end of President Obama's second term when Leah detected a shift in Emily's behavior. From visit to visit, she was increasingly rancorous, often grousing about one thing or another. It was usually Obama, whom she'd voted for twice but now appeared to despise. There was nothing she wished to discuss more than how he was running the country into the ground at the expense of "hardworking Americans" like her. Leah would sit at the dinner table, her food barely touched, listening to the woman who had taught her to always advocate for others—who had gone into law to fight for the less fortunate—now fuming about the taxes she was required to pay to support people on welfare.

Every time Leah pointed out the hypocrisy, Emily would snap that she had simply opened her eyes to reality. She even grumbled over the phone about the Obamacare provision barring insurance companies from denying coverage to those with preexisting health conditions, which had resulted in higher premiums and out-of-pocket costs for her. Leah couldn't believe what she was hearing. For the first eighteen years of her life, she had relied on a legal framework enabling children with certain disabilities to be covered under Medicaid. Without it, she wouldn't have gotten the care she needed. She hung up the call in disgust.

These talking points, Leah soon discovered, were coming straight from Fox News. She drove home for a visit one weekend to find it playing on the TV, and then it just never turned off. Emily kept it on all the time, replacing *Jeopardy!* and *Lost* with a lineup of frowning faces huffing about Obama golfing away their tax dollars. Trying to change the channel only ever provoked an argument.

On Facebook, where it was evident that Emily was also spending more of her free time, she started posting a steady stream of right-wing clickbait fulminating against the Left more broadly. She was combative and even rude in the comment sections when people criticized or questioned her content. Her kids were mortified. Emily was known to have a temper at times, but this was something else.

Engrossed in the stress of establishing their respective careers, Leah, Adam, and Jessica could only reason that as a small business owner, Emily had gotten so caught up in the financial challenges of running a solo law practice that she'd lost sight of her values. Whenever any of them tried to confront her, gently or bluntly, she was quick to remind them in no uncertain terms who was the parent and who was the child. Calls and visits became more upsetting and less frequent.

By 2016, their lifelong-Democrat mother, once a progressive beacon in their dark-red Tennessee county, was openly supporting Donald Trump for president of the United States.

Victims of the Establishment

Emily had been brainwashed, Adam was sure of it. Up in Chicago, diving into his first job as an associate attorney, he deleted his Facebook account, buried himself in his work, and went months at a time barely speaking to her, desperate to preserve in his mind the parent he used to know. She was the only one he had left. Communicating his concerns to her had gotten him nowhere; he hoped his silence would say more. Really, though, it only left him feeling guilty, and itching to gamble.

Adam and his sisters couldn't make sense of what had happened to her. In their view, Trump embodied everything she'd taught them to stand against. The question wasn't *how* it had happened; the Fox-and-Facebook saga was spilling into public view as half of America grappled with its new president. The real question was *why*.

One piece of the puzzle, the siblings suspected, had to be loneliness. By the time Adam had moved out, Emily hadn't lived on her own in decades. She'd gone from having a husband and kids at home with her to just three kids, to one, to no one. It wasn't what she'd envisioned for that stage of her life. She and Dan were supposed to grow old and see the world together. Instead, he had abandoned her, taking her happy, easy life away from her in a flash. On the rare occasions when she talked about him, she did so from a place of seemingly still-raw anger. It was too painful for her children to hear. They were her greatest remaining joy in life, she had often told them, and now they had all left her too.

Facebook helped fill the void. *FarmVille,* specifically, to start. The viral farming-simulation game debuted on the platform less than a year after Adam left for college in 2009. It became a craze almost overnight. On computer screens all over the world, blue-overalled avatars descended upon pixelated pastures, perma-grins stretched across their oversized heads as they cultivated little square patches of bell peppers, eggplants, and soybeans. There was almost no escaping it. Even for nonplayers, logging onto Facebook, for a time, meant scrolling through spammy posts and updates from FarmVillians engaging with each other or trying to recruit newcomers.

Adam was surprised when he noticed that some of the *FarmVille* posts cluttering his newsfeed were from his mother, who'd hardly ever used her Facebook account. She'd been stubbornly averse to social media for as long as it had been around, preferring to spend her free time out on the property with her animals, and, previously, with her children. In *FarmVille,* at least, she could raise virtual livestock. Adam observed from her posts that she had developed a nightly habit of playing before bed, the time when they used to watch TV or movies together.

Before long, her Facebook use was increasing, even outside of her digital crop fields. She'd often share pictures of her kids, bragging about them and their many accomplishments to the point of embarrassment, as parents do, and lots of farming content. She posted more and more as time went on, mixing in heartwarming quotes she found on the site. Between those kinds of status updates ("Hanging out with your adult children is like visiting with the most beautiful and precious part of your life") and her auto-generated *FarmVille* ones ("Emily found a lonely Pink Cow on their farm. Oh no! Adopt the Pink Cow!"), her feed was pretty wholesome, at first. Cringeworthy in the best way. And, later, in the worst.

Facebook's recommendation engine had surely played a hidden hand in Emily's rightward pivot. But it didn't randomly go from feeding people farm memes to Breitbart articles. While the platform had a disturbing pattern of recommending progressively extreme content to its users and siloing them into echo chambers, it did so in line with the things they'd already been clicking on and searching for.

Fox, then, had to be the root of it all, Adam supposed. He would never know what had made his mother change the channel in the first place. Maybe she had flicked it on by accident one day. As for what had kept her watching all this time, though . . . that was the hardest part to swallow. She seemed seduced by the network's Manichaean narrative of victimhood.

Tucker Carlson quickly became Emily's favorite prime-time host, Leah reported to her siblings. In his nightly monologues, he'd warn his millions of viewers that "the ruling class" or "the regime" or "the establishment," as he'd call it, was out to get them.

"They hate you," "They want to control you," "They want to hurt you," he'd hiss, austere and unblinking. Carlson's "they" was a reference to a supposed cadre of leftists in varying positions of power—from Democratic politicians and mainstream media journalists to progressive actors, athletes, and academics.

Adam loathed the man. It was rich listening to *him*—Tucker Swanson McNear Carlson, a multimillionaire, prep school–educated, carefully coiffed trust fund baby who summered in Maine—position himself squarely among the downtrodden, shoulder to shoulder with his viewers, decrying plots by "the elites" against "the rest of us plebes." Fox's overwhelmingly white audience was hardly the oppressed underclass Carlson made them out to be. Especially Emily, an epitome of privilege: She was a wealthy, successful lawyer residing in a McMansion. Some of her farm equipment cost tens of thousands of dollars. And somehow, Carlson appeared to have convinced her that "the powers that be" were conspiring to take it all away from her, along with everything else she valued in life.

Adam was right to worry that a sustained and strictly partisan media diet could have an effect similar to brainwashing, or could radically alter the way that people like his mom thought. A pair of political scientists would later attempt to reverse-engineer this effect by paying hundreds of Fox News watchers to switch to CNN for a month. By the end, the participants' opinions on hot-button issues, from racial justice to voting by mail, had shifted significantly. The experiment revealed not only that Fox played a major role in shaping its viewers' beliefs, as Adam understood, but also, on a more hopeful note for him and his sisters, that such beliefs remained malleable.

What the siblings couldn't have foreseen was that Emily's "brainwashing" had only just begun—that Carlson and his colleagues, through an IV drip of victim mentality rhetoric, were priming her for a transformation much more extreme than simply switching political parties. It was far easier to believe in antiestablishment conspiracy theories after being conditioned to identify as a victim of the establishment.

The Descent

"Um, hello?"

Jessica had no idea why her friend was calling her. It wasn't even 7 a.m.; she was still in bed checking work emails.

"Jess, hi—are you okay?"

"Yes. . . . Why wouldn't I be?"

"I just saw your mom's Facebook post—"

Jessica let out a long, exasperated sigh and lifted her palm to her face. "What now?"

Like her brother, Jessica had gotten rid of her Facebook account. She didn't need the constant reminders of her mom's slow-motion descent into MAGAland. She and Emily had recently gotten into a heated political disagreement over the phone; now Emily was apparently asking her Facebook friends to please "pray" for Jessica. Only in response to a flurry of alarmed comments did she clarify what was ailing her daughter: liberal indoctrination. By that point, in early 2020, Emily's grievances with the Left had grown far beyond money and taxes. Her Facebook posts were becoming more God centered, anti-immigrant, and bizarrely obsessed with pedophilia. She had sent Jessica a blog post months earlier positing that the tunnels beneath the Denver International Airport were some sort of labyrinth used to traffic kids.

Jessica abruptly ended the call with her friend, leapt out of bed, then dialed Emily to demand that she delete the post asking for prayers. The voice on the other end was unrecognizable. Half-screeching, half-crying, Emily wailed that her "own fucking child" was a socialist and a Marxist, which she now seemingly equated with being a Democrat. Jessica was speechless. Her mom wasn't speaking to her from MAGAland anymore. She had reached somewhere far darker.

Panic set in a short time later, when Emily texted all three of her children a series of garbled tweets from random accounts claiming, among other things, that Mike Pence had been cloned in a test tube, Michelle Obama was a man, and George W. Bush was behind 9/11. Adam hadn't even realized that Emily was back on Twitter, which she had previously used to promote her law practice. Given her Facebook activity, he was afraid of what he'd find there.

It was worse than he'd feared. In her Twitter bio, Emily now declared that she was waiting for "#THEGREATAWAKENING," and for JFK, Jr.—who'd been dead and gone for more than twenty years—to join Trump in the White House as his vice president. When Adam looked at her latest tweets, his heart sank.

Bring on the Galatic Federation to CRUSH SATANIC MON-STERS!!!!

@AOC You are an ignorant entitled little fraud with a evil core. Your eyes little devil give you away. Not the flotsam coming out of your red lips. Where are your #redshoes?

Pallets of CASH, OBAMA BIDEN, ALL THE CRONIES. PROOF, ALL OF IT, BQQM!

There were hundreds of them—all utter nonsense, as if some lunatic had stolen Emily's phone and mashed out fragmented, blood-lusting gibberish. His mouth agape, Adam scrolled in a zombie-like daze until he reached her old, beautifully boring tweets, tiny digital footprints from the attorney at law he had idolized for his entire adult life.

Trust our attorneys to help you decide on the best course of action for your family's well-being.

Check out some cars with the most frequent personal injury claims. Contact us for legal consultations.

Here's what you need to know about Distracted Driving Awareness Month.

Adam sat in silence for a long time. He could feel a lump in his throat as his ears began to ring and tears welled in his eyes. This was just crazy. Completely fucking crazy. What had happened to his brilliant lawyer mother? When had it gotten *this* bad?

He'd been more than distracted lately. Just a few months earlier, he'd moved to San Francisco to start a new job as an associate at a prestigious global law firm. Being in the big leagues, professionally, was a thrilling but brutally taxing rat race—or, as his colleagues put it, a pie-eating contest in which the prize was more pie. Compounding his stress was the looming California bar exam, which his new firm was expecting him to take as soon as possible. In Illinois, he'd passed the bar without studying all that hard, as was the norm for him. But California's was notoriously the most difficult in the country.

Now Adam had something new hanging over his head. As he paced the length of his eighteenth-floor luxury apartment, poring over his mother's recent, nauseating tweets, he noticed that several contained a curious yet consistent typo: the letter Q. Then, like a hard kick to the gut, it hit him.

She was a fucking QAnon believer.

Adam had heard of QAnon in the news. He knew the gist: Some psycho Trump superfans on the internet were convinced that the president was engaged in a clandestine battle against a pedophiliac, cannibalistic cabal at the helm of global power. For the siblings to learn that their own mother was one of them was completely horrifying. In a frenetic group chat, they considered their options. Adam proposed a family intervention, but his sisters thought it was much too late for that. They believed that a call to a psych ward could be warranted.

Leah sent Emily's tweets to a friend from school who was now a psychiatrist. In response, she advised Leah to do some research into "delusional disorder," a rare form of psychosis that normally emerged in adulthood, in which an individual experienced delusions but otherwise continued to function normally. In a similar vein, Leah found, others online speculated more generally that some QAnon followers could have a syndrome called "folie à deux" (madness of two) or, in wider contexts, "folie à plusieurs" (madness of several). It involved one person transmitting delusions to another—just like a virus, except not necessarily via in-person interaction—and was most common among those experiencing prolonged social isolation. Though not confirmed, folie à deux was widely believed to be a driving factor in a nationally shocking 2014 assault in which two twelve-year-old Wisconsin girls lured their friend out into the woods, pinned her down, and stabbed her nineteen times in an attempt to appease "Slender Man," a tall, mythical creature with no face.

Adam resented the notion that Emily needed to be admitted or diagnosed. He didn't want to believe that she had truly lost her mind. But most people—including him, until now—looked at QAnon adherents en masse as certifiably insane. It was a temptingly simple explanation for a deeply complex phenomenon. Media coverage was partly responsible for this unevidenced perception: It tended to spotlight QAnon's most gobsmacking beliefs, leaving people mystified as to how any sane individual could fall for something so crazy. But that obscured the process. Believers weren't drawn to QAnon through lurid tales of cannibalism, infanticide, or satanic sex abuse rituals. They started out consuming lighter, more digestible conspiracy theory hors d'oeuvres with kernels of truth baked in, like rumors about corrupt elites, then gradually developed an appetite for wilder and wilder claims. There was a variety of potential issues at play, and insanity wasn't necessarily one of them. Researchers would later find a positive correlation between conspiracy theory belief and depression—most prevalent, interestingly, among the relatively privileged: white people, high-income earners, and those with college educations. Psychological stress as well as state (situation-based) and trait (personality-based) anxiety were also determined to be precursors, suggesting a circumstantial vulnerability in some cases rather than a mental disorder.

Jessica's therapist had a different thought. Nita knew the Porters' tragic family history well. She knew that Emily's behavior had been of increasing concern since a few years after her kids moved out. It was possible, Nita suggested, that Fox News, and now QAnon, supplied Emily with external grievances through which to channel her internal anger and sadness. Those grievances, like supposed threats to finances and freedoms, could be highly gripping for her in particular. Emotional trauma had the power to permanently alter the brain: It could cause the amygdala—the alarm center controlling emotional responses such as fear, anxiety, and aggression—to become overactive. Social isolation and loneliness, as well, were known to fuel hypervigilance toward perceived threats, in addition to cognitive decline.

Nita also speculated that Emily's rage, sensitivity, and victim complex, as described by Jessica, could be signs of narcissistic personality disorder, a condition that was typically present to some degree from childhood or adolescence but could become more apparent later in life as a delayed response to trauma. Narcissism was one of very few personality traits that was a robust predictor of conspiracy theory thinking. To narcissists, espousing such views offered validation that people had it in for them, scapegoats upon which to blame their own misfortunes, and a coveted sense of uniqueness. This was also true of collective narcissism, the belief that one's community—like a political party, QAnon, or what Carlson called "legacy Americans"—was superior and at risk, breeding suspicions of other groups.

Adam pushed back. Emily wasn't insane or self-obsessed, he told his sisters. She had just been cooped up by herself for too long, marinating inside the pressure cooker of the internet with Fox News blaring in the background. This was being done *to* her, not *by* her, he insisted.

She was a victim—just not in the ways she thought.

Adam knew he should be using his precious little free time to prepare for the bar, but he decided there was something more pressing he needed to study instead. The more he understood about QAnon, he figured, the better equipped he would be to pull his mother back out of it. So he dove headfirst down the rabbit hole after her.

A *NOTEBOOK* ROMANCE

—Doris—

Once upon a time, a young man named Dale was on his last first date. Though he didn't know Doris well, a part of him knew that she was the one. She was beautiful, yes: doe-eyed and radiant, and nearly as tall as he was thanks to her Jackie O. bouffant. But it was something about her elegance and her calm, quiet confidence that drew him to her so magnetically. So after carefully combing his black curls to the side, tucking his button-down shirt into his freshly pressed slacks, and fastening his tie in the mirror just right, he set off in his old blue Chevy to take her out for an evening they would never forget.

The two had first met earlier that fall, in 1968, during a literary event at a college in New Orleans, where Doris worked as an administrative assistant and Dale taught classes in American literature and philosophy. In his buttery, distinctive southern drawl, an uncanny echo of renowned American novelist Shelby Foote, Dale performed a reading for the audience. He selected a passage from one of his favorite works, Richard Wright's *Black Boy*, a memoir about racism and poverty in the Jim Crow South. Among the captive listeners were Doris and a few of her friends. Twenty-eight-year-old Dale could talk endlessly about history and prose, but talking to an enchanting woman could leave him tongue-tied.

He did his best the next time he saw her, at a local pizza joint. Some mutual friends had arranged a group night out, pushing tables together in the restaurant so all ten of them could share slices from each other's pies. The surrounding chatter and clangs of salad forks against ceramic plates made it difficult to have much of a conversation, but Dale jumped at the chance to pay for Doris's meal after she realized she had forgotten her change purse. A few days later, to his pleasant surprise, he found an envelope in his mailbox addressed from her. Inside was a nickel and a quarter, money for the pizza right down to the cent. Her message seemed clear: If he was going to buy her dinner, it would have to be a proper date. Just like that, Dale was smitten—he couldn't get Doris out of his head.

He took her to Tony's, a hole-in-the-wall Italian spot outside the city with tacky gold wallpaper and delicious spaghetti and meatballs, hoping to impress her. (Only years later would she confess that it had long been one of her favorites.) Seated across from her in their booth, tongue-tied once more, Dale worried that they would have little in common. He was a humble country boy; she was a glamorous city girl from a well-to-do family and four years his junior. But two hours flew by, and by the time their tiramisu arrived, they had discovered their shared passion for animals, the environment, social justice, and the arts. Neither wanted the night to end. After escorting Doris to her doorstep, Dale gave her a bashful peck on the cheek in the moonlight, looked deep into her dark brown eyes, and asked her to go steady.

From that point on, Dale and Doris were officially *Dale and Doris*. They were inseparable. On weekends they could be found out on the town, locked in each other's embrace inside jazz clubs and the community theater. After saying goodbye, they would get home and call each other on their rotary-dial telephones until one or both fell asleep. Doris spent many weeknights using her typewriter to help Dale prepare lesson plans for his students, who in one class were learning about Marshall McLuhan, a philosopher arguing that the entire world was becoming one big "global village" interconnected by new media technologies. It was quite a concept for Dale, who'd grown up on a working farm in a town of no more than five hundred people. Though Doris was from an entirely different walk of life, the two of them just fit together: They both enjoyed the thrill of a party and the quiet of nature, and longed for the company of others but shied from the spotlight.

Less than a year into dating, Dale asked Doris to marry him. There was no grand speech, trail of red rose petals, or gimmicky proposal; the question flew out of his mouth as naturally as their first "I love you" while they were alone one day at his place. His elated bride-to-be began to plan their wedding immediately. They tied the knot on an unseasonably warm winter day in 1970 in an old wooden church with Palladian windows and oak pews packed full of friends, family, and Dale's former students. Dale wore a sharp black tux and Doris a white lace gown with embroidered flowers down the sleeves.

Up at the altar, holding Doris's small hands tightly in his own, Dale knew this was the beginning of their Happily Ever After.

They settled into married life in a red-brick bungalow they bought for $35,000. It had two fireplaces, front-facing picture windows, and a nearby peach orchard they could ride to on their bicycles. Doris decorated the interior and Dale tended to the gardening and yard work. They got to know many of his students well, like nieces and nephews, and would keep in touch with several for years, even decades. They co-chaperoned a school trip with eighteen of them through western Europe in 1973, returning home in the midst of the Watergate hearings. Both had considered themselves to be rather apolitical Republicans, but sitting before their black-and-white television set, learning in dismay of President Nixon's flagrant corruption, flipped them decidedly into Democrats.

In the '80s, Dale and Doris moved into a white house with chestnut paneling in the den and a stone-laid walkway to the front door, which they lined with boxwoods on either side. Surrounded by tiered magenta gardens of azaleas and tulips, a lone cucumber tree stood in the yard. It reminded Dale of a Thomas Holley Chivers poem:

> Like the sweet, golden goblet found growing
> On the wild emerald cucumber tree
> Rich, brilliant, like chrysoprase glowing
> Was my beautiful Rosalie Lee
> My lamb-like Rosalie Lee
> My dove-like Rosalie Lee

As Doris sat beneath the tree on a lazy afternoon, wearing the long white dress Dale's mother had crocheted for her and a touch of plum-red lipstick while caressing their cat, who lay asleep in the grass, Dale was overcome by her beauty. He was seeing her for the first time once more. She looked tender and serene: his very own lamb-like, dove-like Rosalie Lee.

Theirs was a love story as pure and as beautiful as any Nicholas Sparks novel: a real-life *Notebook* romance, without the disapproving parents or years of forlorn separation. Doris was the Allie to Dale's Noah—only it wasn't dementia that eventually took her mind.

The Global Village

It's difficult for Dale to pinpoint when, exactly, Doris slipped away from him. The changes in her behavior were subtle and gradual. Maybe he was too close to see them at first; dust accumulates unnoticed until an opaque layer coats the mantel. He thinks it began with a trip to the doctor. He knows it spiraled with Facebook.

One day in 2016 in Tuscaloosa, Alabama, where Dale and Doris had retired, they went to see a new physician for a checkup about Doris's type 2 diabetes. She expected the usual rundown: Maintain a healthy diet, exercise regularly, and so forth. Instead, he told her she had pancreatic cancer.

As Doris sobbed hysterically in his office and Dale stood frozen in shock, the doctor urged her to begin chemotherapy right away. He would prescribe her a daily regimen of medications to treat the side effects of the chemo, and medications to treat the side effects of those medications, he said. Doris managed to compose herself enough to explain that she would like to do some research and get a second opinion. He scowled, plainly indignant that she would question his diagnosis. She didn't have time to wait, he said: The survival rate was 10 percent—in the early stages.

Doris did not have cancer.

Maybe her test results were inaccurate. Maybe the doctor misread them. Or maybe, as she would come to suspect, he was a dime-a-dozen Big Pharma shill who fabricated the diagnosis to try to lure his latest victim into a lengthy, costly, unnecessary treatment plan.

Had this happened a decade earlier, it would have simply been a traumatizing experience with an awful physician that soured Doris's trust in the medical system, perhaps even permanently. But because it happened in the age of the social media–wired *global village,* Dale believes it became a launchpad into a world of commodified paranoia.

Doris started searching online for others who had encountered seemingly predatory healthcare professionals. She found *lots* of them, brought together in Facebook groups from all over the country and far beyond, who posted heartrending stories about debilitating treatments, adverse reactions to prescribed pills, and even deaths. They offered Doris their sympathy and shared in her anger. In her seventy-two years, she had come across only that one bad-apple doctor, but inside these digital echo chambers, brimming with highly emotional (and unfalsifiable) anecdotes, medical malfeasance began to look like an epidemic.

Stories there trumped studies and statistics, and were the basis upon which many people made raging accusations against the "medical establishment" at large. Those who did so the loudest were often in the business of alternative medicine, or in the wellness industry, Dale observed. They advertised all-natural cures for everything from the common cold to cancer. It was they who seemed like the predatory ones, at least to him. Even as an avid believer in natural wellness, and a shrewd skeptic of Big Pharma, he considered the new herbal remedies and supplements that had started to crowd Doris's medicine cabinet to be pseudoscientific junk. But Dale didn't worry much about his wife's new online network, unaware at the time of who and what it was expanding to include. He knew that she was seeking comfort, community, and validation, which she had clearly found.

He thought that was a good thing.

Dale's own experience on Facebook was the kind that Mark Zuckerberg and other Big Tech CEOs loved to point to while romanticizing social media as a tool for bringing the people of the world closer together. For a senior citizen, Dale was remarkably popular on the platform, a reflection of the great care he put into staying actively connected to so many people there. He cherished all his friendships, tending to them like flowers in a virtual garden, with just-because check-ins, personalized birthday wishes, and updates of his own. His beaming selfies could garner more than three hundred likes and draw in dozens of comments, including several from former students across multiple generations who still called him "Professor." Dale always replied to each one, taking the time to inquire about the lives they were leading far away from his. But just as social media could bring people together, it could also drive them apart. It was there, on Facebook, that Dale and Doris's shared reality began to fracture.

From the time they were born in the 1940s, through the first half of their lives, Dale and Doris got most of their news and information from just three dominant television networks: CBS, ABC, and NBC. The "Big

Three" delivered to Americans of all backgrounds a common set of facts. In households young and old, coastal and central, blue- and white-collared, there was a general consensus that up was up and down was down. As a married couple, Dale and Doris also read the paper together. They liked to sit at their kitchen table on weekends and exchange sections of *The New York Times* over their morning coffee. The news stories inside were, of course, always the same for him as they were for her.

On Facebook, that wasn't the case.

After browsing the platform, each could log off with a radically different impression of what was happening in the world around them. It was unlike anything they'd experienced in all their decades: Users were tracked and catered to in real time, individualizing their online experiences. Instead of flipping through standardized, prewritten pages of the paper, Dale and Doris scrolled through their personal newsfeeds in a choose-your-own-adventure manner, the content on their screens gradually recalibrating on the basis of their every click. In time, it was Facebook that did much of the choosing for them.

Dale, part of the Silent Generation, and Doris, on the cusp of being a Baby Boomer, belonged to the fastest-growing group of users on Facebook. The number of seniors on the site nearly doubled between 2012 and 2019. A concerning feature of their online behavior quickly became apparent: They were consuming and disseminating information with relatively limited skepticism—in fact, they were four times more likely than "digital natives" to share fake news. This heightened vulnerability to online falsehoods could be due in some cases to cognitive aging, researchers determined, but also, to a limited understanding of how social media platforms operate behind the scenes. A third of "digital immigrants" over sixty-five believed that the news articles in their Facebook feeds were selected by a group of company employees, just as a team of editors would decide which stories to put in the *Times*. Only 18 percent were aware that it was done by machine-learning programs curating posts specifically for them.

Without knowledge of that technology, there was no wariness of the insidious ways that Facebook could warp individual users' perceptions of society—and of each other—in pursuit of corporate profit. Unseen was a business model built around social media companies' most prized commodity: human attention. The longer they could keep people engaged on their platforms, the more ads they could show them and the more money they could make. While for Dale that meant lots of cat videos and *Atlantic* articles artificially amplified in his feeds, for myriad other Americans—now including his wife—it meant a deluge of propaganda mirroring and magnifying their existing fears to keep them hooked.

In turn, for the creators of that content perched higher up the information food chain, it meant big opportunity.

Enter the Influencers

It was a few months after the misdiagnosis that Dale started hearing the name "Debbie" a lot.

His wife talked about Debbie all the time. Debbie was "so smart," "so fearless," and "such a breath of fresh air." America *needed* Debbie. The woman of whom Doris spoke was Deborah Lusignan, a Massachusetts-based vlogger in her midforties who talked with her hands and shot from the hip in her searing, sometimes expletive-laden polemics against the pharmaceutical industry. But lately she was turning her focus—and Doris's attention—to the 2016 presidential primaries, which she claimed were wildly rigged. Branding herself the "Sane Progressive," Lusignan was anti-Republican, anti-Democrat, anti-Trump, and fervently anti-Clinton.

Doris appeared entranced. She admired Lusignan's brash willingness to call a spade a spade and her commitment to cutting through the nastiness of partisan politics to deliver the unvarnished truth. Though Doris was a longtime liberal who had enjoyed several of Hillary Clinton's books, she told Dale that she'd been rethinking things as of late. Her worldview was shifting, and her resentful distrust of the medical industry was bleeding into her perception of all bodies of power.

While Dale posted links on Facebook like "19 Cats Who Had No Idea You'd Be Home So Early," an old BuzzFeed photo listicle of startled-looking pets caught being silly, Doris covered her page in "Sane Progressive" YouTube videos exposing the hidden agenda of the "corporate regime" and its collusion with the "bought and paid for media." In Lusignan, Doris raved to her husband, she saw a martyr: an ordinary woman brave enough to stand up to both Big Pharma and corrupt politicians at her own risk.

The way Doris spoke of and posted about "Debbie," on a first-name basis and with pure adulation, was perplexing to Dale. It was as if his wife felt like she knew this loud, angry woman on her screen personally. She often tried to write to Lusignan: "I know you are a brave lady, and I admire you SO much for speaking the truth!" seventy-three-year-old Doris posted on her own Facebook page in 2017, evidently unaware that Lusignan would never see it there. Praising Lusignan's continued election fraud content, Doris added, "We simply have to figure out a way to get it out [to] the majority of Americans. I just hope it does not cost you your life."

Lusignan had no official expertise in election integrity or evidence-based research; she simply scoured the internet for "intel" and drew conclusions based on her sleuthing, often blending conspiracy theories into her analysis, like her impassioned assertion that the 2017 Las Vegas massacre was "the largest false flag since 9/11." Yet Doris was growing to trust her more than any other news source. This trust was a product of parasocial attachment, a one-sided, illusory relationship in which an audience member comes to think of a public persona, whom they've observed from afar for a long time, as a friend. It was a common phenomenon, particularly in the age of online influencers, who put their lives on display like animals at a zoo to create a semblance of intimacy with the strangers who followed them. Over time, these unrequited psychological bonds could become remarkably strong—and persuasive. Influencer marketing was already a booming, multi-billion-dollar industry built off online starlets convincing their adoring fans to buy the ThighMasters and facial cleansers and energy drinks they were shilling.

But parasocial dynamics could be used to sell ideas too. And coming from a friend figure, like "Debbie," conspiracy theories could start to sound less like conspiracy theories.

Older adults were more susceptible to this kind of influence. Interpersonal trust had been found to increase with age, and adapting to a shifting media landscape came with unique challenges for seniors in discerning whom to believe online: After growing up pre-internet, with Walter Cronkite and just a select few other dependable faces delivering the news, they were parachuted into the social media era, where for every Judy Woodruff or Lester Holt there were suddenly countless "Debbies" clawing for their attention with unchecked narratives and undisclosed interests. Worse, algorithmic megaphones were handed not to the most credible voices, necessarily, but often to the most incendiary—giving "Debbie" types outsized visibility and a veneer of legitimacy.

When Doris was making her way down the virtual rabbit hole, it was a Wild West. Lusignan was drawing her into YouTube, where algorithmically promoted content—which generated more than 70 percent of all user traffic—was particularly egregious. Conspiracy theory videos were showered with billions upon billions of views. Alex Jones's Infowars became one of the most artificially recommended political channels on the site, while videos labeling school shooting survivors as "crisis actors" soared to the top spot on the trending page. It was symbiotic: To mine users' attention like gold from the earth, YouTube wasn't just blasting bad actors like Jones into virality—it was *paying them,* doling out a cut of the ad revenue via its broader "Partner Program" as an incentive to keep the content coming.

This helped give rise to a new class of profiteering influencers effectively trained to churn out fearmongering clickbait and wholesale falsehoods in exchange for greater exposure. In many instances, their sinister distortions of major breaking news events outperformed professionally reported media coverage shared to the same platforms. It was disinformation industrialized, and a windfall in both directions: Tech giants were fanning the flames of chaos spreading like wildfire across their sites and beyond while raking in the ad dollars. Creators were falling over themselves watching their most unhinged videos erupt with monetizable traffic, turning QAnon decoding into a cottage industry of its own. And caught in the middle of it all, searching for truth, were people like Doris.

Doris found Lusignan the same way she found Claudia Stauber, an off-the-grid environmentalist vlogger who made her own "toothpowder" and believed the U.S. government was committing "global genocide" by poisoning the soil with chemtrails; Laura Eisenhower, the great-granddaughter of President Dwight Eisenhower who claimed to be in contact with numerous alien species and "sky beings"; and a growing cast of other perceived mavericks whom she came to trust and respect after many hours spent consuming their content on social media. In fact, it wasn't Doris who found them, but almost the other way around: Each was recommended to her by Facebook or YouTube, which gradually nudged her along from alternative medicine spaces deeper into the fringe.

To Dale, some, like Lusignan, appeared to be motivated by a genuine belief in the theories they touted, while others spewed unadulterated, money-grubbing disinformation trumpeted as gallant citizen journalism. In many cases, though, he detected a mix of both: a foundational conviction that some form of malevolence had occurred, and an increasing willingness to hyperbolize, fabricate, and lie as money flowed in. It was those people, the believers-turned-opportunists, who seemed the most compelling—and the most dangerous.

In addition to Lusignan, Doris's most trusted new influencer was antivaxxer Del Bigtree, an eccentric daytime television producer with tousled gray curls, drilling blue eyes, and no medical training whatsoever. After working on *Dr. Phil,* Bigtree had moved to the talk show *The Doctors,* where he was pained by stories from parents who said their kids had fallen ill from pediatric shots. It compelled him to cowrite and produce *Vaxxed,* a newly released documentary falsely alleging a connection between the childhood MMR vaccine and autism. There was no initial prospect of serious money in making the film. It was preemptively yanked from the Tribeca Film Festival lineup in response to public outcry, instead premiering before an audience of only a few dozen. But as the offline world was initially hostile, the online world opened its arms. On Facebook—where, as on YouTube, vaccine falsehoods were not only allowed but amplified—the *Vaxxed* page gained hundreds of thousands of followers. Bigtree promptly launched his own antivaccine show on both platforms, bringing in tens of millions of views with untold earnings, and founded an advocacy group, through which he was making a rising salary of nearly $150,000 by its second year.

As his influence—and income—swelled, so did the breadth of his claims. Vaccines didn't just cause autism anymore, they were part of a heinous conspiracy led by the government and the pharmaceutical industry to harm children. Bigtree's original cause of warning parents about MMR shots was twisting into a cash-cow mission to convince his burgeoning audience that the people in charge were their oppressors. He even started wearing the Nazi-era yellow Star of David on his lapel to drive the point home, despite not being Jewish, claiming to show solidarity with the Hasidic community. He was well on his way toward QAnon territory—and bringing Doris right along with him.

"I just can't believe it," she'd say again and again, shaking her head while watching his videos. But she did. She appeared to believe it all, even taking it upon herself to caution people she knew personally against mainstream medicine. Dale was horrified when she advised one of their friends, who was dying from cancer, to forgo chemotherapy in favor of apricot seeds and an organic diet—a "cure" she'd apparently heard about on Facebook.

Something in Doris was changing right before Dale's eyes, and it wasn't just her beliefs. A kindling was starting to burn. Mark her words, she'd tell him, it was heroes like "Deb and Del" who were going to wake up the world.

Deborah Lusignan didn't get the chance. She died just a few years later, affirming Doris's worst suspicions. "Sane Progressive" fans drew their own conclusions about the cause of death, carrying on speculating even after Lusignan's grieving family publicly pleaded for them to stop. Some suggested that she was really in hiding. One wrote a four-thousand-word blog post implying that she'd been assassinated. But as the world battled a new virus called SARS-CoV-2, most agreed on what must have killed her: the vaccine.

Dale and Doris were already nearing a crisis point by the time the coronavirus pandemic hit.

Though his hair was mostly gone, save for a thinning white combover, Dale was still the same gentle soul who'd fallen in love in the fall of 1968: a man who literally stopped to smell the roses, and used words like *swell* and *golly.*

It was Doris who'd changed.

As in *The Notebook,* where an elderly Noah attempted day after day to wrest his dear wife from the grips of dementia, Dale found himself spending his twilight years desperately trying to pry Doris from a spell of delusion. It felt like she'd been stolen from him.

In her dark brown eyes, now hooded and creased, he could still see the woman he'd loved for half a century. He had hope. One day, he believed, they could find a way back to their Happily Ever After.

4

THE PERFECT STORM

—Alice—

Alice hunched over her computer, clicking intently through the Photoshop color wheel. She was trying to choose a background shade for the little postcard flyers she was designing. Plain white was too boring. Navy blue was too serious. She landed on bright canary yellow. *Perfect.*

At the top of her pop art–style masterpiece, she had written, "FEEL THE BERN!" and at the bottom, "BE THE CHANGE!!!" Sandwiched in the middle, beneath a black-and-white cutout of a grinning Bernie Sanders head with small red stars, there were twenty-three bullet points. Each displayed one of the Vermont senator's presidential campaign promises, including closing corporate tax loopholes and dismantling institutional racism from the inside out.

After making a few final tweaks, Alice dashed off to a printing shop with her new boyfriend, Christopher, and made five hundred copies. They spent the afternoon handing them out and tucking them under windshield wipers at the local college campus just outside Santa Cruz.

It was May of 2016, and Sanders was the hero Alice had been waiting for. A self-styled "New Age hippie" in her early forties with a nose ring and wild auburn curls that matched her free spirit, she wore her heart on her sleeve and the weight of the world on her shoulders. And the world, as she saw it, was not as she wanted it to be: Greed and corruption had sunk their talons deep into American democracy, causing vast, needless suffering.

Alice had lost her faith in the established systems of power long ago, and for good reason. Many, in fact. The U.S. government's documented breaches of public trust were copious and egregious, from spying on the American people via mass surveillance programs to MKUltra, the CIA's top-secret mind-control program involving psychological torture and sexual abuse. She had wept in disgust over the bald-faced lies that the Bush administration had cooked up to justify its catastrophic invasion of Iraq—which, like Sanders, she had vehemently opposed from the start. But what incensed her the most, and left her feeling utterly, crushingly powerless, wasn't any singular case of deceit or cover-up. It was the insidious profits-over-people governance model making the country sicker, poorer, and more polluted to line the pockets of the 1 percent.

Sanders was its greatest threat, and her greatest hope. His presidency would bring an end to lawmakers' shady dealings with Wall Street, pharmaceutical giants, fossil fuel companies, and "billionaire oligarchs," as he called them. He was, in Alice's eyes, a once-in-a-generation politician: unshackled by private interests, unafraid of the powers that be, and unwilling to accept the status quo. That was why, despite her low hourly wage at a friend's nonprofit, she was donating $100 per month to his campaign. It was the first time that real change had felt within reach: A future with Sanders at the helm, she imagined, would reflect what her favorite writer, Charles Eisenstein, described as "the more beautiful world our hearts know is possible"—one in which Alice's teenage son, Dawson, could live without fear of crippling student debt, insurmountable medical bills, or a planet wrecked by climate change.

It was Bernie or bust.

When he lost, Alice fell apart. She didn't know what to do with herself other than cry, mourning a dream that had felt so real only to be ripped away. For a few weeks, like so many other shell-shocked Sanders supporters, she tried to convince herself that it wasn't true—that somehow, despite the delegate counts, he could still come back and clinch the nomination. But eventually, denial turned to despair. And when a cache of hacked emails later revealed Democratic Party officials' extraordinary bias against Sanders—including discussion of undermining his campaign, and attempts to manipulate press coverage in favor of Hillary Clinton—despair turned to despondence. The revolution, it seemed, was over before it began.

On the day of the 2016 Democratic National Convention, Alice opened Facebook in search of solace. She scrolled upon a live-stream video of Mikki Willis, a progressive filmmaker she had long admired for the heartwarming content he shared of himself with his two little boys, including a clip reposted by Ellen DeGeneres in which he had praised his eldest son for picking out a princess doll at the toy store to play with. In this latest video, Willis was standing next to Claudia Stauber, an environmentalist YouTuber with a thick German accent and wavy white-blond hair, whom Alice also recognized. Both well-known, diehard "Berniecrats," Willis and Stauber had run into each other in Philadelphia outside the convention center. They were taking turns speaking selfie-style to the camera, urging their audiences not to lose faith.

"The fight continues," a teary-eyed Willis encouraged. "The movement continues."

He insisted that change was still possible, if not through Sanders, then some other way. For the sake of his children, he wasn't giving up.

"We'll figure out the next step," Stauber assured. "And good finally will win over evil."

Alice couldn't muster the hope they preached. It was abundantly clear to her that the people at the top were far too powerful to ever allow a true change-maker into their ranks. Her vision for the future had gone up in flames.

Crisis Mode

Alice first heard about Covid-19 a month before it changed the world forever.

She and Christopher were engaged and living together in the San Francisco Bay Area. Things were at once terrific and terrifying: On one hand, she was in love, had a wonderful, uber-progressive community of friends, was in good health, and immensely enjoyed her job as a life coach. On the other, existential dread was slowly closing in around her like smoke, making it harder and harder to breathe. She loathed Donald Trump with a simmering passion; he was a lying, racist, misogynistic, xenophobic, climate change–denying tyrant, as far as she was concerned, and he had plunged the nation into a state of white-hot polarization unprecedented in her lifetime. With surging numbers of hate crimes under his tenure, including a boom in racially motivated attacks right there in San Francisco, she worried that the societal damage he was inflicting might be too grave to heal. On top of that, officials had already warned that California was in store for its worst wildfire season on record. The news had become so overwhelming that Alice had stopped watching. Sometimes she wished she could tuck into herself like a turtle and hide.

Like an estimated 20 to 30 percent of the global population, Alice was a "highly sensitive person," the clinical term for an individual prone to intense emotional reactions, including acute anxiety. Where she diverged from others on the "HSP" spectrum was in her social tendencies— especially in her longing for physical touch. She was a hugger and a holder, and she and Christopher took every opportunity to get out of the house and be with friends, whether for a hike, a brunch, or a party. Professionally, though, many of Alice's relationships were virtual.

In early February of 2020 she was attending an online workshop for practitioners of "compassionate communication," a conflict resolution strategy she employed with her clients. Participants were asked to take part in an empathy-focused group exercise by talking about things that frightened them. Alice didn't need to think twice. Part of her was petrified that Trump could actually be reelected, a fear espoused by several people on the call. One man, Calvin, was particularly eager to share. He had two big concerns. The first was 5G cell tower radiation, which he believed was behind his mysterious fatigue and dizziness. He had already taken measures to protect himself, he said, pointing to the blue beanie on his head. Its interior lining supposedly defended his brain from radio-frequency electromagnetic exposure. He added that he was connected to the internet using an ethernet port instead of Wi-Fi and had even coated his house in a pitch-black 5G "shielding paint."

People nodded along politely in their little Skype squares, but no one seemed overly troubled by Calvin's warning. Alice, however, was disturbed, despite his eccentricity. She had heard compelling claims from trusted friends and influencers in the natural wellness space about 5G causing cancer and weakening the human immune system over time.

Calvin was also concerned about a deadly new coronavirus tearing through China. He suspected it could be part of a covert conspiracy to mandate harmful vaccines down the road. Gemma, a young Chinese woman, cut in. The virus was something they should all be afraid of, she said. Her parents back home were living a nightmare: Hundreds of millions of people in different parts of the country were trapped inside their houses under draconian lockdown measures. Flights were grounded. Police drones surveilled the streets. Entire cities were quarantined—some literally barricaded and guarded. Rule-breakers faced criminal penalties.

Alice was horrified. A whirlwind of questions raced through her mind. *What if the coronavirus became a threat inside the United States? Dawson was away at college; would she still be able to see him? What about her dad? He lived on a tropical island with his wife; what if the virus made its way there? How would they escape?*

Christopher, whom she called her "beloved," tried to gently calm her down. As an executive at a life sciences firm, he was a grounded, level-headed voice of reason who was always well informed, and the reports he'd read said the fatality rate was extremely low. But on March 11, with more than 118,000 infections and a spiking total of well over four thousand deaths worldwide, the World Health Organization declared a global pandemic. Four days later, Bay Area officials issued a shelter-in-place order. Then the rest of America closed down.

Everything Alice had feared was turning into a reality. She went into fight-or-flight mode—and there was nowhere to flee. In a mad dash to the grocery store, she filled her cart with as many nonperishable food items as she could fit, then individually sanitized each one. Basic necessities like toilet paper had already been completely cleared out by frenzied crowds stockpiling anything and everything they could.

Pacing back and forth across her living room floor, Alice devoured news stories as if her life depended on it. For all she knew, it did. She needed to know how to protect herself and her loved ones. Doctors in Italy, she read, were so inundated with patients that they were forced to choose which of them to save and which to abandon. It was usually the least likely to survive—the elderly—who were left to die, scared and alone until their lungs gave out. Alice sobbed as she thought of her parents and her grandmother, who was ninety-seven. She was even worried for Christopher, who, at fifteen years older than her, was nearing sixty.

There was no cure for Covid-19, no clear understanding of how it spread, and no indicators of what the long-term effects could be for those who survived. The guidance Alice was hearing seemed to change from one day to the next and from one source to another. Experts lined up on cable news oscillated between declaring that the crisis was overblown to warning that it was just getting started. The CDC appeared to be making rules up on the fly. First, face masks were discouraged; then, suddenly, they were compulsory—at which point they'd been scooped up by price gougers. Trump regularly contradicted his administration's own infectious disease specialist, Dr. Anthony Fauci. And not long after his initial assessment that Covid was "like a flu," he did a 180: "It's not the flu. It's vicious."

Alice's existential dread had erupted from a looming angst over "someday" threats into a debilitating panic over what would happen tomorrow. As with fear of the dark or deep bodies of water, it was the *not knowing* that was the hardest. She was desperate for answers.

In May, she got them.

Truth in the Darkness

Within hours of its release, *Plandemic* went viral.

The slickly produced documentary was a tall, chilling tale of how "the minions of Big Pharma" had muzzled sixty-two-year-old Judy Mikovits— "one of the most accomplished scientists of her generation," it proclaimed— from exposing their dirty secrets for nearly a decade. Now, at last, she had a platform to speak out, even if it meant risking her life. It was a risk she was willing to take, she said: People deserved to know the real story behind Covid-19 before it was too late. (*Plandemic* was only the beginning; for the rest, they could buy her new book.)

"So," the film began in an interview, "you made a discovery that conflicted with the agreed-upon narrative?"

"Correct," Mikovits, small and silver-haired, nodded with a meek smile.

"And for that, they did everything in their powers to destroy your life?"

Her face fell.

"Correct."

The creator and on-camera interviewer was none other than Mikki Willis, the Sanders-supporting filmmaker Alice had followed online and respected for years. Alice watched in shock as Mikovits accused Fauci, Bill Gates, and other powerful "forces" of what would amount to genocide: planning the pandemic—which had already killed more than a quarter-million people—in order to profit off the eventual vaccines. Alice could feel the distress in Willis's frowning blue eyes as Mikovits told him that these same forces were withholding lifesaving treatments from the public.

By the end, Alice's head was spinning. It all sounded legitimate. Big Pharma had a long history of unscrupulous crimes, like wittingly misleading the medical community about the dangers of opioids in order to fuel and capitalize on what became a deadly epidemic. But Christopher said *Plandemic* was just "a bunch of fearmongering and conspiracy theories" being promoted on the right to steer blame for America's Covid failures away from Trump, who'd been sinking in the polls. Alice didn't know what to believe. She trusted Willis. She also trusted her beloved. She *hated* Trump.

While she bounced off the walls in restless trepidation, Christopher moped around the house in a funk. Prepandemic, he had traveled monthly for work. He hated being cooped up and he missed his own adult children. Then, in an atrocity caught on camera for all to bear witness, George Floyd was murdered. Watching a Black man wheezing in agony under the knee of a white police officer like a dog in the street for eight minutes and forty-six seconds left Christopher speechless and shaking. He was, like much of the rest of white America, coming to understand that living under the threat of state violence was still part of the Black American experience. Alice had already spent years educating herself about racist police brutality in the United States and was heartbroken—though not surprised in the least—by what had happened. But Christopher was newly ashamed of his country and his own blind spots.

Confined under the same roof day in and day out with no end to the crisis in sight, the two of them were smothering each other and drifting apart at the same time. Their clashing hysteria and depression were a disaster waiting to happen. Before long, it did, on a miserable Saturday afternoon. They blew up at one another in a tearful screaming match that had been weeks in the making.

Alice needed space to ground herself. She went upstairs to their room, shut the door, and crawled into bed. Then she opened Facebook on her phone and saw a message from her friend of fifteen years, Tracy, who was also a Sanders supporter. For the past couple weeks, Tracy had been going on about a ten-part docuseries on YouTube called *The Fall of the Cabal*, which had apparently left her questioning everything she thought she knew about the way the world worked. She was aching for someone to talk to about it, she said. Alice had been too preoccupied with global calamity to watch, but today she welcomed the distraction.

It began with a silent text-on-screen message that instantly inspired her trust to a degree: "I urge you to accept nothing as the truth. Please do your own research and double-check everything I present to you. That is the only way to truly wake up and become an independent thinker."

Overnight, Alice's life changed.

The videos struck a chord right off the bat with heart-wrenching images from California wildfires of years gone by. The creator and narrator, Janet Ossebaard, an intelligent-sounding Dutch woman who claimed that she'd had a "leftist" upbringing, pointed out that completely blackened, scorched houses in the blazes' path of destruction were surrounded by curiously green, unburnt trees. Alice had never noticed that before. She examined the photos closely. They looked real and unedited. *What the hell?*

"Are you sure these are ordinary forest fires?" Ossebaard asked.

It wasn't clear what, exactly, she was implying; however, a quick Google search would have surfaced news articles with the hardly extraordinary truth: Gusting winds had pushed the burning embers along so quickly that they had never had a chance to rise into the trees, many of which had regionally adapted over time to survive wildfires by developing thicker bark and higher, moister foliage. But Ossebaard repeatedly stressed the need to avoid the mainstream media at all costs, claiming that it was a mouthpiece for rich and powerful elites. (A little research into her, too, might have raised some cause for skepticism: The fifty-four-year-old had spent decades trying to prove that crop circles were crafted by supernatural forces.)

If viewers wanted to know what was *really* going on, Ossebaard urged, they needed to figure it out for themselves using alternative, independent sources, as she herself had done. Even fact-checking organizations were not to be trusted.

The entire hours-long series followed the same pattern: Again and again, with striking visuals, Ossebaard made outright false or misleading claims and insinuations—like her conflation of geoengineering aerosols, a proposed intervention to reduce global warming, with "chemtrails," toxic chemicals rumored to be sprayed by airplanes to harm the public. Then she chastised the media for failing to report "the truth."

Some parts left Alice uncomfortably second-guessing her own beliefs, especially when Ossebaard acknowledged that she too had initially dismissed certain ideas as mere "conspiracy theories." The videos also raised new suspicions surrounding issues that Alice was already familiar with, including spyware surveilling private citizens and the monopolistic corporate power of Monsanto, a genetically modified crops producer.

Although certain points gave Alice pause—such as when Ossebaard emphasized that the French phrase "J'aime les enfants" (I love children) was similar to the name of James Alefantis, who owned the pizzeria at the center of the "Pizzagate" child-trafficking rumors—many of the bombshells were as staggering to her as those unburnt trees. The deeper into the series she got, the more outrageous the claims became, but they were stacking in her mind like building blocks: *If this one crazy thing was true, couldn't this other, slightly crazier thing also be true?*

The craziest was the existence of an "institutionalized pedophile ring" inside which a "huge" number of kids were brutalized and harvested for their blood. Beyond the gruesome absurdity of it all, Alice thought, the notion that something like that could be kept under wraps was implausible. But then again . . . for two decades unabated, billionaire financier Jeffrey Epstein had trafficked girls as young as eleven for sex on his private island in the Caribbean, all the while hosting members of the highest ranks of society. That wasn't just a conspiracy theory.

Behind this plague of depravity, Ossebaard said, was a singular, all-powerful enemy: the Deep State Cabal. And working to end its reign of corruption in a day of justice to be known as "the Great Awakening" was a grassroots movement of dreamers called QAnon.

As Alice listened in awe to Ossebaard describing the inner workings of both groups, and QAnon's battle to radically shift the balance of power in society, she realized that she'd heard this story before—even lived it. She just hadn't made it to the happy ending.

The specifics laid out in *The Fall of the Cabal* were more extreme—vastly so—but many of the themes were spot on: A rigged system. Suffering innocents. Billionaire elites. Corporate oligarchs. Top-down conspiracy. Information gatekeepers. The military-industrial complex. Revolutionary justice for the everyman. And, above all, hope for the future.

"Q portrays a better world without wars, treason, and corruption," Ossebaard said, bringing an involuntary smile to Alice's face. "And whether you like it or not, the task to get there has been put in the hands of Donald J. Trump."

Wait. *Trump?!*

Her smile vanished.

"Now, normally when I say this to people, I get the most vicious of looks," Ossebaard explained. "Thanks to the mainstream media . . . people believe Trump to be a narcissistic dictator. But hey, let's talk some facts here, shall we?"

The president wasn't the monster the press made him out to be; Ossebaard was adamant about this. Following orders from above, journalists twisted his words, concealed his accomplishments, and blamed him for everything, she said, including the raging societal divides that the media itself had stoked. She proceeded to list off Trump's many apparent feats that had purportedly gotten not a peep of news coverage, including signing a major bill to clean up the oceans—a cause near and dear to Alice's environmentalist heart.

Alice shook her head. *Nope. No way that's true.* When it came to the planet, Trump was an enemy, not an advocate, and his army of America First fanatics certainly didn't seem to care about the earth or its creatures, so why would he do that? She left YouTube to do a quick Google search just to prove herself right, then gasped at the results.

Trump had authorized $50 million over five years to go toward the prevention and removal of marine debris. Why *hadn't* she heard about that in the news?

She thought about Sanders. In scathing condemnations of the "corporate media," he had accused major news conglomerates and legacy outlets like the Jeff Bezos–owned *Washington Post* of targeting him with overly critical, misrepresentative coverage. He was a threat to the bosses' private interests, he had implied, so they wielded their power to turn the narrative—and public opinion—against him . . .

Alice raised her hand to her mouth in a moment of sobering revelation. Was the same thing really happening to Trump? And had it worked on *her*?

It was 12:51 a.m. and she was wide awake, sitting straight upright next to her now-slumbering beloved, her face illuminated by the glow of her iPhone. On her dresser, she could make out the little blue and white figurine owl that she had crafted out of wax and tiny plastic beads earlier that year. It symbolized seeing truth in the darkness, like the wise, nocturnal owl. She wrote back to Tracy about *The Fall of the Cabal* with trembling fingers.

"Holy fucking shit . . . could all that be true???!!!!"

If it was, it would mean that the evils humanity was up against were far worse than Alice and her fellow "Berniecrats" had grasped. But it would also mean that real change was *still* possible, even though Sanders couldn't get his foot in the door to make it happen.

Trump was already in.

There it was, peeking out through the clouds of despair once again: the more beautiful world her heart knew was possible.

Pandemonium

Under ordinary circumstances, it would have taken more than a docuseries on YouTube to flip Alice's political worldview upside down. But 2020 was no ordinary year, and what happened to Alice was no isolated occurrence. Against the backdrop of an exceptionally contentious presidential election season, Americans faced the deadliest public health catastrophe in a century, the most dire recession since the Great Depression, the worst California wildfires in recorded history, and a nationwide uprising for racial justice that exploded to the fore of the culture wars.

This perfect storm of chaos did two things: It made everyday people like Alice more vulnerable—and it made disinformation peddlers like QAnon more powerful.

In times of unrest and uncertainty throughout history, people have turned to conspiracy theories—some valid, many not—to make sense of what was happening. Cold War–fueled fears of communist espionage gave rise to McCarthyism. 9/11 was followed by sweeping suspicion that the U.S. government had played a part in the carnage. In the bigger picture of America's long, waxing and waning track record of mass delusions, and despite claims to the contrary, the Covid-19 pandemic was not an unprecedented era of paranoia. But on social media, where the average American spent more than five hundred hours in 2020, falsehoods spread like viruses themselves. And when the world shut down, people's immunity against them deteriorated.

Tens of millions of Americans abruptly lost their jobs or were forced to work or study from home, where they remained in isolation for months upon months as end dates to the lockdowns were extended again and again. Like Alice, many were lonely and scared and had little to do in their downtime but go online, where a firehose of information blending truths, opinions, and lies awaited them. It was, as the World Health Organization declared, an "infodemic." It was also a race against time: Key facts behind the outbreak were slow to emerge as scientists scrambled to study a mutating coronavirus previously unknown in humans. But as people's anxieties over losing their income, businesses, personal freedoms, and even loved ones soared, their patience rapidly dwindled. With QAnon, they didn't have to wait. It had an explanation for everything.

Amplified by social media algorithms and echoed by a cacophony of right-wing media stars, pundits, and politicians, QAnon influencers swooped in to fill the information void with their own twisted version of events: A cabal of liberal, globalist elites was plotting a New World Order. Covid-19—whether it was a Chinese bioweapon, akin to the flu, or something else entirely—was part of the elites' scheme to subdue the masses through fear. They inflated death tolls, cranked out alarmist news coverage, and silenced dissenters through social media censorship. Lockdowns, curfews, mask mandates, and social distancing rules were oppressive measures to yield public subservience. The same was true of the coming vaccines, which could also be tools to implant location-tracking microchips or to wipe out humanity—only time would tell. Cabal-commanded telecom giants were rolling out 5G technology to make people sick. Black Lives Matter rallies and protests in the wake of Floyd's death (a false flag) weren't really about racial justice at all; they were orchestrated by antifa to stymie Trump's rising support among the Black electorate.

Everything—*everything*—could be contorted to fit the conspiracy theory.

That was the lens through which Alice and myriad others came to view their suddenly frightening, uncertain world. More than a quarter of Americans believed the microchipping theory at the time. Close to a third thought that the virus was "purposely created and released" and that the threat it posed was being "exaggerated by political groups" who sought to damage Trump.

Trump leaned into these sentiments without evidence to support them, going so far as to suggest that he was being sabotaged by members of his own administration. His reference to the State Department as "the Deep State Department" during a press briefing provoked what appeared to be an incredulous facepalm from Dr. Fauci, who, to Trump's ire, had already repeatedly publicly corrected him. (A Cornell University study would later find the president to be the single largest superspreader of Covid-19-related falsehoods.)

With a simple retweet asserting that it was "time to #FireFauci"— originally posted by a QAnon promoter—Trump flicked a match and sparked an inferno. Just like that, the crisis had its villain: a five-foot-seven, seventy-nine-year-old veteran immunologist from Brooklyn with an accent to match who'd served every president since Ronald Reagan. More importantly, though, Fauci was a face and a name to attach to the elite, anti-Trump forces supposedly conspiring from the shadows, giving people a clear enemy to oppose as they stewed in their collective powerlessness.

Fox News anchors quickly ginned up populist suspicion about Fauci's motivations. Despite the strictly advisory nature of his role, Tucker Carlson likened him to a "dictator," while Sean Hannity suggested that he was handing the Democrats exactly what they desired: "massive restrictions with no end in sight." The QAnon–to–Fox News pipeline was spewing all sorts of Far Right disinformation into the mainstream discourse— including that Black Lives Matter was a front to launder money for Democrats, as repeated by prime-time host Jesse Watters and retweeted by Trump.

The impact was clear: As the narrative that Fauci had a leftist agenda to undermine his boss and devastate the economy took off, and his shifting public health advice was construed as nefarious rather than adaptive, polls found trust in him souring among millions of Americans.

Alice was one of them. Christopher looked at her like she was losing her mind, but she hadn't felt this lucid in ages. Everything was *finally* making sense.

"Someone who does what he does . . . I would put it in the category of crimes against humanity," she wrote on Facebook of Fauci. "Justice will catch up to him. And in the meanwhile, he will need security."

He did. Fauci and his wife and daughters were so inundated with death threats that they required a round-the-clock security detail.

. . .

Inside the QAnon labyrinth, opposition was celebrated as validation. So the less Alice trusted the press, the more she trusted the people it debunked and criticized. If the media said someone was wrong, she believed, then he or she must *really* be onto something.

This kind of thinking was encouraged by Trump and others on the right more broadly, creating epistemic pandemonium. Joined by homeopaths, miracle healers, and fellow pushers of pseudoscience, a groundswell of discredited scientists and fringe doctors came out of the woodwork as Covid truthers. They proudly identified as independent thinkers pulling away from the herd (often while clamoring for donations or shilling unproven remedies). Their appeal, in turn, generally hinged upon their status as dissenters rather than the legitimacy of their dissent, while their professional reprimands, malpractice complaints, and fact-checked Facebook posts were touted as badges of honor.

That was how Alice had come to see Judy Mikovits. Almost immediately, *Plandemic* had made her a star—a hero—and her book a bestseller. Perhaps its biggest selling point was her shocking backstory: Her breakout research paper about chronic fatigue had been retracted, and she had been arrested, fired, and sued for stealing research materials from her employer. It was all part of a plot to muzzle her, she claimed. So when *Plandemic* was scrubbed from social media for promoting false information, Alice was convinced that Mikovits and Willis were being censored by the Cabal for unveiling the truth. And when Facebook, YouTube, and Twitter purged QAnon from their sites, she was proud to be part of the movement.

The bans did little to curb the spread of QAnon's conspiracy theories. By that point, anons had already seeded them inside other communities on those platforms, like parenting networks and wellness groups, where fears about child trafficking, grooming, 5G, and vaccines resonated deeply. The damage was done: Mommy bloggers and healthy-living influencers started becoming QAnon evangelists themselves, bringing the falsehoods back to their trusting, parasocially attached audiences.

Compelled in many cases by a sense of maternal duty, women—in particular, suburban white women—were flooding into the movement in such large numbers it gave rise to the term *QAmom*, reminiscent of the "Mama Grizzlies" of Tea Party populism. As the pandemic intensified, anons co-opted the slogan "Save Our Children," the name of a political coalition formed in 1977 by Anita Bryant, a white American singer and mother, in her crusade against gay schoolteachers, whom she believed to be potential child molesters. The timing couldn't have been better: QAnon's messaging hit home inside quarantined households nationwide as the already-disproportionate burden of caregiving on women dramatically increased. It also promised community, purpose, and excitement at a time when many friends and hobbies were out of reach. Not least of all, being a QAmom could be empowering, with the self-serving allure of identifying as a protector of the innocent while projecting the image of virtuous white femininity through digital activism.

It was stunning to behold. Between vegan smoothie recipes, kiddie craft ideas, yoga videos, and filtered selfies, social media starlets and local soccer moms were suddenly posting about Bill Gates slurping down babies' blood or cooking up killer Covid shots.

"[The Deep State has] been trying to depopulate humanity for a very long time," one influencer-turned-conspiracy theorist, a "mindset" guru with beachy blond waves and a Yorkie named Peanut, declared to her one hundred thousand Instagram followers. She had pivoted from posting brand-sponsored health and beauty product endorsements to selling QAnon merchandise, including baby-blue water bottles displaying the text "WWG1WGA" and "Save Our Children." After labeling herself an expert on government operations, "frequencies and energies," and the human immune system, she took a sip of her iced vanilla latte and added: "I've been learning so much crazy stuff lately, you guys. This is why we have diseases. Legit."

In its wildest fantasy, QAnon couldn't have dreamed up better messengers. They repackaged and redistributed its propaganda using pretty pastel colors, delicate fonts, and emoji-laden messages, like "It's time to #WakeUp, mamas!" With their aesthetic touch, even the most ludicrous claims could become palatable—and, coming from them, *believable*.

Alice wanted to spread the word of Q too.

She wanted to get back on Photoshop and create bright pop art flyers to slip into mailboxes all over town to let people know that they didn't need to be afraid anymore: *It was all going to be okay.* The Great Awakening was coming. Maybe they'd cry tears of comfort and joy, as she had. Or maybe . . . they'd think she was crazy.

Instead, Alice began by sharing a Q Drop on Facebook, to start gradually sprinkling QAnon's ideas into people's newsfeeds. Printed atop the ethereal image of a heart emitting twinkling stars and beams of light in muted purples, oranges, and yellows, it could have easily been mistaken for a run-of-the-mill inspirational quote.

> Division is man-made.
> Division is designed to keep you powerless.
> Division is designed to keep you fighting each other.
> Division is designed to keep you enslaved.
> The Narrative Has You.

5

WHITE WORLD

—Kendra—

Tayshia and Kendra stood in front of their new school and begged their mother not to make them go inside.

"What if there are bullies?" they squealed. "What if nobody likes us?"

It was the spring of 1990, already partway through the school year. Tayshia, in fourth grade, and Kendra, in third, were dreading being the new kids. They felt ridiculous in the itchy sweaters and matching plaid skirts they were required to wear, and wanted nothing more than to go home. But their mother tugged them along by their hands, up the steps and through the tall glass doors.

Students and teachers streamed through the hallway as the sisters timidly trailed behind her, their eyes flitting around the building in search of an escape route. They quickly noticed that they were the only Black people in sight. It was nothing like their old inner-city school, from which they'd been plucked against their will upon receiving special state vouchers for underprivileged students covering their tuition here.

Tayshia and Kendra were used to change; it was already a defining feature of their childhood. But this would be a big one.

Their family moved all the time, cycling through Milwaukee's lowest-income neighborhoods. Before they could read, the girls knew that a paper taped to their door meant that it was time to start packing again. Sometimes they'd sleep at family friends' places; once in a while they'd stay on rollout cots or bunk beds at the Salvation Army shelter. At their last house, a multifamily home in a Laotian enclave, they had watched in horror as their neighbor bled to death on the street in broad daylight. He'd been stabbed by his wife, who worked with Tayshia and Kendra's mother, Brandy, as a packer at the Ambrosia Chocolate factory.

A single parent caring for the girls and their two little cousins on her own, Brandy worked a second job at Kentucky Fried Chicken to keep food on the table. She was usually gone sixteen hours a day, leaving before 5 a.m. and returning at around 9 p.m. Even though nine-year-old Tayshia was the oldest by just eleven months, she was in charge of taking care of the other children whenever they were home alone.

When they were hungry, Tayshia would heat up pastries with the little white toaster oven her mom taught her how to use. The brown sugar ones were her favorite, except on the rare occasions that they'd have actual Pop-Tarts in the cupboard. Some days she'd make cereal with water and powdered milk, sneaking out to ask neighbors for sugar if her baby cousins refused to eat it. Another go-to was a snack she called "cheese bread," her version of a grilled cheese sandwich, which was just cheese on an untoasted slice of bread with a squiggle of ketchup. They didn't have a washing machine, so she would clean clothes in the bathtub and hang them up to dry. Brandy's KFC uniform reeked so strongly of grease that it made Tayshia feel sick to her stomach, but she was still excited when her mom came home with Chicken Little sandwiches for dinner.

In the snippets of their childhood when the kids could just be kids, they liked to play jump rope, four square, and hopscotch around whatever neighborhood they were living in at the time, never straying too far from home or staying out past dark. Tayshia and Kendra told each other everything, as little girls do. They were so close in age that they called themselves "twin best friends." Kendra's birthday was in late July, but because money was extra tight by the end of the month, the sisters celebrated their special days together on Tayshia's birthday, in mid-August. It was their favorite time of year. Going to this new, strange school was less scary knowing that they had each other.

Their first field trip was a multigrade visit to the Milwaukee County Zoo. After filing off the bus with the other students, Tayshia and Kendra were surprised to see their mom waiting for them in the zoo parking lot. A teacher had called Brandy because the girls had come to school without lunches again, so she had rushed over from work with a bag of McDonald's. Inside were two Big Macs, an unexpected treat on an already exciting day.

As Tayshia and Kendra wandered past animals from all over the world just beyond arm's reach, their fearful shyness gave way to unguarded wonder. They had never been to the zoo before. They oohed and ahhed and giggled playfully with the other students, temporarily distracted from the sense of otherness they'd been feeling since that first day. But toward the end of the trip, as their group spilled into the primate exhibit, an older boy started laughing at them.

"Look! It's your mom!" he shouted, pointing at one of the apes before jumping around and scratching his armpits, to the great amusement of his peers.

In an instant, Tayshia and Kendra's joy evaporated. Brandy was overweight; they thought the boy was making fun of her size. But the racism they experienced as little Black girls in a white world became impossible to miss as time went on—like when kids teased that they might melt into chocolate milk, or when a man leaned out his truck window, shouted, "Go home!" and chucked a beer can at Kendra's feet while they were waiting for the bus.

For Tayshia, the most traumatizing incident happened one afternoon during science class. The students were crafting little devices with wires and other materials to learn how batteries worked. Out of nowhere, a boy came up behind her and twisted his contraption into her hair—*hard*. She could feel her face turn hot with a flush of embarrassment while she tried, frantically, to wriggle it loose as her classmates crowded around.

Tayshia loved her hair. She had been growing it out for so long that it hung down to the middle of her back. Brandy had styled it into thin, sleek braids with white and purple beads that clicked when Tayshia walked and made her feel pretty. The teacher, a slight, blonde woman, tried tugging the device out too, provoking laughter from around the classroom. So she sent Tayshia to see the principal, a bald man in a tweed jacket who always had a sour expression on his face. He attempted to remove it with one quick yank downward, causing Tayshia to yelp in pain. Then, before she knew what was happening behind her, he grabbed a big pair of scissors from his desk and cut off a fistful of her braids.

Tayshia burst into tears as they fell to the ground. She dropped to her hands and knees to gather her beads as they scattered in every direction, gasping between sobs as she tucked them into her socks and skirt pockets.

That night, Brandy had to cut her hair all the way up to her chin to even it out while she wailed in protest.

For years, Tayshia and Kendra traveled back and forth between jarringly different realities. Their days were spent surrounded by white kids whose parents would pick them up in Audis and BMWs to dash them off to dance class or soccer practice. Then the two of them would bus home to food stamps and middle-of-the-night gunshots on the impoverished north side of Milwaukee, one of the most hypersegregated cities in America. It ingrained firmly into their young brains that life wasn't fair for people with dark skin.

The sisters had been living through the same struggle day by day and side by side for as long as they'd both been alive, but that grim realization sent them careening down drastically divergent paths into adulthood.

It lit a fire in Tayshia, who decided that she was going to make the world a better place for people like her. On her eighteenth birthday, she took three buses to City Hall to register to vote. She was her mother's daughter in that regard. Before life had gotten in the way, Brandy had been an activist for her community and for the planet, and she encouraged her daughters and little niece and nephew to stand up for what they believed in too. So after completing college in Michigan, Tayshia got involved in local progressive politics in the state, working to help elect candidates committed to racial justice. It felt like her calling. She worked different jobs to pay the bills and spent her free hours knocking on doors, starting petitions, setting up meetings with public representatives, and, eventually, organizing Black Lives Matter rallies, emerging as a prominent activist in her area.

Fighting for change gave Tayshia hope for the future. But in Kendra's view, her sister was a dreamer and she was a realist, she'd say. Any hope she had seemed to be doused by the time Brandy, the hardest-working person she'd ever known, had a stroke before fifty that slowly killed her, cutting far too short a life of unrelenting hardship and disadvantage. The only change Kendra spoke of was that things were getting *worse*. And they were: When Brandy had entered the workforce, the median income of a Black Milwaukee resident was just 58.3 percent of a white resident's.

By the time Kendra did, that number had fallen to 49.6 percent. Then it kept falling, reflecting a nationally widening racial income disparity.

What was the point of trying to make something of herself in a world that was stacked against her? She had endured enough disappointment for one lifetime. So instead of fantasizing about positive change, Kendra found solace in a web of antiestablishment conspiracy theories that vindicated her seething distrust in the government and cemented her understanding that the system was rigged—that she'd never stood a chance.

Disinformation and the Disaffected

Kendra and her sons lived in a small, shoebox-shaped house with faded yellow-green vinyl siding in the outskirts of Detroit. A gravel-covered alley stretched along the right side, past the little chain-link-fenced yard out back. Tayshia was just ten minutes down the road, not wanting to be far from the boys, seven-year-old Jonah and thirteen-year-old Jayden. She stopped by at least once a week to check in on them and to say hi to her sister, though the two had drifted apart over the years.

During a visit on an overcast Saturday afternoon in early August of 2020, Jonah was telling Aunt Tayshia all about his new battle royale video game, *Apex Legends*. He wanted to play, but his mom was using the TV to watch YouTube again. It was a flat-screen smart TV that Kendra had purchased for that exact purpose. She was between jobs, so she'd sit in front of it day in and day out, bingeing videos that purported to unveil "Deep State" subterfuge. Though the specific subject matter varied, they all sounded more or less the same to Tayshia. Each projected a common message: *You've been wronged.*

Kendra's repertoire of conspiracy theories had been building for a long time. She and her boyfriend were convinced that his severely autistic teenage son, from a previous relationship, had been injected with the disorder via a pediatric vaccine in a covert experiment on Black babies. Following the 2015 death of Sandra Bland, the young Black woman found hanging from a garbage-bag noose in her jail cell three days after she was pulled over for a minor traffic violation, Kendra insisted that Bland was already dead in her mugshot (her eyes having been propped open by cops who'd killed her before she ever reached the jail).

But lately, her beliefs were becoming more extreme and, for Tayshia, more distressing and perplexing. Kendra was now adamant that the police were an ally to the Black community, alongside Trump and the GOP, and that Black Lives Matter was a communist organization.

Tayshia looked over at her sister. At five-foot-two, she was sprawled across the length of her small couch in a pilling gray sweatsuit and a hair bonnet, her head propped on her palm, completely engrossed.

"So, have you registered to vote?" Tayshia asked her, already knowing the answer. She'd spent the morning going door to door around the neighborhood, a predominantly Black area, asking resident after resident that same question. The response was often one of disaffected disinterest: *Why would I bother? My vote doesn't count.*

"I'm gonna vote for Trump!" Jonah interjected, beaming at his mom like a puppy waiting for praise. Kendra smiled, her eyes still on the screen.

Just then, the front door swung open and three of her friends walked in. All were Black. None said hello, so Tayshia introduced herself.

"Oh, this is *her*?" the first to enter, a pretty woman in dark clothes and a baseball cap, asked Kendra. She looked Tayshia up and down.

"Mm-hm, this is her," Kendra smirked, sitting up and rolling her eyes. "My Trump-hating, Biden-supporting sister."

The energy in the house was suddenly tense and uncomfortable. Feeling outnumbered, Tayshia hoped humor would help.

"It's not that I don't like Trump. I just have a problem with people who wanna grab my pussy and not pay me for it!"

Only her nephews laughed.

"Y'all just believe everything y'all hear," the first woman sighed. She sat down on the couch next to Kendra and pulled out her phone. A YouTube video was already queued up.

"Girl, have you seen this?"

It was a viral clip of Stella Immanuel, a Cameroonian American pastor and physician, speaking on the steps of the Supreme Court days earlier. She was flanked by a motley crew of other white-lab-coated doctors who'd all been quietly summoned to D.C. by Republican operatives to deliver a press conference echoing Trump's pandemic talking points.

"I'm here to say it: that America, there is a cure for Covid!" shouted Immanuel, who ran a tiny clinic out of a Houston strip mall. "All this foolishness does not need to happen!"

She was talking about hydroxychloroquine, an antimalarial drug. It had first caught the president's attention after a blockchain investor and a lawyer falsely claiming to be affiliated with Stanford University heralded its use in a non-peer-reviewed paper they self-published as a Google Doc. Their conclusion was based upon a single French study that had tested the drug on twenty-six Covid patients (three of whom had ended up in intensive care, and one of whom had died). But Immanuel argued that no further research was needed.

"Let me tell you something—all you fake doctors out there that tell me, 'Yeah, I want a double-blinded study'—I just tell you: Quit sounding like a computer! 'Double-blinded, double-blinded.' I don't know whether your chips are malfunctioning, but I'm a real doctor!"

Within hours, The Daily Beast had uncovered Immanuel's history of supremely bizarre claims, including that vaginal cysts were caused by having sex with demons while dreaming, and that "reptilians" had infiltrated the U.S. government. Soon after the news broke, a brigade of right-wing media personalities condemned as racist those questioning Immanuel's credibility: "The Left is trying to destroy her," Rush Limbaugh scoffed on his talk radio show. "Wait a minute! I thought it was the right wing that had all the mean-spirited, racist bigots. So I asked myself, 'When are the American people gonna wake up and realize it's the Democrats—it's the American Left—trying to destroy a Black, immigrant, female doctor?' It ain't us," he proclaimed, labeling Democrats "the party of Black Lives Matter."

Kendra and her friends were hanging on Immanuel's every word as she suggested that she might literally be killed for speaking out. (By whom, she didn't say.) Once the clip ended, all four of them had their phones out, each wanting to show off other videos. The boys hovered by the couch, craning their necks to get a look.

What transpired over the next forty minutes felt like a fever dream. Tayshia sat in silence, dumbfounded by what she was hearing as phones changed hands. It was surreal: *Joe Biden rapes and eats children. Covid-19 isn't real. The Jews control the media. George Floyd's killing was a hoax. Trump is a savior for Black people. A war is coming.*

Not only was it crazy . . . some of it was plainly racist and hateful. Tayshia wanted to knock the phone out of Kendra's hand and shake her, like: *Hello? Have you forgotten that you're Black?* Those kinds of conspiracy theories, she thought, were only for the likes of rural, white, gun-toting Baby Boomers who watched Tucker Carlson and lived in fear of immigrant invasions—the sorts of people whose car locks suddenly beeped when she walked by in parking lots. Not her urban, millennial sister of color.

But Kendra and her friends were hardly the outliers Tayshia presumed them to be. Black Americans, as well as Hispanics, were in fact statistically more likely than their white counterparts to believe in QAnon's central claims. And despite its roots in white supremacist lore and antisemitic myths, they were overrepresented in the movement relative to their makeup of the U.S. populace. There was even a small contingent of Asian Americans in QAnon, mainly from the Chinese dissident diaspora, who had found in its online arenas a home for their anger toward the Chinese Communist Party.

The allure of conspiracy theories transcended race and other demographic boxes: At a basic level, they appealed to people with a sense of powerlessness—perceived or valid. White nationalists who felt victimized by multiculturalism had found a boogeyman in George Soros, who they maintained was paying caravans of Central Americans to storm the U.S. border, just as Second Amendment fanatics who felt threatened by gun control efforts routinely accused the Jewish billionaire of bankrolling false-flag shooting sprees. Kendra's belief in the illogical was—comparatively—quite logical.

Minority communities, where feelings of powerlessness were often deeply entrenched from generations of acute, *legitimate* oppression, were ripe for conspiracy theory thinking stemming from rational hypervigilance: an adaptive, deceive-me-once type of learned suspicion to avoid further suffering. In America, for the Black population, such distrust was well founded. Kendra and her boyfriend's belief that his son had been harmed by a racist medical experiment could be backed up by historical fact: The infamous Tuskegee Study of the twentieth century saw the federal government lie to hundreds of Black men with syphilis about the nature of their conditions and wittingly withhold a cure, leaving scores to go blind, lose their minds, and slowly die. Notably, members of marginalized groups weren't just more receptive to rumors about plots to hurt *them;* chronic social devaluation had been found to make them more apprehensive in general.

As made clear by her sister's interest in QAnon falsehoods, Tayshia's perception of the movement as a magnet for white supremacists was an oversimplification. Hateful conspiracy theories could, in effect, both attract and produce bigots. Researchers had newly determined that exposure to conspiracy theories vilifying Jewish people, for instance, could foment antisemitism—and, indirectly, a broader suspicion of other, unimplicated outgroups, such as Arabs and people on welfare.

Tayshia would come to think of QAnon as having a "Clayton Bigsby" effect on Kendra. It was a reference to the Dave Chappelle skit in which the comedian played a blind white supremacist who didn't know that he was Black. But in Kendra's case, it wasn't her Blackness that she was blind to; it was, to Tayshia, her anti-Blackness.

Carefully Targeted Lies

Kendra pulled up one last video.

"Watch this," she said. "Candace tells it like it is."

From her phone emanated the mile-a-minute voice of Candace Owens, a glamorous, unflinching YouTuber-turned-conservative firebrand. To critics, she was a Black apologist for white supremacy; to fans like Kendra, she was a brilliant martyr unmasking the truth. Over the past year or two, Owens's sardonic, Limbaugh-esque vlogs had reshaped Kendra's understanding of Trumpism and what it meant to be Black in modern America, helping to lift her from a state of apolitical despondence into aggrieved conservatism.

Both in their thirties, they had more in common than Kendra likely knew. Owens's childhood was shrouded in poverty as well. Her family of six had rented a three-bedroom apartment in a dilapidated building crawling with cockroaches in southern Connecticut. As a student, Owens, too, was a target of racist bullies. Three girls were charged in a hate crime after beating her and berating her with racial epithets. And, in what became a nationally publicized scandal at the time, a group of boys—including the mayor's son—left her a series of voicemails calling her a "fucking nigger" and threatening to kill her. (Owens's family sued the school board for failing to protect her, triggering online trolls to call her a race-baiter.)

Kendra also likely didn't know how fervently—or recently—her new icon had disavowed the MAGA principles that she now appeared to so boldly champion. After leaving Connecticut, Owens had journeyed into progressive activism. She launched a blog in 2015 where writers penned a mishmash of liberal essays and woke musings, including comparisons of Trump to Hitler. In one post, Owens herself wrote of "good news": Republicans would "eventually die off (peacefully in their sleep, we hope), and then we can get right on with the OBVIOUS social change that needs to happen, IMMEDIATELY."

It was only in 2016, after the crushing public downfall of Owens's next social justice venture—a website people could use to essentially dox their trolls, to make them "think twice before they exercise their First Amendment rights online as a means to hurt others," in her words—that she abruptly changed her tune. In what she would later describe as "hit pieces" by "the Left," mainstream news outlets pointed out her project's glaring flaws, like how it could easily misidentify innocent people and ruin their lives. The overwhelmingly critical coverage precipitated Owens's sudden "red-pill moment," she subsequently recalled, steering her into the open arms of a political Right keen to have an influential woman of color sing its praises to other Black Americans—a pivotal voting bloc long out of reach.

Thus began a thriving symbiotic relationship. Owens's time came to be spent pinballing between GOP fundraisers, Fox News sit-downs, and college campus events, where she would rebuke Democrats as the true anti-Black party and mock Black Lives Matter activists, once calling them "a bunch of whiny toddlers" who were "pretending to be oppressed for attention." Within a couple years, Trump had dubbed Owens "the hottest thing out there right now." She also founded BLEXIT, a foundation encouraging Black liberals to cross over and vote red, grossing more than $7 million in its second year. Meanwhile, online, she batted around fevered disinformation, such as the debunked allegation that Bill Gates had used "African tribal children" as "human guinea pigs" for unapproved vaccinations.

Now here Owens was on Kendra's phone, repeating QAnon's false claim that Soros was paying Black people to protest in honor of Floyd. (In fact, it would soon be revealed that BLEXIT was paying travel and lodging costs for Black people to attend Trump campaign events.) Watching in quiet dismay over her sister's shoulder, Tayshia saw two women consumed by conspiracy theories: one cooking them up while becoming wealthy and powerful, the other devouring them whole while becoming angry and hateful.

When Kendra watched Owens declare that Black people were tired of being manipulated and lied to, approvingly nodding along at her screen, she didn't seem to see the irony in it. Not only were marginalized communities in some ways uniquely susceptible to conspiracy theories—they were also specifically, aggressively targeted with them by people like Owens and other partisan interests seeking to activate or extinguish their voting power as a group.

The Internet Research Agency, Russia's army of online trolls, targeted "no single group of Americans" more than Black people in its infamous information warfare operation to install Trump in 2016, a bipartisan senate intelligence committee investigation found. Foreign agents disguised as Black Lives Matter activists flooded social media with fake news and propaganda to deter them from supporting Hillary Clinton, such as a YouTube video titled "HILLARY RECEIVED $20,000 DONATION FROM KKK TOWARDS HER CAMPAIGN," or to convince them that their votes were worthless.

Already, in 2020, partisan lies exploiting trauma among exiles of communist and socialist regimes were ripping through Florida at such staggering volumes that state representative Debbie Mucarsel-Powell would soon call on the FBI to investigate the eruption of "far-right conspiracy theories relating to 'QAnon' or other fringe ideologies designed to manipulate Latino voters." Trump would even launch a Spanish YouTube ad in the crucial swing state making the explosive false claim that Biden was the preferred candidate of Venezuela's Chavistas.

Campaigns to manipulate minorities as political currency often weren't successful in deceiving them, to be sure. But the sheer onslaught of false and misleading information made it ever more difficult to discern what to believe at all, widely eroding trust in even credible sources, and laying the groundwork for groups like QAnon to ensnare people like Kendra. The proof was staring Tayshia in the face, grumbling from the couch about protests against police brutality in the wake of Floyd's murder.

"Black Lives Matter can kiss my Black ass," Kendra muttered to her friends.

Tayshia's heart ached. She thought back to the little girl she had called her "twin best friend" while they were growing up in Milwaukee—back to the beer can hurled at Kendra's feet when she was just eight years old—and was at a loss.

"Don't you think your life matters?" she asked, breaking her silence.

Everyone turned to look at her.

"All lives matter!" Kendra snapped. "And you know, I've been pulled over by the police and I've never been shot. If they all just did what they were told they'd be fine."

Tayshia couldn't believe the words coming out of her sister's mouth. It was as if her conspiracy theories had rewritten her own lived history in her mind.

"You're one of the lucky ones. Remember that. What happens if things turn south for you one day, who's gonna stick up for you then? God forbid, what if it happens to the boys?"

"Uh-uh. 'Cause I teach my boys to put their hands up and be quiet."

"That's not how it works," Tayshia sputtered, raising her hands to her temples. "We grew up in the same neighborhood. We've seen it happen before our eyes. How could you forget that?"

"I didn't forget," Kendra said. "I just understand it different now."

6

DIGITAL SOLDIERS

—Matt—

In a way, Matt's road to radicalization began with a mysterious pain in his groin.

It was early 2015, months before Donald Trump descended his golden escalator to announce his candidacy for president, and years before QAnon was born in the online fever swamps. Matt and Andrea had settled into a routine of happy chaos familiar to any parents of two kids under six. On sunny days they'd bring Abby and Hayden to the playground near their home in small-town Missouri; once a week they'd escape for low-key date nights after work while Grandma and Grandpa babysat. Sundays were for church.

Then one morning, that all changed. Matt woke up feeling as if someone had tried to rip his left leg right off in his sleep, like a kid with a Ken doll. Andrea took him to the ER for an ultrasound, the first of many scans that would come back inconclusive over the months to follow. As excruciating as it was baffling, the sensation persisted so intensely that even sitting down for more than a few minutes at a time was unbearable. Matt's only relief came from lying back with his legs elevated above his waist. This mostly confined him to an old beige recliner for restless days and nights on end as his medical team of orthopedists, urologists, and a lineup of other specialists struggled to produce a diagnosis.

Day-to-day life devolved into a series of challenges that made Matt feel like a burden on his family. Unable to drive, he relied on Andrea to chauffeur him to one doctor's appointment after another as he rode in the back of their van with his feet up on the collapsed front passenger seat. His job as a producer and morning news announcer with the radio station became physically taxing too, even from home. After hoisting himself from his recliner over to his desk, he'd deliver his rundown of the day's biggest headlines with his leg awkwardly propped up on a stool, grimacing through the pain without breaking his voice. It made his back ache so badly he had to take partial disability leave.

Most of Matt's time was spent idle and immobile in an empty home until the kids got back from school and Andrea returned from work. Video games, a longtime vice, became a necessary distraction from the nothingness. *Assassin's Creed* was one of his favorites: Players joined a brotherhood of warriors who decoded secret messages and solved mysteries throughout their battle to save mankind from the Templars, a shadowy organization of wealthy tyrants. Though the feeling was fleeting, it was nice to be a protagonist for part of his day instead of a guy stuck in a chair. Watching Andrea take on the lion's share of household errands on top of her job as a middle-school librarian sent Matt ricocheting between self-loathing and self-pity. She never once complained, but as she cooked and carried his meals to him, vacuumed around him, and corralled the kids by herself while he sat there in front of the TV, he was sure that her resentment was brewing. He could only say "Thank you, I'm sorry" so many times in a day before it felt meaningless.

Getting up each morning was becoming as big of a mental challenge as a physical one. Days went by when Matt didn't change out of his pajamas as his beard grew long and unkempt. He hated being unable to provide for his family in the ways that he used to: unable to mow the lawn, to squash the spiders, to pick up his children, to romance his wife. Before his injury, he hadn't realized just how integral such simple acts were to his sense of self—or how deep of a hole he would feel without doing them. If he couldn't fulfill his roles as a partner and a parent, who was he? But Matt was unwilling to come to terms with his circumstances and try to adapt; that would require him to accept that his disability could be permanent. Instead, he prayed to God daily for his pain to go away.

Eventually, and suddenly, it did, when in 2018 a nurse practitioner recommended a tricyclic antidepressant that was also commonly prescribed to treat persistent nerve pain. Like the flip of a switch, the world beyond Matt's recliner opened back up. Yet while physically he was better (albeit thirty pounds heavier), psychologically he was scarred. Spending three years in relative social isolation—unsure when or if his life would return to normal, and unable to partake in many of the joys and duties that made him feel whole—had given him an unwelcome preview of the early-pandemic conditions that would help prime so many others for their own descent into conspiracy theories.

Matt was healed but broken, mobile again but stuck all the same. Re-entering the world from a place of badly diminished self-worth was daunting. Andrea had established her own system of doing things around the house without him, and the kids, now nine and six, had stopped waiting for him to play catch and frisbee long ago. They had their friends, it seemed, and didn't need him like they used to. Even the radio station had gotten along just fine without having him working full-time in the job he'd held for sixteen years.

It wasn't long after his recovery that Matt stumbled upon Aunt Carol's Facebook post and down the QAnon rabbit hole, ripe to join an online brotherhood of anons saving humanity from a cabal of real-life Templars.

Raison d'Être

The first QAnon luminary Matt took a shine to was a fellow Christian man named Dave Hayes. Bald and stocky with a blinking gaze and a soothing voice, fifty-six-year-old Hayes was better known as "Praying Medic," a reference to his purported faith-healing abilities. Matt was immediately intrigued. A quiet, wistful part of him had long wondered if faith healing could have saved his father from prostate cancer.

He was also gripped by Hayes's backstory. It began in 2008, when Hayes, who was working as a paramedic in Washington State, had his first dream in twenty-five years. God appeared and started teaching him how to cure people through the power of prayer. Hayes was skeptical, initially, but after nearly a year of dream lessons, it happened: On a blisteringly hot summer day at the deli counter of a Safeway in Tacoma, he cleared his mind while standing in line and was startled by a vision from the Holy Spirit. It was the image of a middle-aged blonde woman along with the word *headaches*. Hayes looked up to find that very woman, an employee at the supermarket, standing before him.

"I'm here to help you get rid of those headaches," he told her, explaining that God had sent him. She gasped and wept with joy; she had been suffering from chronic migraines, she said. He placed his palm on her forehead and commanded, in the name of the Lord, that the "spirit of pain" leave her body. Just like that, she was healed.

In the years since then, Hayes had humbly fixed everything from broken bones to PTSD to cancer in mere seconds with his prayers. Miracles, for him, were all in a day's work.

At least, that was how Hayes told it. And he'd told it a lot: in promotions for his $120 video lessons on "divine healing" and "seeing in the spirit"; in his many self-published books teaching much of the same; on a live-studio audience talk show, which spent seven of twenty-eight minutes airing commercials for his spiritual coaching materials; in his blog posts about the countless alleged beneficiaries of his miracles (who by the final paragraphs were often reduced to tears of gratitude); and in pleas for donations to his tax-exempt online ministry.

The details of Hayes's spiritual journey varied a bit over years of repetition, but the takeaway remained the same: He was a bona fide miracle worker, *and you could be too!*—if you just followed his divine teachings, which were conveniently available for purchase. Hayes wasn't just selling Pentecostal how-to manuals. With grand promises of personal transformation for even the most average of Joes, he was dangling a carrot far more enticing—something people could spend a lifetime chasing: A sense of purpose. A raison d'être. A chance to *be somebody.*

As Praying Medic, Hayes made his living commodifying people's innate longing for a higher calling. After he'd spent years professing that, for a price, he could teach anyone to cure the incurable, God purportedly came to him in 2017 in yet another dream and told him to become a decoder in the QAnon movement, a hotbed for opportunists exploiting the aimless and unfulfilled. Hayes had been leading anons into battle against the Deep State ever since, with keyboards for weapons and screens for shields.

From the social media trenches, he trained his brigade of "digital soldiers" how to advance the Plan and prepare for the Storm. Most of his directives—often echoes of the propagandizing and wild-goose chases ordered by Q on 8chan—could be accomplished from a smartphone: spreading strategic narratives online to counter mainstream news reporting; recruiting new anons into the movement; scouring the internet for "clues"; and one of Q's favorites, engaging in "meme warfare" targeted at journalists and other supposed Deep State agents on Twitter.

Q would even call upon anons to take a QAnon "oath," a slight twist on the official oath of office, leading scores to bare their solemn faces in videos posted online showing them with their hands over their hearts dutifully pledging their allegiance to the movement. It was the first real unmasking of who was behind Q's sprawling online army: There was a middle-aged woman with a pixie cut and bright pink lipstick who said she'd been living alone for twenty-three years; a Mexican immigrant with tears in his eyes and an American flag pinned up behind him; a clean-cut young man in a combat uniform who affirmed that he was ready to die for the cause, if need be; a millennial mom behind a beauty filter in Ray-Bans and a push-up bra; a lonely-looking old man in a MAGA hat clutching his rifle in a dark room—all brought together from across the country to *serve*.

Being in the movement, Hayes would tell his growing audience, was like "being in the special forces" under the joint command of God, Trump, and Q; he was but a drill sergeant.

"Whether you are writing a blog, writing tweets, doing a broadcast on Periscope—whatever it is that you want to do. You are a digital soldier, and many of you are going to be having more followers [and] more listeners than CNN in a couple months!"

Through this work, Hayes's Praying Medic persona made him a QAnon celebrity, attracting an influx of followers and cash as his star rose. Within his first year of posting QAnon videos to his YouTube channel, which he'd created previously for healing-related content, his subscriber count soared by nearly 2,500 percent and he amassed almost twenty million views. On top of his other QAnon-linked revenue streams, a single fundraiser Hayes launched to help himself conquer "forces of evil" seeking to "silence the voices of truth" pulled in hundreds of thousands of dollars. Several donors left messages accompanying their contributions that read like dispatches from a war zone.

"Hoping that all of your hard work motivates others to get into this epic battle," one man wrote to Hayes, sharing that he was doing his part "hammering hard against the Deep State" from Austin, Texas.

Another said that serving as an anon had given his life meaning.

That was perhaps the greatest gift QAnon could offer its adherents. Man's desire for meaning was intrinsic and intoxicating; famed psychiatrist Viktor Frankl had called it the primary motivation of human existence. It was also elusive—only one in four American adults had a strong sense of life purpose—and the pursuit had led some down dark paths. Extremist groups, cults, and many a religious grifter were masters in making their followers feel righteous and special. Conspiracy theories could do the same: By identifying villains to unite against, they gave believers a chance to feel like they were on the right side of history.

QAnon, for many, was a journey to self-actualization through collective action, not unlike standing up to legitimate abusers of power. Just as environmental advocates could find fulfillment in marching against Big Oil corporations for the sake of the planet, anons who mobilized online against the Deep State for the sake of the children could derive from their efforts a validating sense of purpose.

When Matt fell under Praying Medic's tutelage, there was little he craved more in the world.

"Are You Ready to Be Part of History?"

QAnon made Matt feel as if he'd been living in the Matrix. Everything he thought he knew was turning out to be a carefully constructed lie stitched into one cosmic delusion. The more he learned about the Plan to overthrow the Deep State, the more he wanted to know. YouTube was ready and waiting to meet his demand. It was his second Bible; the decoder videos he watched there were giving him a new understanding of the world around him. They were also pulling him away from it.

After escaping his recliner, Matt had simply moved to a different chair. He was spending all his free time down in his basement office inhaling QAnon content like a college student cramming for an exam the night before. But for Matt, it was every night, and the prospect of ever being caught up was farcical. The information supply was endless. His obsession had taken hold quickly, within mere weeks of watching "The Plan to Save the World," the video that had started it all. Something about being an anon just felt right to him—like he'd been needing it.

With his head immersed in the QAnon fishbowl for hours every day, coming up for air was disorienting. The narrow staircase from the basement transported him up to a disparate realm, one in which his family had movie nights and baked cookies and bickered like any other. Matt arrived there each evening for dinner wanting to talk about nothing other than things like the latest covert executions at Guantanamo Bay. Instead, he sat down, smiled vacantly across the table, and asked, "So, how was school today?"

Every minute spent away from his research felt like time wasted. His idea of being there for his family—of being a man—had come to mean keeping them safe from ever-imminent danger. As the Storm loomed and the Cabal panicked, Praying Medic and other decoders regularly implored anons to prepare for power grid failures, economic shutdowns, and worse, appealing to patriarchal masculine ideals of heroism and protector roles.

Matt felt like he was privy to potentially lifesaving intel that few others on the planet even knew to look for. But things changed quickly, and he couldn't keep his loved ones out of harm's way if he wasn't constantly in the know. He started tuning into Patriots' Soapbox, a 24/7 QAnon network live-streamed on YouTube that, visually and otherwise, was pure chaos. In the middle of the screen was a fevered rotation of talking heads trying to fill the round-the-clock broadcast; on the bottom right was a running display of Trump's newest tweets; on the bottom left were the most recent Q Drops; on the top left was a live chat log whipping through comments from any number of the channel's roughly fifty thousand subscribers in real time; and along the very bottom was a scrolling news banner and a clock.

"[The elites] have built throughout the centuries an evil power structure rooted in ancient, secret religions, and growing through secret societies, secret oaths, infiltration, and indoctrination," it warned in a video played on-stream by the hosts at 2 a.m. one Friday in October, while Matt was watching. "Like an octopus coming from another world, this power structure has spread its tentacles, placing its numerous puppets in our school system, our places of worship, and our administrations to devour everything we value and to destroy everything that is good."

Patriots' Soapbox both satisfied and intensified Matt's budding FOMO. At work, when he wasn't on-air, he kept it playing in a small window on his computer screen just to stay in the loop. The show also replaced his go-to video-game podcast he listened to while sitting bumper to bumper in the school pickup line waiting for Abby and Hayden. It engrossed him so deeply that every time the car door swung open and they tossed their backpacks inside, he'd jump to turn it off.

Parked there day after day, watching silently as students wandered past to his private soundtrack of Far Right fearmongering, Matt grew paranoid that the Deep State was trying to brainwash his children through public schooling. He wanted to give them a real education, one free from a woke, liberal curriculum and revisionist history lessons designed to instill blind trust in the system from a young age. Homeschooling seemed like the best solution, but he knew Andrea would never go for it. She was a public school librarian, after all—an unwitting cog in a corrupt system.

Matt kept Andrea in the dark about QAnon. She wasn't ready, he decided; it was for the best. Still, he knew that he was causing his wife pain. He could sense her lingering stares and building anxiety as he strayed deeper into YouTube and further from her. She had started asking him to be "more present" and attentive. She just didn't know that by serving the Plan, he was being the best husband and father he could be, he told himself. If she could hang on *a little longer,* it would all be okay. With the Storm, a beautiful new beginning awaited them; he wished he could tell her that. But their marriage still hadn't fully recovered from the strain of his disability, and he worried that his honesty would only make things worse. He knew that the premise of QAnon sounded batshit crazy at first.

Andrea didn't care much for politics or world affairs—certainly not enough to invest the time needed to understand the byzantine operation unfurling in the shadows. Matt had already tried bouncing some theories off her just to see how she'd react, like the rumor that special counsel Robert Mueller, who was publicly investigating Trump's alleged electoral collusion with Russia, was actually working privately *with* the president to expose far worse crimes committed by Democrats. But each one was met with the same uninterested nod or "hmm" Andrea gave when Matt talked about gaming. On Twitter, he had seen anons recount how they had excitedly endeavored to wake up their own family members, only to be labeled as insane conspiracy theorists in return. Q had warned about this too, in a Drop.

Do not force those not yet ready.

The FAKE NEWS narrative (make-believe) has been ingrained
for a long time.
Do not isolate yourself within your own family . . .
Q

Timing was everything. Matt had been counting down the days until Andrea and everyone else would be unplugged from the Matrix, and the wait was nearly over.

The Storm was coming.

Q had been dropping not-so-subtle hints for months, declaring that America would be "UNIFIED AGAIN" on "11.11.18," and that that date would bring "a parade that will never be forgotten"—a sure reference to Trump's military parading Hillary Clinton, Barack Obama, and all their cronies through the streets of Washington, D.C., in shackles. Veterans' Day, it seemed, would see justice unleashed on the Cabal at last.

"Are you ready to be part of history?" Q asked in a Drop as the date approached.

The eleventh day of November, a Sunday, finally arrived. Like his fellow anons, Matt was glued to his phone, practically vibrating with anticipation. The news could break at any moment. He'd been rehearsing in his head how he would explain everything to Andrea. While he'd been gradually eased into it all by watching "The Plan to Save the World" and following guidance from decoders, she would go to bed knowing a different reality than the one she'd woken up to. They could figure out together how to tell the kids.

Yet as the hours ticked by . . . nothing happened. There was no triumphant tweet from Trump, no emergency news broadcast—no sign of metaphorical storm clouds whatsoever. Matt's hope faded with the daylight. By midnight, he realized that the morning news roundup he would deliver in a few hours for the radio station would be as ordinary as any other.

The primary reaction online was one of denial. Anons and decoders swiftly assembled to spin together theories of what had gone wrong, or how they had misinterpreted Q's messages.

"I was thinking," pondered the Twitter user @WWG1WGAmama, "11:11 ('A Parade that will not be forgotten') Could that mean 11/22 (11+11)? On Thanksgiving Day there is a parade."

Many resorted to a common refrain: Q had lied on purpose, using a "military deception" tactic to throw the Deep State off the trail. But amid the mental gymnastics, some were angry. This was far from the first hyped-up date that had turned out to be a dud.

"WHAT HAPPENED TO 11/11/18 UNIFIED AMERICA DAY YOU DISGUSTING LIAR FRAUD???" a rattled anon fumed on 8chan in a rare display of doubt in Q.

Q's response, in a Drop, was predictably puzzling.

"Think WAVES," it read in part. "[Controlled] moment activated? [17] Do you believe in coincidences?"

Praying Medic offered a translation two days later, based on a discovery from a diligent anon. On November 18, he explained in a decode video, mysterious seismic waves had circled the globe in seventeen-second interval pulses. (The seventeenth letter of the alphabet, as anons knew by heart, was Q.) He also shared a link to a *National Geographic* article. Sure enough, it was headlined "Strange Waves Rippled Around the World, and Nobody Knows Why." It called the event a "geologic conundrum."

Matt got chills. The Plan's failure to materialize didn't undermine QAnon's legitimacy—it revealed just how big of a threat the movement posed to the Deep State, and the extraordinary measures the elites were taking to prevent their own demise.

How, exactly, low-intensity seismic wave activity had disrupted the military's ability to carry out sweeping arrests that had supposedly been in the works for years wasn't clear—nor was the logic behind the Q-interval pulse connection. Matt didn't question it. As Q and Praying Medic had stressed over and over, there was no such thing as coincidences. *Everything* had meaning; some things just required a little more creativity to comprehend.

What had felt to Matt like an epiphany, however, was in fact an *apophany*: a Rorschachian conclusion drawn from dots that have no business being connected. Apophenia is a natural phenomenon; the human brain is hardwired to scan for patterns, even where they don't exist. It's also a bedrock of conspiracy theory thinking, wherein illusory patterns perceived in random noise are held up as evidence of nefarious activity.

In QAnon, apophenia was the name of the game. Conclusions were laid out unsupported; anons were then tasked with hunting down proof via independent "research," instilling in them a feeling of duty—and potentially, accomplishment—while helping to keep the movement alive. After Q hinted that Disney was a pedophiliac corporation, eagle-eyed anons inspected classic childhood films frame by frame and found phallic-shaped objects—supposed subliminal messaging—like a side view of Minnie Mouse's puff-sleeved dress. And after Q told anons to "Think Google," they realized that Google's graphics processing unit was called "Adreno" and its browser was called "Chrome"—sure corroboration of the theory that the Deep State terrorized kidnapped children to trigger their bodies' fear-induced production of the chemical compound adrenochrome, turning their bloodstreams into immortality elixirs to be slurped down by their captors.

It was a heuristic, self-fulfilling prophecy: If you looked hard enough for a missing puzzle piece, you'd find something that fit. That was part of the thrill.

Reporting for Duty

By December, Matt was gearing up for battle. The Storm was coming—for real, this time—and he was going to be ready.

His QAnon feeds had been abuzz lately with frantic talk of the "ten days of darkness," an apocalypse-like blackout period during which the power grid would shut off (an event that appeared to have been lifted straight from the sci-fi blockbuster *Blade Runner 2049* into QAnon mythology). The chaos would culminate in a Trump-led military takeover, bringing an end to the Deep State's reign and an eradication of evil on earth. Q had suggested that it would occur during a federal government shutdown; the next was slated to begin on December 22. Those who were unprepared would be in for a hellish holiday, scrambling to secure nonperishable food items to get by. Matt envisioned a scene out of *The Walking Dead* with barren shelves inside ransacked grocery stores.

It was time to take action.

After work slowed down one afternoon, Matt slipped out of the house to do an emergency supplies run at Sam's Club. Though he'd been there countless times before, he strode through the sliding glass doors with fresh eyes and a rush of adrenaline. He felt like he was on a secret mission.

As he rounded the aisles, loading his cart with big bags of beef jerky, boxes of bottled water, and a Chef Boyardee variety pack, he took stock of the people around him. There was an older man deciding between toilet paper brands, a lady with a cart full of junk food, an employee at a sample booth who looked like she'd rather be anywhere else. They were all oblivious, completely unaware of what was coming. Matt felt sorry for them but distinctly pleased with himself. Whatever happened, his family would be prepared.

Yet again, though, nothing transpired. The ten days came and went. Christmas, while cold and gray, was not at all apocalyptic, nor remotely Stormy. The only gift Matt had been hoping for never came. Instead, the new year arrived and the world kept on spinning, still firmly in the clutches of the Deep State.

Decoders were quick to chide those who expressed frustration.

"Everyone I know who has lost faith is focused on the arrests. Everyone I know who still trusts the plan is not," Praying Medic finger-wagged on Twitter, where he himself had made repeated predictions about Cabal members' pending incarcerations.

Matt was no quitter. He'd had unwavering faith in a higher, unseen power all his life. He doubled down. By mid-2019, he was spending some eight hours a day mainlining QAnon content, sometimes through a single headphone at the dinner table. When it was revealed that summer that the FBI had classified the movement as a domestic terror threat, following numerous acts of violence by anons, it further cemented his belief that the Cabal was growing desperate as the walls closed in. Unbeknownst to his wife, he bought a 9mm handgun and hid it in a safe in their bedroom closet, just in case. It was soon accompanied by twin piles of silver and gold coins, which he purchased for bartering purposes with a home equity line of credit of $35,000—well over half their annual household income, taken out in secret. It was the right thing to do for his family, Matt told himself. His trusted decoders, who were running paid ads for precious metals retailers on their YouTube channels, had aggressively warned of an imminent "financial reset" under a New World Order. Existing debt would be forgiven and cash would be worthless, they had claimed, pushing credulous anons toward financial ruin.

Matt was in so deep he'd lost sight of how he got there. The theories were getting wilder and the evidence was getting thinner, but at the same time he was trekking further into an echo chamber of believers, increasingly isolated from facts and dissenting voices.

Looking to Praying Medic's faith-led example of QAnon evangelism, Matt felt compelled to step up in his own role. Being an anon meant supporting the cause by whatever means possible. Driven by this sense of duty, he eyed an opportunity in his access to the radio station's listeners, a syndicated audience of nearly a million. He began aggregating his morning news broadcasts from the Trump-obsessed, QAnon-promoting *Epoch Times*, doing as much as one man could to wake up the nation from down in his basement. He felt like he was making a difference. And that felt damn good.

Swept up in his hero's quest fantasy, Matt didn't give much thought to his wife's new habit of dressing up and going out on her own. It was to see friends, she'd say. Andrea's pleas for him to unplug and be present had proved futile so many times she'd stopped asking. Her affectionate playfulness, meanwhile, had hardened into poorly feigned indifference, betrayed in part by the meticulous hair and makeup she'd been wearing around the house, unappreciated. Their relationship was dying in slow motion, and, as she'd later sob in marriage counseling, she was the only one grieving. A young Christian conservative woman who'd married in her early twenties, Andrea was experiencing the secondhand effects of Matt's identity crisis. He was her other half; being his wife had become a core pillar of who she was. As it crumbled, leaving her feeling like a single mother, she did her best to erect new ones to prop herself back up.

She poured her energy into LuLaRoe, a multilevel marketing firm known for its brightly patterned leggings and widespread allegations of pyramid-scheme conduct. Likened to cults by a growing pool of researchers (and plaintiffs), MLMs courted new independent sellers—many of them millennial moms—by inviting them to unleash their untapped potential and turn against the system by taking their financial freedom into their own hands. It would often start with some variation of the faux-feminist "boss babe" or "mompreneur" pitch: *Take charge of your life! Become a boss babe and build the future you've always wanted!* In reality, pay-to-play costs and heaping piles of unmovable inventory had tumbled countless aspiring boss babes into debt, while the very few individuals perched atop the pyramid—referred to by rank titles such as Queens, Double Rubies, and Royal Crown Diamonds, depending on the company— could juice the downlines for millions. The majority of sellers never turned a profit.

Andrea was no exception. To join LuLaRoe, she had to buy in for several thousand dollars and purchase its clothing in bulk to resell, all the while recruiting more base-level sellers. She created Facebook groups, she made calls, she held pop-up sales at local shops with a smile on her face. But the vision she'd been sold never came to fruition. In its place, racks of unpurchased pink, purple, and orange garments lined the basement next to Matt's dust-coated emergency supplies endlessly awaiting the Storm. Still, like so many struggling sellers, Andrea kept at it. MLMs came with the promise of self-made success that was always just around the corner, making them enticing to join and difficult to leave—even in the face of unrelenting disappointment.

That was something Matt understood well. Many nights, he'd crawl into bed after Andrea had fallen asleep, bleary-eyed and wired from hours of research. Other times, they'd lie awake beside each other with their heads bowed over their phones, a boss babe and a digital soldier hustling in their own handheld worlds. The wider the chasm between them grew, the closer their family inched toward its impending implosion. Both were sucked into systems designed to make them feel fulfilled while enriching the Royal Crown Diamonds and Praying Medics at the top.

Matt had no interest in getting out. To be an anon was to belong to a band of patriotic underdogs: a collective David to the Deep State's Goliath. It made him walk with his head a little higher. With each Storm-that-wasn't, if there was a voice in his head that knew he was being lied to, it was drowned out by a louder, more persuasive one charged in emotion rather than logic. He was pulled from bed each morning by a sense of purpose. Since his injury, that feeling hadn't been easy to come by—or to let go of. So he looked past the failed predictions and gaping factual holes in the conspiracy theories he was fed, and focused instead on the apophanies that seemed to affirm his new belief system.

He wasn't ready to hang up his armor.

PART II

CONSPIRACY CRUTCH

HOOKED

—Emily—

GreatAwakening.win was the bleakest place on the internet Adam had ever visited.

To open the Far Right message board was to enter a dystopian alternate reality in which risible nonsense was met with a chorus of cultish credulity. In threads filed beneath a banner displaying a large "Q" in dark-blue storm clouds, Pizzagate was a national tragedy, Princess Diana was still alive, and Wayfair, the online furniture retailer, was selling storage cabinets with missing children locked inside. Spending just an hour skimming the latest content from the site's tens of thousands of users was enough to make even the most logically inclined question their sanity— not for the absurdity of the conspiracy theories themselves, but for the near-unanimous conviction with which they were embraced.

This had become part of Adam's daily routine. Before and after work— and, increasingly, during work hours—he ventured madly and miserably through the paranoiac underbelly of the web. It was a grim kind of field research. Holed up in his San Francisco high rise as a firestorm of Covid-19 and sociopolitical chaos raged outside his walls, Adam was engulfed in a crisis of his own: His mother was slipping away in the QAnon quicksands. So from across the country, he had hatched a three-part plan to save her before she was too far gone. Part one was simple: Learn everything there was to know about QAnon. *Stat.*

After rolling over in bed to silence his phone's morning alarm, Adam typically swiped straight to Telegram, a barely moderated encrypted messaging app he'd mostly forgotten about after downloading it back in law school at the request of his weed dealer. To Adam's dismay, it had since become a quiet breeding ground for QAnon channels, where like mushrooms they sprouted and multiplied in the dark. Other times, he started his day on GreatAwakening.win or 8kun, the rebranded 8chan, trying to stomach his cereal while reading grisly tales of cannibalism and child rape. It was as sickening as it was painful. Adam often pictured his mother—the once-revered *Emily Porter, attorney at law*—surfing through the same content inside her big empty house in Tennessee. It was no mystery how she'd been spending her time. Almost without fail, a day or two after the latest Far Right conspiracy theory started making the rounds online, Emily would be spewing it back out all over her own social media pages, and in stupefying texts to her children that landed in their pockets like live grenades ready to ruin their days.

Stationed on his couch in gym shorts as weeks blended together and virus death tolls skyrocketed, Adam devoured news articles written by extremism reporters who'd been studying QAnon from its early stages, his blue eyes scanning longingly for useful information to share with his sisters. He, Leah, and Jessica had been texting frantically across three time zones with links and screenshots between bouts of venting. It was primarily for Leah's benefit. Like most other doctors at her overwhelmed, understaffed Arkansas hospital, she'd been abruptly reassigned to treating the throngs of Covid-19 patients flooding into the ICU. The hours were so long and the breaks so few that by the time she finally peeled off her N95 mask at the end of each shift, red and purple marks were etched into her skin in its place. She didn't have time to read about the Deep State's army of clones or the return of JFK, Jr.

Adam didn't really have time either. He was still a new hire at his law firm. It was one of the most prestigious in the nation, housed in a glitzy, *Suits*-style skyscraper of an office where associates worked well past sundown before loosening their ties or swapping their heels for flats and escaping to the bars for a nightcap. In the Covid era, though, the camaraderie was no more, and the notion of a 9-to-5 was still laughable. For Adam, moving to California earlier in 2020 for this job had meant starting anew without the chance to make friends or meet colleagues. He'd hardly hit the ground running. From his eighteenth-story one-bed/one-bath-turned-live-in workspace, he was already falling behind in billable hours (and with a rate of hundreds of dollars per hour, "Time is money" was more than a mantra to his employer). Making matters worse, he'd barely studied for the California bar exam, which was just a few months away. The thought of failing and disappointing his new bosses was terrifying. But so was the prospect of leaving his mother to her own devices any longer.

He did his best to straddle both worlds: In the background of his bar review, he binged through the *QAnon Anonymous* podcast, a deep-dive series hosted by a trio of investigative researchers. They broke down the movement's myriad conspiracy theories and traced some back to pre-Q origins, like the centuries-old "blood libel" accusations that Jewish people were ritually abusing Christian children and drinking their blood. The more Adam learned, the deeper his shame. He realized he might never fully understand what had happened to Emily. But he needed to know how to undo it.

Following his QAnon crash course, part two of his plan was to become a self-taught deprogrammer. In his view, the movement was a cult and Emily was its victim—a brainwashed disciple sucked in during a vulnerable period of her life marked by extreme isolation, loneliness, and too much screen time. The closest person she had to a friend outside of QAnon was Mary, her older sister up in the Northeast, with whom she'd recently reconnected after spending many years out of touch. As an introvert who'd mostly been on her own since her husband's suicide, maybe Emily was seeking community in QAnon, Adam reasoned to his sisters.

Jessica was less forgiving. She believed, as her therapist had suggested, that their mother's stubborn refusal to work through her trauma had manifested in an irrational anger at the world that was conveniently validated by antiestablishment conspiracy theories. The siblings had argued at length about the best way to approach her, with Adam lobbying for gentle empathy and Jessica pushing for a harsh ultimatum: QAnon or her kids. Adam pleaded with his sister to give him time. The literature on prying people from cults didn't inspire much confidence, however, and the limited advice for people in his position was inconsistent and often seemed contradictory: *Question the cult member's beliefs but don't make them feel attacked. Approach them with compassion but don't enable their behavior. Give them their space but not too much.* And last: *Accept that they may never come back—no buts.*

Adam tried not to feel discouraged. After tailing his mother down the rabbit hole, he was as ready as he could be for the final, most daunting part of his plan: Lead her back out.

Drag her, if necessary.

One-Tribe Mind

There exists in the American legal framework a fundamental principle called the "best evidence rule." In essence, it holds original documentation as the superior form of proof. This, Adam decided, would be his springboard into action to save his mother. While they no longer saw eye-to-eye on politics—among other things—they still shared a profound respect for the law.

So early on a summer morning, when out of the blue, Emily sent him a text gloating about the imminent arrests of several high-profile Democrats who were set to be hauled off to the Gitmo gallows for treason and worse, he tested the waters.

"Hey Mom. Wow," he responded. Then, prodding her as delicately as he could, he added: "Where'd you hear that?"

He watched intently as three gray dots danced on his screen in an iMessage bubble to reveal her answer—a nonanswer.

"Oh my darling son. There are so many things you don't know about."

Adam frowned. It was perhaps the most lovingly ominous thing anyone had ever said to him, spiced with a mild aftertaste of condescension. He tried again, asking where, specifically, she had gotten her information. Emily sent him a tweet from a QAnon influencer boldly and baselessly declaring that the arrests were about to drop.

Seizing his moment, Adam reminded his mother of the best evidence rule. He urged her to think like a lawyer. Where were the original public records documenting the charges? And why wasn't this front-page news? Already, his guise of innocent curiosity was wearing off. It was clear what he was trying to do.

Like a spooked animal, Emily suddenly flipped onto the defensive. The indictments were still sealed, she replied curtly, and the mainstream media was actively covering up the truth. If he was too much of a "sheep" to question the official narrative, that was his problem. Even through texts, Adam could hear her snapping at him, as if his questions were the most ridiculous she'd ever heard. She proceeded to bombard him with links to YouTube videos about the mainstream media, the Clinton Foundation, Dr. Fauci, and a handful of other tangentially related topics, ranging from a few minutes in length to over an hour, to help him "wake up."

Getting through them all would consume the rest of his workday, Adam reckoned, glancing wearily at his laptop.

He did it anyway. If he wanted her to engage in good faith, he knew he should do the same. So applying the "issue-spotting" techniques he'd learned in law school, he examined each video closely, pausing every minute or so to jot down notes and fact-check the core claims. He recognized a couple of the creators from his QAnon research. They were masters at their grift who knew all the right buzzwords to drop and anxieties to exploit to work their viewers into a populist fury. It was almost formulaic, a dismally predictable series of conspiracy theory Mad Libs drawing from pools of leftist evildoers and ludicrous evil deeds. Adam wanted to lean through his screen, look them dead in the eyes, and ask if they felt any remorse for what they were doing to people like his mother—if they even understood the extent of the damage and agony they were causing. If they even cared.

Some of their theories were so outlandish they left him shaking his head, while several were at least partially accurate but deceptively mis-contextualized, requiring nuance to debunk. This was the benefit of texting over calling, Adam figured: He could take his time to get the facts in order, as if he were preparing to litigate a case. After hours spent painstakingly formulating concise, carefully sourced bullet points exposing the holes in the videos' assertions—and the creators' credibility—he was ready to present the evidence to his jury-of-one over in the Southeast, where it was getting late. He'd share just the bare facts, sans opinions and unneeded commentary. If nothing else, this would give her pause, he thought, tired yet tingling with cautious optimism. It was time to crack the foundation of her new belief system.

But as Adam started to lay out his findings point by point, sharing links to articles and reports for Emily to review in return at her leisure, she breezed right past them. From *The New York Times* to the CDC website, his "Deep State" sources couldn't be trusted, she chided, suggesting that he ought to have known better. In mere seconds she'd thrown out a near-full day's efforts that could have been spent catching up on work or studying. Before he could get a word in, the gray dots appeared again, followed by a new fleet of YouTube videos. One thumbnail featured a poorly edited image of Michelle "Michael" Obama with a five o'clock shadow. Adam's heart sank.

"Are you fucking *kidding me*?" he hissed alone in his living room, aglow in the golden hues of twilight now streaming through his windows.

He began typing an exasperated response pointing out the hypocrisy of rejecting legitimate journalism and science for the rantings and ravings of random YouTubers, but he caught himself and deleted it. Anger wasn't productive. Instead, he told his mother that he wished she'd participate in an actual dialogue. Without acknowledging what he'd said, she carried on delving into her latest batch of theories.

Adam kept going. Their conversation had veered off course, but he wasn't jumping ship. Skipping ahead several steps in his deprogramming strategy, he tried candor.

"I know who you are. You're educated, you're smart, you're successful, you're accomplished. But mom, you've been brainwashed by propaganda designed to manipulate and deceive you."

The dots paused for a moment. Then, briefly, they returned.

"I feel the same of you."

Adam's weeks and months to follow brought a lot of the same: The same bland white walls. The same looping news cycle of the Left calling to "slow the spread" and the Right calling to reopen the country. The same creeping dread as the increasingly fraught presidential election—and the bar exam—drew nearer. The same maddening arguments with his mother.

All they did was argue. Even when Adam deliberately brought up her pre-QAnon interests, like farming and painting, Emily could reroute the conversation right back to conspiracy theories. No topic was safe. She seemed to revel in her rage, fuming on and on about the "traitors" and "monsters" who would soon get what was coming to them. She could be snide and antagonistic—cruel, even. When speaking of her perceived enemies, she sometimes used vile nicknames; Kamala Harris was "Kamal Toe." If Adam dared to push back, that wrath was directed at him. In heated moments, she had told him he was arrogant, disgusting, and a "terrible person" for closing his eyes to "the truth," cutting him deeper with each jab. Talking to her had become akin to screaming into a void. No matter how damning the evidence he showed her to disprove her claims—like the original, unedited photo of the former First Lady—she'd dismiss it outright or pivot to something new.

It wasn't just her, Adam observed. During his still-daily visits to Great-Awakening.win and various QAnon Telegram channels, he was no longer merely lurking. He'd been going undercover, using burner accounts to pretend to be an anon himself so he could engage with true believers from a place of common ground. After indulging their theories and even reciting some himself to build rapport, he'd pose an innocuous question, like, *Wait . . . Angela Merkel was born nine years after Hitler died—how could he possibly be her father?* But if Adam deviated too far from the collectively embraced narrative, he'd be promptly ejected from the channel or banned from the forum. For people who prided themselves on being champions of "free speech" and "the truth," they cared very little for dissent and facts.

In this regard, QAnon was a microcosm of the Trumpian Right: a more extreme and insular product of harmonized lies from right-wing politicians, media figures, and influencers, which were repeated until they sounded believable—a phenomenon known as the "validity effect." Inside their at-times cult-like ideological echo chamber, they, and they alone, dictated what was true. Loyalty trumped logic, while an entrenched with-us-or-against-us mentality cast outsiders as enemies: Reporters, scientists, field experts, and other external purveyors of information were never to be trusted. This kind of "tribal epistemology," a term coined by journalist David Roberts, was apparent from Trump's first full day in office, when White House press secretary Sean Spicer falsely claimed that his boss had drawn "the largest audience to ever witness an inauguration." Trump's crowd size was actually a fraction of Obama's, which was immediately obvious from looking at aerial photos of both events. Yet when researchers presented those images to people who voted for Trump, 15 percent still bafflingly pointed to his ceremony as having the greater turnout. Already, Trump's hold over an expanding portion of his base—his tribe—was more powerful than black-and-white, smack-you-in-the-face reality itself; facts be damned. Standing with the tribe was more important than standing for the truth when one's ideology became their identity.

Emily seemed to live and breathe QAnon. She preached her beliefs to anyone who would listen—even to her hairstylist, prattling on about satanic elites between blasts of the blow-dryer. She found an open ear in Mary, the sister with whom she'd recently reconnected, a highly religious woman in her seventies who put great stock in the words of her brilliant *lawyer* sister down in the Bible Belt. But Emily's main audience was her begrudging children, who categorically refuted almost everything she said. And when people's firmly held beliefs are challenged—particularly those tied to their sense of self—the brain reacts the same way it would to a physical threat, ready to defend those beliefs as if they were part of the body. Adrenaline courses through the bloodstream, the heart races, and the prefrontal cortex, the brain's logic center, is functionally compromised. It can make people impulsive and irrational.

Cruel, even.

Adam took the two-day virtual bar exam on October 5 and 6. All his life, he'd been an A student without having to put in much effort. This was different. He was sleep-deprived, distracted, and acutely depressed. He submitted the final portion, one hundred multiple-choice questions and a written performance test, with an unfamiliar sense of anxiety. It was the same day Facebook announced that it was banning QAnon content from its platforms, a move so woefully overdue it seemed almost pointless. The movement had already swelled to include millions of followers and had successfully blasted a slew of pandemic-related conspiracy theories into virality, dumping gasoline on the open flames of a public health catastrophe. And, Adam feared, it had already robbed him of his mother.

But the following week, less than a month out from the election, something astonishing occurred that restored some of his hope. It happened after Emily texted him a pair of viral YouTube videos. They were from a monetized channel with millions of viewers called The Next News Network, a professional-sounding name belying its function as a right-wing conspiracy theory mill. In these clips, the tied and suited host, Gary Franchi, sat stern-faced with gel-slicked hair at an anchor's desk before a floor-to-ceiling display of the Manhattan skyline and dropped a bombshell: New "hard evidence" proved that Joe Biden and his cronies had executed the entire SEAL Team Six to cover up the fact that Osama bin Laden was still alive. Franchi cited an article published to an obscure Far Right media website by a self-identified "Homeschool Mom in North Carolina," which had already been posted to Twitter by a QAnon account and retweeted by Trump.

Adam wanted to hurl his phone at the wall. From the social media outrage factories to the Oval Office, these unscrupulous opportunists were shepherding democracy off a cliff for their own gain, and there was his mother: racing toward the edge at their command while calling her kids "sheep." He took a breath and sent her a *Forbes* article debunking this latest nonsense—certain that she wouldn't bother to read it—and, like a broken record, urged her to use more reliable sources. His patience was wearing thin.

"That you believe absolutely baseless conspiracy theories on YouTube is incredibly troubling," Adam told her.

"They have ALL THE DOCUMENTS!" Emily replied.

"Oh what documents mom? how are you a lawyer? My god."

Adam could feel his blood pressure rising. They sparred for nearly an hour before landing back on one of Emily's favorite topics: the ever-pending arrests of Deep State elites, which were now supposed to happen before the start of Trump's second term. Obama, Biden, and Hillary Clinton would be put to death on the spot, she said.

"When none of it happens," Adam wrote back to her, "I expect you to admit that it was all bullshit?"

Then, in her most shocking comment yet, Emily cracked open a window of opportunity.

"Deal."

There was no version of QAnon's "Plan" in which Trump failed to be re-elected. Its foundational claim was that he had become president in the first place for the sole purpose of banding with the military to conquer the Cabal, which he still hadn't done. Even Emily seemed to understand that if he lost, she would *have* to accept that she'd been duped, Adam explained to his sisters. He was trying to convince himself as much as them.

Meanwhile, Trump and his allies were trying to convince America of their own fantasy. Despite evidence to the contrary, they jointly, incessantly declared that he was far and away the preferred candidate—so if he were to lose, it could mean only one thing: The election had been rigged. Memes went viral misleadingly comparing packed Trump rallies to sparsely populated Biden events, where attendance was purposely restricted and seating socially distanced. They were constructing a fail-safe narrative to preemptively undermine the likely reality of losing. And in a striking display of tribal epistemology in full force, *it worked*. The polls hadn't even closed on November 3 when cries of "Stop the steal!" started ringing out online. The truth never stood a chance.

When Biden won, conspiracy theorists doubled down hard. Posts on GreatAwakening.win became less crazy than scary; talk of violence and uprisings and martial law abounded. GOPers who didn't immediately get on board with Trump's charade were lambasted as "RINOs" (Republicans In Name Only)—and even, baselessly, as pedophiles. Emily dug in deeper too, convinced that it was in fact all part of the Plan.

"PATRIOTS, SIT BACK AND RELAX," she tweeted. "WE GOT THEM ALL RED HANDED. GOD BLESS OUR PRESIDENT DON-ALD J. TRUMP!!!Q!Q!"

In Too Deep

Adam was not okay.

He felt helpless: His mother was turning into a stranger, slipping right through his fingers. The harder he tried to save her, the more hostile she became. Fearing that he was causing more harm than good, he dialed back his interaction with her, resisting the urge to fact-check or even reply to many of the theories she lobbed at him. But he continued to closely monitor her on social media. Telegram displayed on each user's profile a note showing when they were last active, and when she wasn't online, Emily's always showed the same three words: "Last seen recently." Adam longed for the day that he would read "Last seen within a week," meaning she'd taken a break from her QAnon channels there for at least forty-eight consecutive hours. The disappointment he endured each time he checked sent him spiraling.

Weed helped. So did online gambling, at least in the moment. He'd take a serotonin boost wherever he could get it, and mobile betting apps made it dangerously quick and easy. Gambling was in Adam's genes; it was a compulsion he'd been battling his entire adult life—a dependable distraction when everything became too much. As his mental health deteriorated, the frequency and magnitude of his bets soared. He was gambling on credit cards, maxing them out and opening new ones while chasing his losses into a tailspin. Even with a quarter-million-dollar salary, Adam was steadily inching toward insolvency.

Long averse to therapy, like his mother, Adam could confide only in Jessica and Leah. Emily's delusions were too embarrassing to talk about openly; as QAnon exploded into a household name, people he knew personally had delighted in mocking followers as "lunatics" and "inbreeds." The few friends he'd opened up to about Emily just didn't get it, shrugging off his concerns with comments like "Boomers on the internet, man. They're crazy!"

But Jessica was moving on. In her telling, Emily had crossed a line: After numerous mother-daughter screaming matches over the phone about their vastly different takes on current events, Emily had started questioning the "story" surrounding George Floyd's murder, and the motivations of the Black Lives Matter movement. Jessica was done right then and there. As far as she was concerned, her mother—the woman who, years earlier, had been in tears over the infamous acquittal of George Zimmerman in Trayvon Martin's killing—was gone, past the point of no return.

Leah, meanwhile, remained swept up on the front lines of Covid-19. Older patients could be admitted to her hospital with a cough on a Friday and leave by Monday for the makeshift morgues and refrigerated trailers that had been set up on the fly to accommodate the crush of infected bodies. The strict no-visitors policy meant that Leah's was one of the last faces many of them saw, her big green eyes peering down at them over her mask as they whimpered out for their loved ones with tubes in their throats. Most often, for their children.

Leah was struggling to keep it together. She ached for her mother, who had once been her rock—the person she could always turn to for comfort or a shoulder to cry on. But to Emily, the "plandemic" was one big conspiracy: The virus was a hoax. Then, instead, a Chinese bioweapon. Then a sinister ploy by Bill Gates, Dr. Fauci, and Big Pharma. Leah's disgust was dulled only by her mental and physical exhaustion. She didn't have the energy to debate the tragic realities she witnessed firsthand every day. She begged her mother, repeatedly, to quit spamming her with YouTube videos featuring quack doctors spouting pseudoscience and lies. To talk about something—*anything*—else. But Emily couldn't seem to stop. She claimed that the vaccines would kill everyone they pricked. She even told her daughter that a prenatal hepatitis B shot was the reason she had been born disabled.

Stealing pained glances at her messages amid the chaos, Leah was reminded of her father. She thought back to the time Dan came to see her in the ICU while she was recovering from a major surgery. It was a brutal procedure for a little kid that kept her hospitalized for weeks, sick from complications and desperate to go home. But seeing her dad didn't help. His mind was clearly elsewhere. He spent most of the time pacing by her bed on the phone, talking in short, animated sentences over the ambient beeps and whirs as she silently looked on. It wasn't the first time she'd felt lonely in his company. Only after his suicide had she come to fully understand that on that day—like so many others that he'd spent anxiously pacing with a phone pinned between his ear and his shoulder—he was gambling, unable to pry himself from calls with his bookies as his young daughter lay ill at his side.

Leah winced. Back in a beeping, whirring ICU more than two decades later, donning not a hospital gown but bright teal scrubs, she was overcome with a familiar sting of abandonment. There was no denying it: Her mother was an addict, and she was choosing QAnon over her own children. It was too excruciating to endure again. She blocked her calls, texts, and emails, following Jessica's lead. But only after firing off one final message.

> *I cannot do this anymore . . . I will not be there when you need me one day just as you have chosen to not be there for me now. I am done.*

Leah's assessment of what was gripping her mother had merit. Like gambling, consuming conspiracy theories could be, quite literally, addictive. A 2018 analysis of the popular r/conspiracy subreddit found that while just 5 percent of its posters actually showed signs of conspiracy theory thinking, they accounted for nearly two-thirds of all comments published there. The most active poster had independently written 896,337 words (picture ten copies of this book stacked on top of each other). Part of the draw has to do with the addictive-by-design social media framework through which conspiracy theory content is typically accessed. But among the other reasons why some people compulsively watch videos about cannibalized babies or stolen elections is the way that doing so makes them feel. Generally: outraged, victimized, vengeful.

Research suggests that harboring grievances—whether they stem from real or perceived offenses—actually makes people feel *good*. Brain-imaging studies have revealed that feeling aggrieved, and in turn, desiring retribution, stimulates the same neural reward-processing circuitry as narcotics. Such desire could manifest in a retaliatory act as simple as Emily rage-tweeting at Biden, or as extreme as laying siege to the U.S. Capitol. But feeling wronged and merely thinking about that release of revenge, perhaps by fantasizing about the Storm, can trigger an intoxicating rush of dopamine—which, incidentally, can make people more prone to seeing illusory patterns, a cornerstone of conspiracy theory thinking.

Whenever Leah missed her mother, she went straight to her Twitter page. It instantly reassured her that she'd made the right decision in cutting off contact. QAnon wasn't just what Emily believed anymore—it was who she was.

"I just reported mom's twitter account," Leah informed her siblings in a text one morning.

Adam responded immediately.

"I'd rather you didn't," he said. "This way we can monitor her activity. Otherwise she'll create another one that may be harder to find."

From afar, Leah and Jessica's concern had shifted from their mother to their little brother. They knew he was compulsively gambling again; he was so nervous about affording his rent that he was considering temporarily moving in with Jessica over in D.C. But they were also troubled by how deeply he was pouring himself into this seemingly futile quest to pull their mother back to reality.

So was Adam. QAnon had taken over not just her life, but his too. As with his gambling, he knew that he was being influenced to a degree by the sunk-cost fallacy: After all the time, energy, and emotion he'd invested, how could he quit now? It haunted him to think that a similar kind of cognitive dissonance could shackle Emily to her conspiracy theories indefinitely. She had sacrificed so much at the altar of Q: her reputation, her dignity, her family. Even if she were to miraculously escape QAnon's clutches, what would she have left to come back to?

Not that there was reason to believe she'd actually get to the point of coming back. Her social media posts were a diary of a woman obsessed. Day after day, week after week, month after month, every time Adam had checked, her Telegram had displayed those same damned three words: *Last seen recently.*

It dawned on him that the same was true of his account.

By the holidays, nine months into his solitary lockdown, Adam felt as if he was trapped in an extended panic attack—paralyzed with dread over his mounting gambling debt, his ailing work performance, and his looming bar results. As his sense of self-worth plummeted to a new low, he shut the world out, too depressed to return worried calls from his sisters.

He was out of moves. He had no more internet-prescribed deprogramming strategies up his sleeve, no more hope that his mother could be saved, no more energy left to try. His three-part plan had failed her. *He* had failed her, he decided. And worse . . . he'd been wrong about her. The whole time that he'd been breathlessly defending her—making one excuse after another to justify her hateful delusions—he'd been deluded himself. Emily was an addict, but she was no victim. The deranged, unrecognizable person she'd become was a product of her own choices, and that person didn't want to be saved. At this stage, he thought, loneliness wasn't to blame; neither was social media, Fox News, Trump, or even QAnon.

Adam wilted. He had arrived at this conclusion some time ago, deep down, but he'd been wrestling with its implications for his own life, which was in freefall. Maybe subconsciously he had believed that if he could "fix" her, he could "fix" himself too—that he could finally begin to heal the underlying damage they both had refused to confront for so long. Maybe he had blamed some of that damage on her. But if she was responsible for her own self-destructive behavior, then he was responsible for his—including his refusal to let her go. He knew it was time.

Part of him felt a hint of relief. Part of him wanted to die. After everything they'd been through—the tragedy, the trauma, the trust they'd built during the years when it was just the two of them living together on the farm—Adam had believed that nothing could break them. He hated his mother for choosing conspiracy theories over him, even if, as an addict himself, he understood on some level. He hated her for being the one to walk away. Hating her made it easier to finally walk away himself. So, mired in torment on the afternoon of December 22, 2020, he wrote her an email expressing exactly how he felt and hit "Send" before he could talk himself out of it.

> *So long as you continue to live in your internet fantasyland of propaganda, misinformation and lies, you are not my mother. You would cause us all far less trauma and pain if you kept to yourself. I want absolutely nothing to do with you.*

Night fell over the West Coast. Adam was relieved, if surprised, to have received no response—unaware that three days earlier, Mary, Emily's elderly sister, had died from Covid. He refreshed his inbox at least every hour until eventually succumbing to a restless sleep.

The next morning, still in bed and barely awake, Adam opened his phone to find Emily's caustic blast waiting for him in a pair of violently cruel emails. They read like a Q Drop novella.

Veering in and out of all-caps text, she excoriated him and disowned him. She told him to shed her DNA.

Adam did nothing all day but read his mother's words. Urgent requests from his clients pushing to close year-end deals went ignored as he read the emails again, and again, and again, studying each line in a haze of masochistic shock. Then he printed them out, filling an entire page with her vitriol, and read them again, gripping the paper so tightly the sides crinkled and tore. Emily was delusional, but she saw him for the failure he perceived himself to be, validating the cruelest voices in his head. She thought that he was a "huge disappointment and utter embarrassment," and that he was destined to meet the same end as his father.

Maybe, for once, she was right.

December 25 brought clouds in northern Tennessee and rain in the Bay Area. On Telegram, QAnon channels were alight with speculation about an early-morning bombing near an AT&T network facility in downtown Nashville, convinced that it was a false flag, or perhaps the work of a heroic anon targeting 5G technology operations. Emily spent her Christmas like any other day, ranting feverishly online to no one in particular.

"Deep state mind control is holding my three highly educated millennial children hostage, with anger and unrecognizable venom," she lamented in a middle-of-the-night musing.

Adam spent his Christmas reading each of the thirty-six tweets she posted that day, between rereading her emails, which were by then all but seared into his memory. One tweet stood out between a pair about the Obamas, calling Barack a "minion rat" and Michelle a "he/she CLONE." It was in response to a random Twitter user's photo of a grumpy-looking French bulldog wearing a little Christmas tree hat with green sequins, shiny red bells, and a yellow star made of felt.

"Is this your pup? Would love the permission to draw/paint this one," Emily had written. "No cost, just my passion . . ."

That tweet hit Adam the hardest. His mother—the one he knew and loved, and so desperately, excruciatingly missed—was still in there. He just couldn't break through to her. Slumped over his kitchen counter, picking absently at his takeout, he pictured her dining all alone in their enormous house, surrounded by empty farmland, where the holidays used to mean feasting cheerfully as a family on her divine Italian cuisine. A home-cooked meal wasn't complete without Emily's signature (slightly singed) garlic bread, which she almost always forgot under the broiler until its mouthwatering scent wafted into the dining room, causing her to spring from her seat like clockwork, to the unfailing amusement of her children. Adam wondered if she was thinking of him too. He wished he didn't care.

Two weeks later, on January 6, a mob of Trump supporters stormed the U.S. Capitol. Chants of "HANG MIKE PENCE!" roared through the grounds as Trump sicced his tribe on his own vice president for refusing to overturn the election results. Emily tweeted that the insurrection was a false flag planned by antifa; Adam teetered on the brink.

On January 8, he got the results from the bar.

He had failed.

Well, you were right. I am just like my father . . . I have made extremely poor decisions and now find myself in a place of unspeakable depression. Despite the countless advantages

and extreme privilege i was given in life, I wasted it all and have nobody to blame but myself. I know my destiny well by now.

Hope that you use your remaining years to reconsider the tremendous damage and pain that you caused to your children.

Be well mom, I'm sorry.

SHADOW PLAY

—Alice—

Deep inside an underground cave, prisoners sit shoulder to shoulder, chained to a partition at their backs. They've lived down there from infancy. Above, unseen, their captors use flames and puppets to cast shadow figures onto the wall ahead. To the prisoners, these illusions are real—the only reality they've ever known. So begins Plato's *Allegory of the Cave*.

One day, a single prisoner is unshackled. He's made to turn around and witness the fiery masquerade over the partition, then he's taken up out of the cave into the blazing sunlight. It overwhelms and temporarily blinds him. But eventually his eyes adjust. And for the very first time, he sees the world as it truly is, in all its brilliant color and depth and detail. He sees the water. The sky. The bright yellow sun beaming down on him.

Alice believed she had seen the sun too.

She was sitting in bed in her Bay Area home with her heart drumming in her chest, her auburn curls in disarray and her mind blown. On her phone, aglow in the dark, played the closing scene of *The Fall of the Cabal*. Bingeing through the ten-part QAnon series had revealed to her that life as she knew it was a spectacle of lies: shadow play projected by the mainstream media and other Deep State puppeteers to an unwitting audience in mental chains. But a brighter reality was within reach. The Great Awakening was coming.

"The world as we know it is about to end," the film concluded. "What is awaiting us is a new era of peace, liberty, equality, and harmony."

Alice took a slow, deep breath, exhaling months of fear and angst that had been bubbling inside her as 2020 erupted into bedlam. She breathed in gleeful new hope. People were inherently good, she truly believed this; it made soothing sense to her that much of humanity's suffering and conflict was contrived by an evil cabal of oligarchs. A society free from their reign would be one without war, corruption, or division—even more utopic than the lost future she'd dreamed of for the Bernie Revolution-that-wasn't. She grinned. What a beautiful thing it would be. Yet as she looked down at her "beloved," Christopher, who was fast asleep by her side, her elation dimmed. Even when he awoke, he wouldn't be *awake*.

In Alice's mind, she had escaped the allegorical cave. But her friends and loved ones were still trapped down there. They were everything to her. She needed to enlighten them.

Plato's liberated prisoner felt a similar duty, so he retreated into the cave to share his incredible discovery with the other captives. They didn't react how he expected. Instead of jubilation or gratitude, they met him with mockery and venom. They thought him a fool, even a threat. The cave was safe and comfortable to them. When he tried to set them free and lead them out into the sunlight, they not only resisted—they attacked.

Slamming the Door

From the time she could walk and talk, Alice had craved human connection like food in her belly.

As a toddler, she would run out past her parents to fling her arms around anyone and everyone who came to their door, from salesmen to Jehovah's Witnesses. Her mother once lost track of her on a train out of Wisconsin when she was a little girl, only to find her clinging to the leg of a bemused stranger standing in the passenger carriage with his hands raised in the air. She had just wanted a hug. Once she was in school, Alice signed up for as many clubs and sports as she could manage: gymnastics, chorus, diving, volleyball, soccer. Being part of a team felt like finding her place in the world. Her social networks remained just as important to her into adulthood, though they centered on other passions: primarily her liberal progressive politics, her spirituality, and her love of yoga and healthy living. California was the perfect place to be. She surrounded herself with like-minded people, each one a pillar in a rock-solid community that was sacred to her.

For Alice, to belong was to feel whole. It was less of a want than a need; in fact, it was humans' most fundamental necessity, outranked only by what was required for subsistence, according to renowned psychologist Abraham Maslow. If it was unfulfilled, in times of feeling isolated or outcast by their social groups, people could quickly grow desperate to find belonging elsewhere—a vulnerability exploited by cults and extremist movements. That was precisely what happened to Alice when, in a bid to warn her treasured community about evils that didn't exist, she destroyed it.

Her beloved was the first pillar to fracture.

When Alice met Christopher, he was in the throes of a midlife crisis. It was 2015 and he was in his midfifties, looking back on his decades with wistful reproach. From the outside, he was to be envied: a handsome, high-flying business executive with a picture-perfect family in breezy California. But with age and retrospection, Christopher couldn't help feeling like he'd lived most of his life from the back seat. He had been the man of the house since he was just fourteen years old, when, in the grief of losing his father, he was thrust into the role of provider and protector for his mother and sisters. And, soon, for his wife. They met in high school and had four children, spinning him into a tireless corporate grind from which he had yet to break free. He loved his kids dearly; raising them had been the single greatest joy of his existence. But they had grown up, and he and his wife had grown apart. They were floundering in the terminal months of a marriage consumed by truculent bickering and mutual resentment. Christopher was coming undone. He wanted to take the wheel, he just didn't know how.

Then Alice came along. She helped him rediscover the magic and the possibility in life. Fifteen years his junior, she was a radiant, spiritual, intensely kind and earnest Burning Man type with a silky-soft voice, elfin beauty, and an endearing innocence about her—the kind of person who still wished for world peace when she blew out the candles, and had the courage to do the things that made her happy. She spoke to a part of Christopher that had been screaming to get out.

During his bitter ensuing divorce, as he was exiled from his social community, Alice welcomed him into her own, a potently progressive bubble of Bernie Sanders–loving, Donald Trump–hating free spirits who happily embraced him. It was a whole new world for a fiscally conservative, traditionally raised suit like himself—and he wasn't looking back.

These were his people now. Being with Alice, and with them, made him feel like a new man.

But behind the magnetic attraction, their differences bred friction too. After years of increasingly frequent and combative arguments with his ex-wife, Christopher could at times be defensive and short-fused, causing his highly sensitive fiancée to shut down. Arguing wasn't in Alice's nature; she had devoted her professional life to the empathy-centered practice of compassionate communication. Another point of contention between them was the naïveté that sometimes bled through Alice's idealism. She had a tendency to take things at face value, not because they were proven to be true, but because she so desperately wanted them to be—whether it was whispers of cancer cures or groundbreaking clean energy sources. Christopher, a thirty-year veteran of the life sciences industry, didn't know what to do with that. While Alice interpreted life through rose-tinted glasses, he saw things in black and white, relying on data and empirical evidence to make sense of the world around him.

So when she came to him one summer morning in 2020 rambling that she'd been wrong all along about Trump, who was secretly saving humanity from dark and powerful forces, Christopher stared back at her blankly, unable to find his words. He had just gotten out of bed to find that she was already up—*still* up, in fact—flitting about with an almost manic energy that immediately put him on edge. He knew her to be overly credulous now and then, but this was unlike anything he'd ever heard from her. He thought she had suffered a psychotic break under her extreme stress from the pandemic.

Alice followed Christopher around the house, pleading with him to watch a video series on YouTube. It would "explain everything," she promised again and again. He could feel his anxiety pulsing through his body as she strung together a web of bizarre claims, from the existence of cannibalistic "spirit cooking" suppers for Hollywood stars to the "planned" sinking of the *Titanic* in 1912. The panic and nervousness that Alice had exuded since the start of the lockdowns had dissipated, replaced by an unsettling excitement. But one thing was still troubling her, she said: Because "the Deep State Cabal" was plotting to make this wildfire season California's most catastrophic ever, the two of them needed to flee the state before their home was reduced to ash. She had heard that the Cabal was armed with space lasers.

"I know I sound crazy right now," Alice cried out. "But please, my love, *please* just watch the videos and you'll understand!"

Christopher snapped at her to calm down. She was scaring him.

"I don't even recognize you right now, Alice!" he shouted over her. "I can't be around you like this. If your energy doesn't change soon, one of us will have to leave."

He stormed into another room, slamming the door behind him.

One of us will have to leave.

Alice sat alone on the couch with tears welling in her eyes and Christopher's words ringing in her ears. They sounded like a threat.

She knew that everything she had just told him seemed absurd at first and, on a surface level, antithetical to her progressive worldview. Maybe she had unloaded too much too quickly. Still, she didn't understand how he could be so dismissive with her. She had expected his doubt and hesitation, but he hadn't even given her that. Learning about the Great Awakening was the greatest natural high she had ever experienced; she just wanted to indulge in it with him—to open his eyes to the magnificent new beginning on the horizon.

Alice paced, caught in a mental tug-of-war of conflicting emotions. So much was changing so quickly. She had somersaulted overnight from loathing Trump to loving him, and from a state of terrifying uncertainty to one of calming clarity. And now, she believed, her beloved—the man who was supposed to protect and cherish her—was threatening to leave her.

Even in their lowest lows, Alice had known Christopher to be wholly committed to her. But she had been wrong about such things before. After her parents split up when she was eight, her father had moved away across the country, leaving her behind in Madison, Wisconsin, in pieces. Alice had been much closer with her father than her mother, yet as his visits became fewer and further between, she started to think of him as an uncle. It dulled the anguish of longing for her papa night after night. She had planned to move out to be near him after graduating high school, but at eighteen she fell in love with a man in Madison and married him shortly thereafter. Then he left too. Within six months of making her a single mother to their infant son, he was preparing to have another baby with another woman.

Both experiences were profoundly traumatizing for Alice. They imbued in her a deep need for stability in her life and her relationships. In their years together, Christopher had done what he could to assuage her fear of abandonment: He had put her onto his life insurance policy. He had added her to the deed of their valley-view home. He had given her a ring. But still mired in the pain of her past, Alice was easily triggered, and her beloved had just slammed the door on her and her new beliefs.

Christopher slept on the couch that night. Above him was a large piece of psychedelic artwork depicting a man and a woman touching foreheads before a beam of light, one of Alice's many tributes to her spirituality that adorned their walls. Filling their bookshelf were titles such as *Sacred Journey of the Peaceful Warrior* and *Speak Peace in a World of Conflict*. Christopher knew Alice's heart. He knew it was in the right place. It was her mind that had strayed.

The next morning, he woke up feeling slightly better about the situation and lousy for the way he had reacted in his initial state of shock. Alice had been there for him in his time of crisis; it was his turn to be there for her. So he went up to his office on the top floor of their home, opened YouTube on his computer, and searched for *The Fall of the Cabal*.

Within minutes, his anxiety came crashing back. The videos were gobsmacking. But they were also emotion driven and solution focused—an intoxicating combination for someone like his fiancée. At every turn, between wild conspiracy theories that were propped up by miscontextualized "evidence" and drenched in alarmist rhetoric, the narrator lauded viewers for being shrewd, independent thinkers willing to step outside of their ideological comfort zones. Christopher sank wearily into his chair. It was no wonder that Alice was so beguiled, he thought. The longer he watched, the more apparent it became that her frenzied behavior was no passing breakdown. They would surely be dealing with "QAnon" for a while.

As the series transitioned from one part to the next, bringing a dip in the ominous audio, Christopher heard a man's voice coming from inside the house. Startled, he jumped from his chair and burst out the door into the walkway overlooking their open-concept living room. Downstairs were two of their male neighbors. Alice darted across the room with her eyes fixed on the floor.

"What's going on here?" Christopher yelled. "Hey! What's going on?" As he rushed toward the stairs, one of the men looked up at him.

"She asked us for our help to move out," he said coolly.

Christopher suddenly noticed that they were carrying OfficeMax boxes. Alice was dragging a suitcase and had her Vitamix tucked under her arm.

"*What?*" he sputtered. "Alice! *Alice?* Where are you going?"

The man stepped into the stairway, lingering there with a box still in his arms.

Christopher froze. Did they think he might hurt her? Did *she* think that? It was a stabbing moment of heartbreak and disbelief. He would never—*could* never—raise a hand to her. Yet she was running away from him escorted by bodyguards.

He stood there, weak-kneed, and watched the woman he loved walk out the door.

Outcast

Alice had a mission. Whether she liked it or not, she believed that it was incumbent upon her to awaken her friends. Withholding a truth this monumental would feel like lying, and to her, the most important part of any relationship was a foundation of trust.

She knew it wouldn't be easy: If there was one thing that everyone in her community shared, it was a complete disdain for Trump. The most shocking of all the bombshells that *The Fall of the Cabal* had dropped in Alice's lap was that the president was a hero, not a villain, despite the Deep State media's coordinated efforts to paint him as such. Spreading the word was her way of supporting the cause; she would just have to be strategic about it.

So, from the empty bedroom of someone she knew across the Bay, Alice tried to guide her friends out into the sunlight that Christopher refused to see. She chose to start with what she assumed would be a politically neutral topic: vaccines. With Facebook as her soapbox, she published a couple posts detailing the shocking things she had learned through her recent research into Dr. Fauci and Bill Gates, including the latter's covert microchipping plans.

"Please take this VERY seriously. We need to wake up before it is too late," Alice wrote in one. Then she eagerly awaited people's comments. Dozens swiftly poured in.

"Nooooo not you too"

"don't become a Trump supporter!!!"

"this is toxic idiocy"

"For fuck sake, knock it off"

"bye! Unfriend!"

"you are being willfully ignorant."

"Seriously, this is pretty gross"

Sitting by herself on her borrowed bed, Alice cradled her phone in her hands, aghast. With each notification came a pang of searing rejection. She felt as if she was surrounded by a pack of bullies who were ganging up on her when she was only trying to help. These people knew her. *How could they think she was malicious or crazy?*

Employing her compassionate communication skills, Alice asked for understanding.

"I do appreciate your concern," she commented back to a torrent of anger over her questions about Gates's motives. "Can you have empathy for where I am coming from? Needing to ask despite the fact that the topic is hella controversial?"

The answer was a resounding "No." People kept piling on, unreservedly expressing their disapproval of Alice's beliefs and suspicions. And, it seemed, of her.

Alice didn't understand. In tears, she turned for sympathy to Tracy, the friend who had introduced her to *The Fall of the Cabal.* Tracy lamented that she was also dealing with stubborn resistance from people she was trying to enlighten, like toddlers plugging their ears and stomping their feet. She encouraged Alice to seek comfort in Facebook's many warm and welcoming QAnon groups. They were growing larger by the day as more people woke up—including, Tracy said, her and Alice's mutual acquaintance in the Bay Area, an outspoken yoga enthusiast named Vera.

Alice felt a sudden flash of shame. Though it seemed like much longer ago, she recalled that she had blocked Vera on Facebook just a week earlier, disturbed at the time that Vera had been posting so many right-wing conspiracy theories.

It was a jarring moment of self-reflection. But in her contrition, Alice found a glimmer of pride. She believed that she'd accomplished something extraordinary: She had opened her mind. She would be relentlessly congratulated for this feat inside her new online circles, where members held each other up as morally superior critical thinkers immune to the brainwashing techniques of the "intolerant Left." Lost on Alice was the irony of her abrupt descent into a Far Right echo chamber.

In reality, she had shifted—not shed—her confirmation bias. Or, more aptly, her "conformation bias," a term coined by social psychologist Péter Krekó to describe a driving force of conspiracy theory belief: "the tendency to seek out information that contributes to justifying the defense of one's own tribe—regardless of veracity." As Alice's existing tribe continued to push her out with apparent scorn and revulsion, she would become frantic to fit in with her new one. The truth, in turn, would appear blurrier and blurrier.

One evening, while eating dinner, Alice received an unprompted text from Sal, a dear, dear friend and roommate from many years ago. It wasn't a friendly check-in. Skipping past pleasantries, he cut straight to the chase.

"Hey, so I need to know what your stance is on qanon at this point," he said. "I need to know if you're on board with what you're implying you are."

Alice was gutted. *Even Sal was turning on her?* Still embroiled in online blowback, and aching from the turmoil with Christopher, she was emotionally exhausted from defending her views—and herself—to people she expected to raise her up, not tear her down. She tried meekly to shrug off Sal's concern. But he kept going. By standing with QAnon, he said, she was supporting racism and antisemitism. He called her "delusions" a "symptom of a greater sickness." Then he ended their friendship with a final blow to the heart.

"I'm sorry. I'm done pretending to be ok with this," he told her. "I can't sit by anymore and be on the wrong side of history."

Nothing could have hurt Alice more. For years, through classes and workshops hosted by other compassionate communication professionals, she had committed herself to examining her own privilege, unconscious biases, and opportunities to create social change. If anything, in her view, she was *anti*-racist, and now she was a target of prejudice herself. Sal's accusations were off-base insults levied from a place of sanctimonious liberal intolerance, she thought. He just didn't like that she no longer agreed with his narrow way of thinking, so he was writing her off as a bad person.

Like other conspiracy theorists in the making, Alice was being conditioned to look at the world as a binary: There was good, and there was evil. Believing that QAnon was on the side of good made it easier for her to look past its most sinister elements, including the intrinsically hateful ones to which Sal had objected. Her ignorance, to him, however, was no excuse, be it willful or not; at the end of the day, she still chose to associate with a group rooted in white supremacy.

All Alice could see was her dream for a just and peaceful society. It was what had driven her to give so much of herself trying to elect Bernie Sanders in 2016, drunk on his populist vision of overhauling the system to give every human being a fair shake at prosperity. But it had failed, crashing down with much of her hope for a better future. Until now.

QAnon was the way forward. If her friends weren't willing to listen to her, maybe they weren't really her friends.

Fighting for the Light

Back at home, Christopher was a mess. Even in Alice's absence, he could feel her everywhere in the house: in the rainbow-colored chakras posters that hung in their living room, in the potted orchids and seashells surrounding their bathtub, in the little white-feathered dream catcher hanging over their bed. Alice had asked for space, but online, Christopher watched her closely. It was devastating: Right before his eyes, like an unending car wreck, she was demolishing the friendships that he knew to be so precious to her. What he couldn't see were the ones she was building.

Finding new community in QAnon happened far more easily and rapidly than Alice had anticipated. There was something uniquely bonding about rallying around a set of forbidden beliefs—especially when it felt like the rest of the world had turned away in disgust. QAnon adherents and adjacent conspiracy theory thinkers saw themselves as a band of misfits. They were united by a perceived higher calling and ostracized by much of society—including, in many cases, those who had once been closest to them. As they became psychos, bigots, and lost causes in the eyes of friends and loved ones, to each other they remained confidants, comrades, and cheerleaders.

"God bless you for being willing to see with open eyes and an open heart. It is not easy nor for the faint of heart," one of Alice's QAnon friends wrote to her privately amid another onslaught of Facebook backlash. "Folks come around or they will leave, but you just keep doing you and speaking truth!!"

So far, for Alice, no one had come around. But she still had two remaining lifelines leading back out of QAnon. One was her seventy-five-year-old father.

Ted was a skinny, indefatigably happy man with the same mystical aura and playful chuckle as Alice. They had begun to mend their relationship long ago, when he took her on a weeklong trip to Sedona, Arizona. Under the sun, the moon, and the stars, they hiked all through the dazzling red rock-scape of Boynton Canyon together. It was a healing experience for both of them that instilled in Alice a lasting love of the area. Subsequent visits to Sedona made her feel connected to Ted, who lived down in the tropics on a small island with his wife.

Long-distance relationships were hard, especially for Alice, but she and Ted committed to speaking frequently over Zoom and Facebook. She felt safe telling him anything. When she confided in him about QAnon and asked him to watch *The Fall of the Cabal* one summer morning, he did so right away, then wrote back with his honest assessment: It appeared to be the work of "a highly intelligent conspiracy theorist."

Alice's heart sank. But Ted wasn't done.

"No matter how far apart we may drift from time to time in terms of thoughts and beliefs . . . you of course have my unswerving adoration and devotion, my darling."

Ted made no attempt to correct or debate her. But he did feel compelled to offer a word of unsolicited caution. He had seen people become consumed by fantasies before.

"The sad outcome all too often is that the conspiracy theory adherent becomes alienated from friends and loved ones alike," he told his daughter, leaving that person "isolated, fighting for the Light in a dark and scary world."

Alice understood this viscerally. Her heart was battling her rewired conscience. The pain of losing her community—of being cast out by people she loved—was among the worst she had experienced, restimulating the traumas of abandonment by her father and then her husband decades earlier. But QAnon had ignited a powerful sense of righteousness within her, a moral duty to stand up for what she now believed to be true. Her new friends thought that was admirable, not shameful.

Christopher, Alice's other lifeline, was trying desperately to get through to her without pushing her further away. On her tenth day out of the house, she allowed him to visit, but could barely look him in the eye when he arrived. The safety and warmth she usually felt in his presence were gone. When he asked if he could hold her, she nodded apprehensively. They climbed onto the bed atop the covers and settled into a stiff, silent embrace across from a mirrored closet. The solemn couple reflected back at them was hardly recognizable.

Alice didn't have anything to say. Neither did Christopher. He pulled out his phone and played an audio file with rolling waves and chirping birds in the background. It was from their trip to Costa Rica a year earlier. Alice had been taking a compassionate communication course at the time, requiring her to record a conversation in which she and a person of her choosing answered a set of questions about why they loved each other.

Over the next fifty minutes, she and her beloved slowly melted into each other's arms on the bed and remembered. Then he stood up to go home, and they parted realities once more.

A week later, Alice agreed to come back to him on three conditions: He needed to be accepting of her beliefs. They needed to fireproof their house. And, until wildfire season was over, they needed to go to Sedona.

The third was no small request. It would mean renting an Airbnb for months on top of paying their $4,000 mortgage at a time when Christopher's salary had been slashed by 25 percent due to the economic downturn. But his relationship was worth the gamble. So he hired someone to cut down the fifteen gorgeous Italian cypress trees that shrouded their property in verdant privacy and had a fire valve installed on their gas line. Then he and Alice loaded up their cars and set off separately for Arizona.

Along the drive, as palm trees turned to cacti, Christopher grappled with creeping doubts. Things with Alice were better but still far from normal. Despite his promise to her to be more open-minded, he knew that he could never truly accept her conspiracy theories, no matter how much he loved her. The world, to him, would always be black and white. He was still holding onto hope that she would eventually break free from her delusions . . . *but what if she didn't?*

He set a private deadline. If they couldn't find their way back to a happy place by the end of the year, he was going to walk away.

Alice was also coming to a fork in the road. Long-distance relationships were hard; those spanning disparate realities were untenable. She knew that soon enough she would need to commit to a choice. In one direction were people she cherished and adored—many for years, even decades—who'd been so quick to turn their backs on her and on the truth, resigned to a life down in darkness. In the other direction were people she was still getting to know, who had immediately embraced her into their community.

The ones who'd seen the sun.

9

BOB & CHAT

—Doris—

There are four lanes at the University of Alabama's indoor recreation pool. Beneath hanging strings of triangular flags in signature crimson and white, the water glistens in natural light pouring in through floor-to-ceiling windows. It's a small, modest facility compared to the school's Olympic-sized natatorium and its outdoor swim complex boasting a thirty-foot slide. But to Dale, an alumnus from the class of 1962, the little rec pool became an escape.

Every morning after an early breakfast, eighty-year-old Dale would make his way there for a dip, sometimes taking mindless detours just to enjoy the campus a bit longer. It was a magical place when the tulips and hydrangeas were in bloom. Dale could talk for hours about his old stomping grounds. As a student, back when he had curly black hair that made the green of his eyes stand out, he could often be found buried in a book in his usual spot on the second floor of the library, or over on Fraternity Row. He had never joined Greek life himself, but that hadn't kept him out of the parties.

Dale's Bama days were among the best of his life. The *schoo-wul,* as he called it in his warm southern accent, was a magnet for alumni. Like him, a number of his classmates had moved away from the Tuscaloosa area only to return later in life. He had done so in his early sixties after retiring from his career as a college professor down in Louisiana. UA would always be his home. He still loved to amble through the lush green Quad to Denny Chimes, the 115-foot, 25-bell campanile tower, which sounded the same to him in 2020 as it had in '62. Crimson Tide victories still filled him with pride.

But most special about UA, to Dale, was the unparalleled camaraderie.

He had been there until just before it desegregated and had since watched it slowly blossom into a more vibrant community, embracing the best parts of southern culture while progressing away from the worst. There was a timeless kinship between students past and present, from the lab geeks to the football stars and sorority sisters across grades and generations. They were one big yet intimate family. Only they could understand the true spirit in crying out *Roll Tide!* at the top of one's lungs, a cheer transcending sports and fandom—or the joy of dashing out between classes to The Strip, the unofficial campus off campus full of charming little shops, bars, and eateries with students on both sides of the register. Going to Bama wasn't just a phase of life; it became part of one's identity. Age would never take that away from Dale. Being back on campus made him feel young again.

When walking out onto the deck of the *poo-wul* each day in his swim trunks, Dale always took a moment to say hello to the lifeguards, greeting them by name. Then he hopped in to do laps of breaststroke with the aid of the blue flotation belt he brought from home. On most weekdays, he first had his water aerobics meet-up. He wished it was every day. For a giddy forty-five minutes or so, a small, tight-knit bunch of seniors gathered in the shallow end and did leg lifts, balanced on pool noodles, and submerged Styrofoam dumbbells. They managed to squeeze in so much chit-chat while their heads were above water that they called the group "Bob & Chat."

Dale credited swimming for his good health. At five feet, eleven-and-a-half inches tall, he weighed 165 pounds and stood straight, without a cane or a walker. He could make it up the stairs without losing his breath and needed just one nap a day. He was proud of that. But his desire to stay in shape wasn't the only thing keeping him in the water. The pool was where his friends were.

There was Eleanor, a former psychologist in her midsixties who had worked with Alzheimer's patients, someone so selfless that Dale couldn't help but feel inspired in her presence. Gord, a retired engineer for a major oil company in his midseventies, whose gentle demeanor Dale had first come to appreciate in a yoga class they took together. Sandra, a freelance writer in her early sixties who used to live in Manhattan, was one of the classiest people Dale knew. Ruth, a former psychology professor in her late sixties with whom Dale never tired of trading stories about their shih tzus. And Anita, a retired history teacher in her early nineties whom Dale had met in a Flannery O'Connor literary discussion group, before her dementia took hold. He found her to be brilliant.

Dale couldn't say enough kind words about his friends. He missed them terribly when the pool shut down in March of 2020 as Covid-19 tore through the country. His community had dissolved in a flash, leaving him floundering and lonelier by the day. On some mornings he drove to campus anyway, just to roam aimlessly by himself.

The townhouse complex where he and Doris lived had turned into a ghost town overnight. They were used to being on their own; as a childless couple, they had cherished their time as a twosome, filling it with long walks and talks and cooking and television. Every now and then they hosted delightful little dinner parties, serving fancy French dishes they prepared together from a tattered old cookbook. Both could be shy around other people—she more than he—though they had always deeply enjoyed social gatherings, content to listen more than speak. It was the company that brought them joy.

Dale was back in the pool as soon as it reopened. He felt comfortable knowing that the chlorine would kill the germs and that safety protocols were strictly enforced. Everyone entering the facility was individually screened for symptoms, and only one person was allowed in a swim lane at a time. The "Bob & Chat" gang was reunited at last, spaced out across the shallow end. They had lots to catch up on. Dale couldn't wait until it was safe enough to attend socially distanced off-campus get-togethers again—something that felt within reach by the spring of 2021, when infections in Alabama had plummeted and the vaccine rollout was well under way.

One day, while out shopping with his mask and gloves, Dale came across a nice bottle of California Bordeaux, a smooth and fruity red wine blend. It made him think of Eleanor, who on several occasions had asked him for recommendations. He gave it to her the next morning at the pool. The following week, when he asked if she'd tried it, she nodded. She had invited Ruth and her husband over for dinner, she said warmly, adding that they'd all enjoyed the Bordeaux very much.

Despair washed across Dale's face before he could try to hide it.

"Oh," he uttered involuntarily, his voice dropping.

He forced a quick smile.

"Well, good! I knew you'd like it."

Dale was crushed to learn that his friends had been hanging out without him. He already had his worries: Just the other day he'd overheard Sandra talking about hosting the group at her place, leaving him eagerly waiting for an invitation that never came. This confirmed it. Standing waist-deep in the cool water, six feet from Eleanor, he felt small, like a kid left out of his peers' after-school plans. Eleanor glanced down, visibly uncomfortable.

"It's just, you know—"

"Sure, of course," Dale cut in softly. "I know."

He didn't need Eleanor to explain why she had excluded him. It was the same reason why he hadn't invited anyone over himself.

It was Doris.

Cargo

When the vaccines first became widely available, there were people who leapt for joy and those who trembled with fear, even rage. Dale was in the first camp. Doris was in the second.

He got his initial Pfizer dose in a drive-through clinic with his arm hanging out his car window and a relieved grin on his face, despite sacrificing his cherished pool time to do so. He had still walked out the front door that morning with his swim bag in hand to keep Doris from knowing where he was going. After a year that had upended his social life and turned trips to the grocery store into life-threatening excursions, getting the shot was an emotional moment: It was his ticket back to freedom and safety.

To Doris, "the jab" represented precisely the opposite. She proclaimed, at first, that the vaccines contained location-tracking microchips. This was in line with her assertion that a "Deep State Cabal" of kleptocratic elites had conjured up the virus in a lab as part of a plot to weaken and control the people of the world. These days, her brain was constantly scanning for conspiracy, like a ravenous bloodhound hunting a phantom scent. All kinds of things smelled fishy to her. In February, when a snowstorm hit parts of western Alabama, glazing their street in a thin sheet of ice, she was convinced that the Cabal had geoengineered the weather by seeding the clouds with biomimetic surfactants.

Dale was beside himself. He feared that seventy-seven-year-old Doris was losing her mental faculties. Only after a series of panicked and rather disturbing Google searches did he learn that nearly all her beliefs could be traced back to a wide-ranging conspiracy theory known as QAnon. Trying to make sense of it was as overwhelming as it was mind-boggling. For an eighty-one-year-old, Dale was quite internet-savvy, but he still didn't know what a Q Drop was or how on earth 8kun worked. Beyond easing his concerns about Doris's cognitive function, having a name for the lunacy coming out of her mouth provided little comfort. He didn't understand how things had suddenly become so dire.

It had been a slow burn at first, stretching back to the traumatic cancer misdiagnosis in 2016 that had sent Doris careening into Facebook's web of alternative medicine groups. At the time, to Dale, her new interest in researching and posting about corruption within the healthcare system had seemed passionate, not problematic, necessarily. He'd read many news reports revealing cozy relationships between drug companies and regulatory officials. His concern surfaced when she became fixated with internet personalities like Del Bigtree, the "vaccine safety" advocate promoting a discredited link between MMR shots and autism. But Dale could see that in speaking out online against the so-called medical establishment, with the support of her new Facebook community, his normally reserved wife was finding her voice. It seemed to bring her a level of genuine fulfillment at a time when other sources of joy and agency in her life were slipping away or gone.

Doris's proud career as an administrative assistant had come to an end, taking with it a piece of who she was. She'd joined the labor force when only a minority of women were working and had even gone on to lead a team at a large company. But by the time she'd retired, the typing skills that had once distinguished her were commonplace. Her body, also, had slowed down considerably with mobility issues exacerbated by a hip injury a few years earlier, mostly keeping her at home. And although she could still take Dale's breath away, her head-turning beauty was turning fewer heads as time marched on. Doris put great care into her health and her appearance; her diet was mostly organic, and she still did herself up as elegantly as ever, with her short hair fluffed and dyed a soft cherry brown and merlot lipstick adorning her face, even around the house. It was as much for her as it was for Dale. But with age came inevitable change, and she seemed to be struggling in ways that he wasn't.

Really, Dale had often asked himself, who did it hurt if she enjoyed encouraging folks to be more skeptical of powerful people and institutions? Aside from the occasional unsolicited, unqualified medical advice she had provided to friends, which she had dialed back at his request, he considered her antiestablishment evangelizing to be harmless. It was a little out there and overzealous at times—increasingly so over the years—but nothing too crazy. Until the pandemic.

In Doris's words, wearing masks and staying home were "signs of submission," and people who complied with such mandates, like her husband, were "sheep" and "Kool-Aid drinkers." She'd leave their townhouse bare-faced, not to go anywhere, just to *go*, strutting undaunted up and down their empty street by herself for a few minutes every day. More than exercise, it was a display of defiance, Dale believed. If he tried to show her news articles correcting her misconceptions about the crisis, she'd click her tongue and chide him for trusting the "corporate media."

The only sources she'd accept were online contrarians like Bigtree, who was still at the top of her list. She tuned in every Thursday afternoon to listen to the talk show producer-turned-antivax rockstar, who spouted increasingly shocking and petrifying nonsense from atop his now multi-million-dollar empire. Like more and more right-wing influencers, he was regurgitating QAnon narratives to his millions of followers without outwardly associating with the movement. Comparing Covid protocols to Nazi rule, and vaccine opponents to the Founding Fathers and Martin Luther King, Jr., Bigtree repeatedly impressed upon his audience that the future of American liberty was in their hands.

"Martial law is coming for us. So what are we gonna do, just roll over and comply?" he boomed in a video. "We have got to make it as difficult as we can because this is not right!"

People had a collective moral obligation to be "superspreaders of truth," he implored. And they needed to *resist*. So that's what Doris did.

One morning, while heading out for the pool, Dale drove past her near their community mailboxes. She was walking over to their neighbor Esther, whose frail, wheelchair-bound husband was severely immunocompromised. A Covid-19 diagnosis would have been his death sentence.

In the rearview mirror, Dale grimaced to see Esther gasp and jerk back-ward as Doris greeted her, unmasked, with outstretched arms for a hug, as if to say, *Look how unafraid I am of this fake virus!*

Her Facebook profile was turning into a buffet of doomsday delusions. Among the many chilling things she posted there was an article from a fake-news website calling vaccination campaigns part of a "mass depopu-lation event" that would make both world wars combined seem like "a Mickey Mouse production."

> *Billions are already condemned to certain, unchangeable and agonising death. Each person who has received the injection will certainly die prematurely, and 3 years is a generous esti-mate for how long they can expect to remain alive.*

Dale choked up reading that. There was no way his wife really, truly, *seriously* believed, in her heart of hearts, that the "vast majority" of hu-manity would soon be dead, as the article went on to claim. Doris knew that all of her and Dale's friends had gotten their shots; if she actually thought each of them was guaranteed to perish in the near future, she would be bedridden with grief, not ranting on Facebook. And yet it was purely on the basis of these preposterous falsehoods that she refused to get vaccinated herself—a decision that could easily send her to an early grave. Deep down, she had to know that too.

Dale understood that broadcasting these beliefs wasn't just about en-lightening "walking zombies" and "sleepers," as Doris liked to say. He knew her better than that. It came with a sense of belonging and value, which was no small thing in a society quick to dismiss seniors as a burden or simply ignore them. As a "superspreader of truth," Doris wasn't an old woman; she was one of the good guys fighting the good fight against a common enemy. But Dale had no idea that she needed her conspiracy theories *this* badly—that she'd literally risk her life to hold onto them.

As Doris had slipped into QAnon, so too had many other seniors. One in every five Americans who agreed with its core conspiracy theories was over sixty-five years old. For some, anxious about the ways in which soci-ety was changing and nostalgic for a distant past, QAnon was a track back to traditional conservative values—a participatory way to help *Make America Great Again*. After living through decades of state and institutional breaches of public trust, from Watergate to the Iran-Contra scandal to the global financial crisis of 2008, traversing a complex social media landscape with limited digital literacy skills only greased the wheels. But what all elderly QAnon believers shared, by virtue of their age, was a natural vulnerability to a diminishing sense of "mattering" as their social roles changed.

Retirement, for Dale, had meant returning to a place that felt like home filled with people who felt like family, where he could swim and socialize every day. The early months of the pandemic had given him a bitter glimpse of what his life would be like without those opportunities and relationships. It was a window into his wife's world, in a sense. As part of a demographic whose perceived societal value had historically been disproportionately linked to sex appeal, Doris faced an additional struggle. Many women in the United States started to feel "invisible" in their fifties, research had found: shoved past in public spaces, ignored in shops and restaurants, talked over in group conversations.

Doris's progressive isolation reflected a reality for much of America's rapidly aging population, and for elderly citizens around the globe. In the Netherlands, one of the fastest-aging countries in western Europe, social scientists seeking to understand the psychological toll of getting older had sat down with seniors who felt that their happiness in life had withered away. Among the most common feelings they described was the pain of "not mattering" anymore. Their kids, once dependent on them, had grown up and moved on. The occupational skills they had honed over decades were no longer put to use. Their independence was waning with the deterioration of their mental and physical abilities. It felt like being alienated and adrift, said one interviewee, an elderly retiree of the shipping industry. He spoke of the raw despair he had recently experienced while on a cruise.

"You know, in the past, when I went aboard ship, I was the superintendent with full authority, carrying out important work," the man reminisced. Only now, "The ship sets sail and everyone has a job, but you just sail along," he said. "I am cargo to them. That's not easy. Not easy."

More than anything, he desired a way to contribute again—to do something of value. But society, it seemed, had no place for him anymore.

"I have no idea in which area someone my age is able to seriously participate. No—that is over."

It wasn't over for Doris.

For six-, seven-, even eight-hour stretches at a time, every single day, she was glued to the computer in a way that Dale had never seen before. She would disappear into their study, her slender frame tense and curled toward the screen with a stressed but electrified look in her eyes. Preaching Covid trutherism on Facebook—"waking people up"—had become her self-appointed job in retirement, one with no barrier to entry and no shortage of work to be done. She was at once a researcher, a journalist, a detective, a watchdog, and a whistleblower, and she took it seriously.

So did Dale. After she suggested offhandedly that people might have to "fight back" with guns when the government knocked down their doors to "forcibly" vaccinate them, he knew things had gone too far. He'd made a point with his college students to be gentle and patient in the way he corrected them, but that hadn't worked on Doris. So he told her unreservedly that her conspiracy theories weren't just wrong, they were dangerous, and that she needed to let them go. It wasn't well received. The very term *conspiracy theory* had been invented by the CIA to shut down conversation, Doris retorted, and she didn't appreciate how dismissive Dale was being of her "research." The two were suddenly arguing in a way they never had before. Their marriage had always been one of compromise and understanding—of *You're right, I'm sorry, dear,* in both directions. But when it came to true and false, there was no room to budge. For days that stretched miserably into weeks, the tension between them just wasn't defusing.

Dale returned home from the pool one afternoon to find Doris sitting in the living room, waiting for him. They needed to talk, she said. The solemn expression on her face worried him. She gestured for him to take a seat in the armchair across from her, so he did.

"Is everything all ri—"

"I need you to listen to me," Doris said. "Don't interrupt."

"Oh. Okay . . ."

"I just feel that you don't respect me and you don't respect my thinking," she intoned.

Then she broke his heart.

"I just feel that you're being verbally abusive."

In all Dale's years, that was the most hurtful thing anyone had ever said to him. *Verbally abusive?* Doris was still talking but he could no longer hear her. *Did she really believe that?* He had never felt so disconnected from her. *Where were they supposed to go from here?*

Apparently she'd already thought about that.

"If this continues," Doris went on, "well . . . I don't know what we'll do about it."

Dale sat there, slack-jawed, trying to process what she'd said and the cautionary tone with which she'd said it. She was studying his reaction, as if to make sure he understood.

He did: His beloved wife of fifty years—his best friend—was threatening to leave him for discounting the claims of a group on the internet called QAnon.

Lonely by Association

Dale stopped challenging Doris's beliefs. He said nothing when he discovered that she had stocked one of their bedroom closets full of canned soups and beans, despite their overflowing pantry. He held his tongue when she refused to see a "Deep State doctor" about an inflamed red rash that had appeared on her arm, hoping desperately to himself that the remedies she had found online would actually work. And when she insisted on spending $10,000 of their retirement savings on a backup generator to prepare for an electrical grid failure, which she expected to occur imminently during some kind of military occupation, he forced himself to think of it as an investment in their safety. The power lines in their neighborhood were buried underground, making the odds of an outage that would merit such a purchase unlikely . . . but, he supposed, not impossible.

For the first time, their marriage felt fragile. The calm safety that Dale had always felt in Doris's presence was replaced with a gnawing uncertainty. He didn't know what she was thinking anymore—or what to say to her—so he said hardly anything at all. He mostly stayed in the bedroom with the door closed, reading and rereading his books for hours each day just to pass the time. It was painfully lonely. They were a wall and a world apart, soulmates-turned-roommates in awkward, uncharted territory. The living room, where they used to curl up to watch their favorite murder mysteries, chat about the news, and read aloud to each other, was no longer a safe space; she might wander out from the study and summon him to come watch another maddening video she'd found on Facebook.

With little else to do beyond reading, Dale was spending more time on Facebook too. But the experience had been tainted: Once a cheerful, care-free place to share snapshots of his life with faraway friends and peer fondly into their worlds, it was now clouded with feelings of shame and sadness. He could barely bring himself to look at Doris's status updates; just knowing that practically everyone in their lives could read them was upsetting enough. Many were affixed with Facebook's "false information" labels, which to Doris was damning proof that Big Tech was out to censor the truth. Dale wished he could post a note on his own page distancing himself from Doris's views without her ever seeing it. She was scaring people away from both of them, taking a pickax to the community they'd spent decades building and nurturing together. In its place, she was har-vesting a new one made up of like-minded strangers she'd met online— people who vocally appreciated her and the work she was doing. Dale wondered if they had influenced her belief that his efforts to fact-check her constituted verbal abuse. Now and then he overheard her talking to some of them on the phone. There was an excitement in her voice that hadn't been there in ages.

As Doris's burgeoning network got bigger, Dale's was only getting smaller. The first person he noticed had unfriended him on Facebook was Ben, one of his former students who was now in his late fifties. Dale and Doris had gotten to know him quite well during the school trip through western Europe that they co-chaperoned in 1973, and had stayed in touch with him over the years. Dale was gutted. He thought of Ben as a friend. When he reached out to delicately ask what he had done to offend him, Ben confirmed his fears: He'd assumed that Dale shared Doris's beliefs, including that the pandemic was a hoax. It was not only ignorant, but also cruel to those who had lost loved ones, Ben said. Upon subsequent in-spection of his "Friends" list, Dale realized that Ben was likely far from the only person who had come to that conclusion. He wanted to cry.

There was only one place where Dale felt at ease anymore. He was al-ways the first to arrive for water aerobics and the last to leave, sticking around after it ended to swim slow, leisurely laps for as long as his body would allow. For a small but cathartic part of his day, he could be with friends and think about something else—at least until the conversation turned to Covid, as it often did, or when they chatted about each other's spouses. Someone would inevitably turn to Dale with an almost pitying smile and ask how Doris was doing, to which he'd reply with a mumbled "She's just fine, thanks," and promptly pivot to another topic. Most awkward were the mornings when the group gathered in the pool following one of their occasional rendezvous without him, still buzzing about the fun they'd had together. Dale understood. No one felt comfortable being around an unvaccinated person—especially someone high-risk, like Doris—or asking Dale to come out but leave her at home. Dale suspected that Doris's increasingly snarky online commentary was also off-putting at a basic, human level. Even in a post-Covid world, he feared, he would still be alienated.

He was grateful for what remained of his social life. He knew it was more than what most people had at his age. But there was a stabbing powerlessness that came with watching the person he loved most drive a wedge between him and his friends.

As intensely as he yearned to get back out into the world, Dale found himself thwarting his opportunities to do so. When Doris suggested that they go out for a treat and get lunch at Rama Jama's, a Strip staple chock-full of Bama memorabilia hanging on the walls and dangling from the ceiling, he pretended he wasn't feeling well. He offered to instead fetch their slaw dogs and fried green tomatoes for takeout. Alabama had lifted its mask requirement, but he worried that the restaurant, where he and Doris had been going for years, might still be asking patrons to wear face coverings while walking to and from their booths. Dale knew how Doris would react to such a request and couldn't bear to watch it unfold. At the vet about a month earlier, while they were picking up medication for their shih tzu, an attendant had politely reminded Doris to put on her mask. She sneered and flashed a little paper card that she had downloaded from the internet supposedly excusing her from wearing one, then reprimanded the frightened-looking woman for "perpetuating a culture of fear." It was humiliating. Dale had to actively fight the urge to apologize. He knew better than to publicly—or privately—oppose his wife. Living under an implied threat of divorce had silenced him.

At home one afternoon, while they were both on Facebook inside their vastly different online universes, Dale scrolled upon a live-streamed video from fifty-five-year-old Phil, one of his former students who had gone on to become a now-retired tennis coach. Phil had been hospitalized for months since contracting Covid-19 while traveling with his wife and exercising little caution, believing then that only those who disobeyed God would be infected. He looked as if he'd aged at least a decade in that time. He'd lost a good twenty pounds, leaving his formerly rosy-cheeked face pallid and gaunt, and his eyes bulging in their sockets. Filming himself from his hospital bed with his phone, Phil thanked everyone for their prayers and gave an update on his health. He'd spent some of his stay comatose and on a ventilator and had suffered severe complications, including partial paralysis and multiorgan failure requiring dialysis.

Praising the Lord, Phil shared with some enthusiasm that earlier in the day, "in a real blessing," he had managed to stand for four full minutes with assistance from a hydraulic lift. Then his voice suddenly trembled and cracked. He let out several involuntary yelps.

"I—I wanna walk. I wanna walk so bad!" he sobbed between rapid, high-pitched gasps, trying to fight back the tears with each quivering word.

He wheezed a frantic goodbye and put his phone down, mistakenly thinking that he'd ended the live stream. With the camera pointed up at the cork-tiled hospital ceiling, in one of the most excruciating scenes Dale had ever witnessed, Phil could be heard whimpering to himself like a child in a dying man's body.

Dale cried with him. He ached for his wife. He missed her touch and her smile and how she made him feel understood in a way no one else ever had. Life without her warmth didn't make sense. He wanted to hold her in his arms and ask her how to fix things. Doris always knew what to do. Surely there had to be some combination of words he could say to break through to her . . . to get back to the way things used to be. Every passing day spent anxiously avoiding her in their own home felt like a wasted gift. At his age, he didn't know how many he had left. He just knew, as she did, that he didn't want to spend them feeling alienated and adrift.

So every morning after breakfast, Dale and Doris escaped to the places where they felt like they belonged. She went into the study and onto Facebook, dutifully immersing herself in her conspiracy theory evangelism while saying little about the angry red rash still creeping down her arm. And he went off to UA, meandering across campus to the pool to spend forty-five precious minutes bobbing and chatting with his friends. Then he slipped into a lane to swim laps by himself, going back and forth in circles until he no longer could.

MOM TOLD ME

—Kendra and Jonah—

The "Stuffler" was a thing of beauty.

Made of smooth, black metal with a silvery sheen and a red rubber handle, it could cook perfectly crispy but tender Belgian waffles stuffed with anything from fried chicken to Reese's Peanut Butter Cups in minutes. As soon as it arrived on Tayshia and her husband Buck's doorstep, their nephews were begging to come over.

She picked them up from her sister's place for a Friday night sleepover a couple weeks before Christmas of 2020. Kendra was in her usual spot, sprawled across the couch, watching a YouTube video on her smart TV about how George Soros had supposedly conspired to install Joe Biden as president. She and Tayshia barely said a word to each other as the boys got ready. Their already-strained relationship had been on thin ice since the election; broaching the topic of politics had become so contentious that Kendra had threatened to withhold access to her sons, so Tayshia was dejectedly backing down.

She dropped thirteen-year-old Jayden off at the house with Buck to do some homework and brought seven-year-old Jonah to their local Meijer supermarket for ingredients to make their waffles in the morning. He was a small, chubby-cheeked kid weighing not even fifty pounds, but his appetite was voracious, especially when it came to sweets. He darted ahead of her through the store, skipping down the aisles and grabbing items off the shelves, like he'd been let loose inside Willy Wonka's chocolate factory. Their grocery cart filled up with everything they'd need for a little boy's idea of a balanced breakfast: marshmallows, peanut butter, whipped cream, maple syrup, chocolate chips, strawberries, and bananas.

As they stepped out through the sliding glass doors with their goodies, a gust of frigid Michigan air hit them so hard that Jonah stumbled backward. The sun had gone down while they were shopping, giving way to a piercing winter night shrouding the long, poorly lit parking lot. Tayshia pointed to the side of the cart and told Jonah to hold on and stay safe before they set off toward her car. He looked up at her and screamed.

"Why? Are they out there?!"

Tayshia turned her head to peer over both shoulders.

"What are you talking about, Jonah?"

"They're gonna get me! I'm not going!"

"Who?"

"The bad people Mom talks about! They eat kids!"

Tayshia gasped, the cold stinging her lungs.

"Hold up. Jonah—you're kidding me, right?"

As he cowered behind the cart with tears spilling from his eyes, she knew he wasn't.

Tayshia had noticed Jonah repeating Kendra's nonsense more and more ever since his school had switched to remote learning. His classroom was now a compact, one-story house in which videos with titles like "COVID 911: The DEEP STATE Insurgency" blared for hours every day. Just the other week, he had pointed at Biden on the TV and called him a "pedo"—a word Tayshia didn't think a second grader should know. He'd even gotten into trouble with his school for telling other students that the coming Covid vaccines would kill them all. But Tayshia hadn't realized just how profoundly these conspiracy theories were affecting him. The look on her nephew's face was one she'd never seen from him.

He was terrified.

"The World's an Evil Place"

It wasn't until her midthirties, when Tayshia met Buck in 2015, that she truly knew how it felt to be taken care of. Her mother had done her best, but as a single parent with two jobs and four kids to support, she was rarely home. Tayshia, from a very early age, was less a daughter than a coparent. She didn't mind. She had nothing to compare it to. Though the scenery changed, rotating through dilapidated apartment complexes and the occasional homeless shelters, her childhood memories were a lot of the same: feeding, nurturing, and watching over her little sister and cousins. Growing up so young was what had shaped her into such a fiercely independent, purpose-driven woman.

Transitioning from caregiver to care receiver wasn't easy at first, especially with someone so fundamentally different from her. Although she and Buck had both grown up in hypersegregated Milwaukee, they had done so nearly two decades apart and had entirely different experiences there. Tayshia was a Black, millennial social justice activist, an animal lover, and a hotel clerk with bright blue hair and butterflies tattooed down her arm. Buck was a divorced, gray-bearded, cigar-smoking U.S. Army vet and hunter in his fifties. And he was white.

They knew how people saw them together. They could feel the stares, and the glares. But they just fit. When she couldn't, he would. As she initially struggled to accept his love, he'd find excuses to dote on her with handmade cards or gifts, like their quarter-anniversary, or "National Squirrel Day"—or just because. He surprised her once with a stunning upholstered vanity stool that he'd made himself with floral purple fabric and strings of dangling beads around the edges. It made her cry. Her love language was food; she baked him his favorite pies and cakes and pastries, trying because of his heart disease to keep them in moderation, but often caving to his pleading sweet tooth. Whenever they parted ways, whether for a workday or a quick errand, it wasn't "See you later" but "Kiss you in a bit."

The sweetness of their love was its silliness. Tayshia had never been able to take life any way but seriously; she'd been in survival mode for much of it. She and Buck both had their own scars from their own battlefields. But when they were together, the mornings were slow and the laughter was endless. They bought a little white house just outside Detroit, near Kendra and the boys, and painted the walls inside bright teals, yellows, blues, and purples. Then they adopted a pair of "fur bastards," a husky named Coco and a tabby named Sylvester, and taught both to play fetch in the grassy backyard. Each had its own pet-sized Detroit Lions jersey. Buck was a diehard fan, so Tayshia became one too. They even brought their big blue foam fingers to their wedding for a photoshoot.

Tayshia wasn't a spiritual person, but she genuinely believed she'd found her soulmate in Buck. It was almost perfect, their life together. They didn't have much, and they didn't need it. Raising a family was their only dream to never become a reality. The pregnancy they'd lost two months earlier, in October, was just the latest to end in heartbreak, leaving an already-assembled white crib collecting more dust inside a spare bedroom-turned-nursery-turned-spare bedroom. But Jayden and Jonah were like sons to them. Tayshia had actually helped raise Jayden during his younger years when Kendra was unable to do so on her own, and the two had remained extremely close. Jayden felt more connected to his aunt than his mother, he'd tell her. He just wanted to grow up, move out, and go to college, like she had.

Little Jonah, meanwhile, was like Buck's shadow, following him around everywhere he went. Buck had jumped out from behind a kitchen corner to spook him one day not long after they'd first met, and right then and there, Jonah had decided that he was the coolest guy ever. His father, Kendra's boyfriend, wasn't around all that often, but the uncle-nephew relationship he had developed with Buck was the most heartwarming thing Tayshia had ever seen. The two had their own special handshake, "hugs and dab," in which they'd wrap their arms around each other, then fling them up angled toward the sky with their heads tucked down. Sometimes Tayshia and Jayden would get to talking for a couple hours, then find them cuddled up on the couch, fast asleep.

Buck and Jonah's favorite thing to do together was work on little fixer projects around the house and property. Jonah was in charge of the toolbox. Buck would reach out from under the sink or from behind the furnace and say "Crescent wrench!" or "Flathead screwdriver!" and Jonah would unfailingly hand him something else. Buck also set up a tire swing out back for the boys. Jonah loved it so much that he'd run straight from the car to the yard every time he came over. Tayshia was inside with Jayden one day when they heard his high-pitched voice squealing "*Uncle Buck! Uncle Buck!*" They rushed out to find Buck laughing and wheezing on his back with the tire and snapped rope beneath him. Jonah had wanted to know if it was strong enough to hold his weight.

Like many kids his age, he wanted to know everything about everything. In response to any new fact he was told, from gravity making things fall to the Lions being the best, he'd ask, "Why?" over and over until Buck would finally exclaim, "Because I said so, my guy!" and throw him over his shoulder to tickle him into a fit of giggles. Almost as boundless as Jonah's curiosity was his ingenuous trust in whatever he was told when it came from a grownup. It was this natural thirst for answers paired with a naïve lack of discernment that made him and other children uniquely susceptible to absorbing false information—from lies about a jolly, red-suited fat man circling the globe in a sleigh to those far less innocent. Worse, with their underdeveloped critical thinking skills, heightened emotional vulnerability, and limited life experience, they were venturing out into an ever-more complex online world, showing up younger and spending more time there than ever. Most American children received their first smartphone before turning eleven. The pandemic saw their social media use climb to unprecedented levels, particularly among those of color and those from low-income households, like Jonah.

Even as digital natives, kids didn't just show up online and figure out how to navigate reality-distorting algorithms or highly sophisticated disinformation, let alone deepfakes. Study after study had found young people to be woefully unable to recognize fake news on the internet, particularly, again, those from disadvantaged backgrounds. Jonah was at an even higher risk of falling for lies and hoaxes than his brother: The cognitive abilities required to evaluate and reject falsehoods only began to emerge at around seven years old, a time of significant neurological development. Children started getting better at problem-solving, logical reasoning, and distinguishing fantasy from reality at that age. They also developed greater skepticism. After turning seven, they were more inclined to rely on firsthand experimentation to test dubious claims themselves, such as feeling a rock with their fingers after being told that it was soft, not hard. A lot of disinformation circulating online, however, was unfalsifiable. There was no way to disprove the existence of child-eating "bad people" lurking out of sight. And to Jonah, his mother's conspiracy theories weren't claims to be evaluated—they were bonding opportunities.

Kendra was obsessed with her YouTube videos and Jonah was obsessed with her, the way any little kid looked up to their mom or dad as a superhero. Tayshia could see it every time she was over at their house for pickups and dropoffs. While other second graders were surely at home playing *Minecraft* or watching *SpongeBob*, Jonah was studying the Deep State and its crooked cast of characters. He would snuggle into Kendra's soft, warm embrace on the couch to watch whatever videos she had on, sometimes visibly frightened, while reflexively nodding and shaking his head when she did and parroting her commentary. When he asked her

"Why?"—*Why do the bad people steal elections? Why do they put poison in vaccines? Why do they eat kids?*—her answer hardly changed.

"Because the world's an evil place, baby."

Kendra's fatalistic anger and anxiety became Jonah's too. QAnon conspiracy theories were serving parent and child in their own ways: For Kendra, they vindicated her distrust in a system that had abjectly failed her since she was a little girl growing up in extreme poverty, with a direct window into the richer, easier, *better* world of her white classmates at the private school she and Tayshia had attended upon receiving their state vouchers. For Jonah, conspiracy theories were a path into his mother's arms. The grim toll it would take on his young life had yet to reveal itself.

It kept Tayshia up at night. Jonah was on a trajectory she'd seen before. Even coming from the same troubled home, she and Kendra had viewed the world in very different lights from a young age. While Tayshia had gone on to find joy and purpose in activism, her sister had taken the opposite route, resigned to the belief that life would never hold any real opportunity for someone like her. Tayshia could already envision that dynamic repeating with the boys, young brothers with two potentially drastically divergent futures ahead of them. Jayden was older with a good head on his shoulders and his own interests. He liked to read and draw anime, and he couldn't wait to make his mark on the world. But Jonah . . .

Tayshia didn't like to think about it. Life wouldn't be easy for either of her nephews. She knew the statistics all too well: Little Black kids were already around four times more likely than their white peers to end up incarcerated, 20 percent less likely to graduate high school, and 60 percent less likely to finish college.

She shuddered to wonder what the odds were for little Black QAnon believers.

Save Our Children

After coaxing Jonah across the long, dark Meijer parking lot and into the car with the ingredients for their "Stuffler" waffles on that cold December night, Tayshia drove him back to her and Buck's home in silence, then tucked him into bed. She promised him he was safe.

Watching him sob and quiver behind the grocery cart had evoked the memory of a deeply scarring incident from when she was his age, back in

Milwaukee. She hadn't thought about it for many years. It was a rainy day, so she and Kendra had been playing inside their multifamily home with their little cousins, Sasha and Benji, when they heard a spine-chilling scream right outside their door. Their mother wasn't home.

The girls looked at each other, unsure of what to do. Tayshia cracked open the door and they both poked their heads out.

The first thing they noticed was the blood.

It washed right by their feet in the rain, swirling down the porch steps and onto the sidewalk. The color was a reddish maroon, so dark that Tayshia didn't know what it was at first. But then she saw him. Right next door, barely six feet away, their neighbor, a Laotian man, was crumpled and motionless on the street, his mouth agape with more blood trickling out.

Kendra shrieked.

It was the first dead body they had ever seen. It wasn't the last.

Their youth was laced with fear and violence. Some had revealed itself only later in life. Not until they were young women did Tayshia and Kendra understand that the man at the shelter where they had sometimes stayed as kids, who gave them graham crackers and chocolates, then took little Sasha by the hand into another room, wasn't really taking her to play. Tayshia had tried to forget most of it. But the terror she and Kendra had experienced on that day with the rain and the dark red blood came rushing back when she saw the same look in Jonah's eyes that she'd seen in his mother's. It was at that moment that she realized Kendra's conspiracy theories weren't just spooking him—they were traumatizing him.

Tayshia hadn't done too much research into QAnon. She knew believers thought Trump was a God-like figure and Biden was a pedophile, and she had seen their #SaveOurChildren hashtags on Facebook. But she wanted to know the extent of what Jonah had been hearing from Kendra and watching on YouTube every day. So she sat down at the computer and read in horror about the movement's most extreme theories centering kids as the victims of satanic, blood-drinking cannibals. When she got to *Frazzledrip*—the rumored dark-web snuff film showing Hillary Clinton filleting the face of a young girl to wear over her own—she wanted to throw up. It was no wonder that Jonah was terrified.

The harm this was causing, at his age, could tragically be permanent. In early childhood specifically, intense and frequent or long-term stress, known as "toxic stress," could literally reshape the still rapidly developing brain, altering its physical architecture in devastating ways. Among the many potential lifelong harms were cognitive difficulties, such as impaired memory function, concentration abilities, and mood control; mental health disorders, including anxiety, depression, and PTSD; and even physical health issues, like heart disease and diabetes. Black children, who were more likely to experience prolonged adversity than white kids, were disproportionately affected by toxic stress.

It was a cycle of intergenerational trauma, Tayshia feared: The toll of a childhood fraught with peril had manifested in Kendra's fixation with antiestablishment conspiracy theories, which were now petrifying her young son. What would happen to *him*?

Tayshia wasn't willing to find out. She and Buck needed to break the cycle and "un-brainwash" Jonah before it was too late, they decided. Confronting Kendra would be too risky; Tayshia worried that her sister would follow through on her threat to keep her from seeing the boys at all. From what she was reading online, one of the worst things to do when trying to deprogram a conspiracy theorist was fact-check their beliefs, which could make them defensive or push them away. One of the best was to get them thinking about other things again by involving them in unrelated activities. So Buck loosened door hinges, detached shutters from windows, and threw huge wads of tissues down the toilet, then called Jonah over every weekend to fix them. If nothing else, it got him away from YouTube for a few hours at a time.

By April, Tayshia and her sister had barely spoken in five months, since the election. But Kendra and her boyfriend were hosting their annual family-and-friends Easter dinner at her place. Tayshia was grateful that she and Buck had still received an invitation; she could only hope that it would go peacefully. She made Rice Krispies treats and he dressed up as the Easter Bunny in a big fuzzy white costume they ordered from Party City. When he hopped his way into the backyard, Jonah screeched with delight and began hopping around behind him. It was too adorable not to smile, immediately easing the tension between Tayshia and Kendra.

While the children scoured the yard for foil-wrapped chocolates with their little woven baskets, Tayshia boiled eggs for them to dye and Kendra finished up the cooking. It was nice to see her focused on something other than her usual doom and gloom. They chatted a little, mostly about Jayden and Jonah, and more like acquaintances than sisters. But it was progress. Through the window they could hear Jonah cry out, "I knew it was you, Uncle Buck! *I knew it!*"

For a few sweet hours, the TV was off and conspiracy theories didn't exist. The only hiccup came during dinner, when Buck accidentally mentioned that Tayshia had signed them up to get their Covid vaccinations the following weekend. He brought it up only to discuss the location: They were going down to a drive-through clinic at the Indianapolis Motor Speedway, home to the annual Indy 500 race, during a trip to see his sister. Tayshia shot him a quick *What the fuck!* across the table with her eyes—returned with a *Shit, my bad!*—then looked nervously over at Kendra, waiting for the ranting to begin. But she just sighed and shook her head, and the conversation moved along.

After stuffing their bellies and clearing their plates, everyone went over to Tayshia and Buck's place. The kids roasted marshmallows over a small bonfire out back while the adults sat around cheerfully sipping Buck's homemade wine. Then Tayshia went over to chat with Jayden about his school life while Buck and Jonah slipped away to discuss plans for their next project: constructing a small pool house to accompany the still-boxed inflatable hot tub that Tayshia had purchased for Christmas. By around 9 p.m., the fire was dying and the night was winding down. Tayshia gave Kendra a tight hug.

"We need to do this more often," Tayshia said. "I've missed you, you know."

"As long as you act right," Kendra teased. "Night, sis."

Buck and Jonah hugged, dabbed, and said goodbye. Then Tayshia nestled her head against her husband's chest in the driveway, beaming as she watched her sister and nephews drive off. It had been a beautiful day.

A couple weeks later, Tayshia was up before the sun for an early-morning work shift. She gave Buck a groggily received peck on the cheek and dashed out the door.

"Kiss you in a bit!"

On her way back home after eight tiring hours, she was stopped at a red light when she got a Ring camera alert on her phone about motion detected at her front door. It was probably Buck, she figured; he'd been planning to go out for some more supplies before Jonah came over to work on the pool house. Tayshia opened the live video feed to say a quick hello through the two-way talk feature. Buck was facing away from the camera, bent down toward his shoes.

"Oh *damn*, baby!" she cheered. "I love that booty!"

Buck didn't respond.

"Can I get a shake?"

He staggered forward, violently plunked down onto the front porch steps, then started crawling back toward the door, clutching his chest.

Tayshia screamed. Cars honked as she sat before a green light, dialed 9-1-1 with trembling hands, and told the dispatcher that her husband was having his third heart attack. Then she raced toward the house, weaving through traffic to cut down the thirty-five-minute drive as much as she possibly could. She was still too late to say goodbye.

When her mom died, in 2009, a part of Tayshia did too.

It was sudden and slow. The stroke took Brandy's memory first, then her life. The kids were all in their twenties when it happened. None had been quite the same since. Kendra did conspiracy theories, Sasha did drugs, and Benji never did much. Tayshia nearly dropped out of her senior year of college, unable to focus on her lectures or finish her readings. The pain was too great. There was no beating it, no escaping it. Eventually, she just embraced it. She carried her grief with her like an anvil on her back, stumbling her way forward until she learned to walk again. Like her mother, she was resilient and inured to hardship. Brandy had taught her to be strong.

Buck had taught her that she didn't have to be.

For more than thirty years, Tayshia had gotten by fine, falling now and then but always getting back up. Then Buck came along and lightened her load. He chipped down her walls and helped carry her pain, bringing her a happiness she'd never even known to wish for. Waking up next to him, curling into his burly chest while he smiled and kissed her forehead, felt like living a dream. He was her Christmas morning every day.

If she could go back to that night in 2015 when they met online and stop herself from ever opening his message, she would. She'd heard the expression that it was "better to have loved and lost than never to have loved at all." Whoever wrote it hadn't known a love like hers. It wasn't a part of her that died with Buck. It was all of her. The light in her soul was out. He'd made her feel safe for the first time in her life, then shattered her completely. There was no getting back up from this.

Once again, Tayshia was alone in the world with no one to take care of her except herself. But she didn't know how to anymore. She contemplated suicide.

Instead of killing herself, she tortured herself, thinking of the dumb shit that only she and Buck could laugh at. Like the April Fools' Day when she snuck out of the house at the crack of dawn to cover his truck in hundreds of multicolored sticky notes, leaving him no choice but to drive to work that way. Or the random texts they'd send each other throughout the day, dropping lines from their favorite shows to watch in bed together. *There's always money in the banana stand!*

For some women, it was long-stemmed red roses and sweet nothings that made them swoon. For Tayshia, besides watching Buck play with Jonah in the yard, it was how every night, at least once—even if it was 3 a.m. and 20 degrees out—he would get out of bed, shuffle across the room in his boxers, open the window, and stick his butt out to fart just so she wouldn't have to smell it.

She couldn't sleep alone in their bedroom even if she tried. She rarely left the couch. Her desperation to feel close to Buck was so intense that she would drape herself in his burial flag and listen to his voicemails on repeat while Coco licked the tears from her face and Sylvester curled up beside her. They were still waiting for him to come home.

Lying on the couch one afternoon, holding one of Buck's cigars under her nose, Tayshia saw that Jayden was calling her phone. She wiped her eyes, cleared her throat, and said hello, trying to steady her voice. It was Jonah.

"I want Uncle Buck's Lions jacket."

"Oh," Tayshia said. "Hey, Jonah. Sure, honey. It's yours."

Something seemed off in her nephew's voice.

"How are you doing, Jonah? Are you feeling—"

"I gotta go."

"Hey, I know it's hard. I'm hurting too. Do you want to talk about it?"

He said nothing.

"Jonah?"

"It's *your* fault!" he blurted out. "You made him get the shot!"

Tayshia's ears started ringing.

"What did you just say?" she whispered.

"You killed him," Jonah cried. "Mom told me."

TRUST THE PLAN

—Matt—

By the fifth time his call went to voicemail, Matt could feel his heart pounding in his chest. It was a sunny Saturday afternoon in July of 2006, and more than an hour had passed since Andrea, his then-fiancée, had left his apartment to make her way to a family friend's home—a thirty-minute drive at most. It wasn't like her to miss a call. Matt paced in his living room, clutching his phone. He was on his way out the door to re-trace her route in his car when, on his tenth call, he finally got an answer.

"Hello?"

It was a man's voice. Matt froze.

"Hello?" the voice said again. "This is Officer Daniels."

Then came the news that Matt had been dreading. He heard it in frag-ments as shock took hold of him: "Serious car accident." "Major head trauma." "Airlifted to the hospital."

"Did you see her?" Matt sputtered. "Will she be all right?"

The line went silent for a moment.

"I think you'd better get to the hospital right away."

Matt and Andrea had spent the morning cozied up on the couch watching *Scrubs* and excitedly discussing their wedding plans. They were due to be wed at a Baptist church in the new year in a big ceremony with white calla lilies, Andrea's favorite. It was supposed to be the long-awaited beginning of their life together: After living apart for the entirety of their relationship to honor their Christian faith, they were finally going to move in and prepare to start a family.

As Matt stood motionless in his doorway, it felt as if everything they'd been dreaming about was slipping away.

Please, God, he prayed as he clambered into his car and sped off for the hospital. *Please, heal her. Send an angel to heal her.*

After arriving at the intensive care unit, Matt was ushered into a near-empty waiting area with windowed, grayish-blue walls and the sterile smell of disinfectants, where he spent the next two hours fidgeting in his seat and walking restless laps of the room.

When he was finally allowed to see Andrea, the sight of her limp, lacerated body left him physically weak. She was intubated and unconscious, hooked up to an IV with two black eyes and cuts all down her arms. The upper left side of her face was caked in dried blood that had oozed from a gaping wound in her scalp, where doctors had shaved back the silky brown hair that she'd tucked behind her ear to kiss Matt goodbye just hours earlier. He stared down at her, unable to speak.

One of the doctors came in to provide a dire update: Although Andrea would likely survive, she wouldn't be the same person when—or if—she regained consciousness. He urged Matt to brace himself for a reality in which she had permanent brain damage, meaning her cognitive function could be acutely compromised, as if she were a toddler in a woman's body.

"We're getting married in January," Matt mumbled numbly to himself.

The doctor gently touched his shoulder.

"We need to be realistic with our expectations," he said. "I don't want to give you false hope."

When Matt got home late that evening, he stood in the shower and sobbed. There was nothing he could do for the woman he loved. He had never felt so helpless. But as he bowed his head and prayed, a deep calmness poured over him. He had faith that everything would be okay, no matter how bleak things seemed at the moment.

God had a plan. He needed to trust it.

The Gospel Truth

In the book of John, after Jesus rose from the dead, He emerged suddenly before His apostles inside a locked room. They marveled and rejoiced at His resurrection. But one apostle, Thomas, was absent. When the others later told Thomas of their Lord's glorious return, he was skeptical that it was truly Jesus they had seen.

"Unless I see the nail marks in His hands and put my finger where the nails were," Thomas said, "I will not believe."

A week later, Jesus appeared once more, this time before all of them. He turned to Thomas and invited him to inspect His crucifixion wounds.

"My Lord and my God!" Thomas cried, his doubts allayed.

Jesus implored him to place his trust not in tangible evidence, but in blind faith.

"Because you have seen me, you have believed," He said. "Blessed are those who have not seen and yet have believed."

John 20:29 held deep resonance for Matt. His faith was the lens through which he understood the world; he'd been taught not to question it. Moments of good fortune in his life were nothing less than divine blessings, he believed. There was no other conceivable explanation for Andrea's recovery. They made it down the aisle as planned just six months after her traumatic brain injury, as if it had never happened at all. That was a true miracle—proof of God above if ever there were any. Not that Matt needed it. When God tested him, through hardships and disappointments, he never wavered, not even when his father slowly succumbed to prostate cancer before his eyes.

Matt's faith gave him answers where there were none to be found and hope when all was lost. When Matt discovered QAnon, the allure was obvious. It was, in so many ways, familiar to what he'd known all his life: a tale of a biblical battle between good and evil that was prophesied to culminate in an apocalyptic day of reckoning. A mission to save the children, drive out satanism, and restore traditional values to society. A path to self-actualization. As he leaned deeper into QAnon dogma, decoders became clergy interpreting the teachings of their deities, Q and Trump. Q Drops, often steeped in scripture, became sacred texts bearing hidden truths. To be a disciple wasn't only about worship or evangelism—it was an invitation to the battlefield.

Matt was heartened by how many other anons appeared to be Christians. Praise for God covered the 8chan message board and filled the comment sections on decoder videos. Qmap.pub, a highly popular Q Drop aggregator website, even had a "Prayer Wall" for anons to come together and share in their faith. It was perhaps unsurprising: Religious belief was significantly positively correlated with conspiracy theory belief, attributed by experts to the service of common psychological needs (certainty, purpose, community) and shared underlying elements (grand narratives, a righteous mission, conviction in the unseen). And while believers of QAnon theories represented only a small minority of Christians overall, they accounted for nearly one in four white Evangelicals; the majority, also, were supporters of Christian nationalism.

Religion was heavily woven into QAnon recruitment propaganda like "The Plan to Save the World," Matt's entry point to the movement. But his faith wasn't just what made it so easy to get in. It was what made it so hard to get out.

As a kid growing up in a rural town outside St. Louis, Matt hadn't cared much for religion or politics. He and his little brother and sister found Sunday service to be boring; minutes into the sermon each week they'd be slumped over in the wooden pews with their cheeks smushed in their palms. At home, they tuned out whenever their parents, a restaurateur and a bookkeeper, turned on Fox News or Rush Limbaugh. Theirs was a quiet household where feelings and emotions were rarely expressed, a home full of introverts who loved each other but seldom said so. When he got a little older, Matt worked as a line cook in his dad's restaurant, an old-fashioned joint with a bizarre but beloved entrée of fried macaroni and cheese balls with gravy. His dad was a laid-back yet hardworking man with a neat brown mustache who loved music, like Matt, and baseball, which Matt learned to love to feel closer to him. They didn't have much money, so they would drive to Busch Stadium and hunt for discarded Cardinals tickets on the ground to try to get into games for free during the later innings.

At school, Matt had few friends; he preferred his Game Boy to extracurriculars. He fit in well with other kids in the youth group at his church, however, giving him a greater appreciation of the community aspect of religion. Seeking new social connections when he got to college, he joined a student ministry group, where he met Andrea and learned more about evangelism. But the depths of Matt's religious teaching happened, of all places, at work.

While completing his degree in audio production, Matt joined the Christian radio station where he would ultimately spend the next almost two decades of his life. It was a close-knit staff of about a dozen twentysomethings who mostly lived nearby and got together on Thursday evenings to watch *The Office*. The owners, a strict, watchful pair, were an independently wealthy middle-aged couple who kept the station afloat with their own money. Joseph, tall and slender with slick black hair, and Dawn, short and round with a blond '80s poof, led a highly private life but wielded considerable public influence: The station's syndicated audience would grow to nearly one million listeners in Matt's time there.

Just about everything Joseph and Dawn did, they did with religious intent—from banning certain topics from discussion on-air to bringing in Chick-fil-A when the fried chicken chain came under boycott for its devout Baptist founder's comments on same-sex marriage and donations to anti-LGBTQ groups. They also saw themselves as spiritual mentors to their young employees. Every Monday, they held a mandatory staff meeting that commenced promptly at 10 a.m. and often dragged through lunch, spiraling from programming matters into hours-long, fear-driven ranting. Society, they'd say, was caving to "Godlessness" at the hands of a powerful enemy: the Left. Liberal Hollywood was conspiring to awaken satanic spirituality in American youth through subliminal messaging in films like *Star Wars* and *Harry Potter*. Democrats were "murdering babies." And Matt and his colleagues, according to their bosses, weren't doing enough to fight back against this secular agenda, as was their "Christian duty."

Though these diatribes provoked subtle eye-roll exchanges between staffers and became fodder for impression acts on *Office* nights, they had a creeping impact on Matt over the years. He cast his first-ever ballot at twenty-three for George W. Bush—newly desperate to keep a Democrat out of the White House, for the sake of humanity—and began to study the Bible closely. The more he read, the better he understood the urgency of Joseph and Dawn's weekly appeals to rise up against the enemy. He just didn't know how.

> Put on the full armor of God, so that you can take your stand
> against the devil's schemes. For our struggle is not against flesh
> and blood, but against the rulers, against the authorities,
> against the powers of this dark world and against the spiritual
> forces of evil in the heavenly realms.
>
> (EPHESIANS 6:11–12)

. . .

QAnon showed Matt the way.

Being a digital soldier was his chance to fulfill his duty. It came with a heuristic sense of immediacy and excitement far exceeding that of traditional Christian eschatology: Against a breakneck news cycle of twists and turns, new clues about the coming Great Awakening were trickling out every day via Trump tweets or Q Drops, filtered through savvy decoders for anons to investigate. QAnon celebrity Dave Hayes, or "Praying Medic," the self-proclaimed faith healer and "mailman" delivering messages from God to Q, even suggested that the president was on the cusp of bringing about "heaven on earth."

When Q's many predictions failed to materialize, Matt was disappointed, but he didn't lose faith. He'd been tested before. Hayes was always right there alongside other QAnon luminaries to repeat the same thought-terminating cliché: *Trust the Plan.*

After dinner on a summer night in 2019, nearly a year into his QAnon pilgrimage, Matt was down in his basement office, combing his fingers through his beard while conducting research per usual as Andrea put the kids to bed by herself. When a guest on Patriots' Soapbox, the God-centered, 24/7 QAnon live-stream channel, mentioned the Beatles, Matt's ears perked up. He had loved the Beatles since he was a boy listening to their songs with his dad. But the man on the live stream angrily declared that Paul, John, George, and Ringo were all satanists and perverts who had tried to indoctrinate their fans. As proof, he revealed the image of the original, banned *Yesterday and Today* album cover photo. Matt had never seen it before. It showed the band members grinning in white butcher coats while holding naked, bloody, decapitated baby dolls.

Matt was gutted. *Not the Beatles.*

He looked up at the *Let It Be* 8-track tape affixed to the drywall over his desk. It was his father's; he had found it in a storage unit along with his baseball cards after he died. Seeing it on the wall next to his Cardinals posters whenever he walked into the room reminded him of their time listening to music together on drives to the stadium to scavenge for tickets.

"This is sick! This is *sick!*" the man on Patriots' Soapbox shouted, calling the Beatles devil worshippers and child sacrificers, and snapping Matt from his nostalgia.

The image on his screen *was* grotesque. There were even slabs of raw pink meat tossed in with the baby parts. Matt was disgusted just looking at it. As he read the comments flooding into the live chat, his disgust turned to indignation.

Anons were feeding off each other's outrage. Many said that they felt ashamed to have ever been fans, and vowed to never listen to another Beatles song for as long as they lived. When a few suggested that they all torch or trash their records, the chat erupted with all-caps enthusiasm and rows upon rows of orange fire emojis.

Matt lunged from his chair, ripped his treasured heirloom off the wall and threw it in the garbage. *Good fucking riddance.*

Aggression was out of character for Matt. He was usually a calm, fairly measured man. But he was, perhaps, not entirely himself in that moment. Mass psychology theory would suggest that he was part of a *collective self* and that his behavior wasn't governed by independent thinking or in service of his own interests. The idea was older than Matt, or even the Beatles: French polymath Gustave Le Bon had argued in his 1895 treatise on herd dynamics that when uniting around an ideology or belief in pursuit of a shared cause, people could come under an almost "hypnotic" influence, freeing them "from the sense of their insignificance and powerlessness" while also making them intellectually weak, impulsive, and gullible. It was a seminal theory that could be interpreted, controversially, to hold such individuals inculpable for their actions. Le Bon's framework would continue to be built upon and applied to the study of certain extreme religious, military, and political groups, like Capitol rioters, and online movements, like QAnon, to dissect the blind fanaticism driving members to act irrationally and to devote their lives to—or destroy them for—a perceived greater good.

"The masses have never thirsted after truth. They turn aside from evidence that is not to their taste," he wrote. "Whoever can supply them with illusions is easily their master; whoever attempts to destroy their illusions is always their victim."

Among the most remarkable things about the man in the mass, Le Bon said, were the extraordinary personal sacrifices he was willing, even eager, to make.

Those sacrifices, for Matt, would be life-changing.

In pursuit of the Great Awakening, like many anons, he was alienating himself from his own family, convinced that in the divine scheme of things—until the Deep State was defeated—his duty as a digital soldier superseded his roles as a husband and a father. Andrea and the kids hardly saw him outside of dinnertime, when he would emerge from the basement to scarf down his food before disappearing back to his research.

In September of 2019, after countless pleas for him to be more attentive, Andrea insisted on marriage counseling. Matt agreed, to placate her, but spent each session thinking about Q's latest intel while she wept about feeling like a "single mother."

The fallout from his QAnon devotion began to reveal itself to him late one night in December. It was Friday the 13th, an unlucky day in Christian superstition: Jesus was crucified on Good Friday following His betrayal by Judas, the thirteenth apostle to arrive to the Last Supper. Retiring to bed after a long day of work on YouTube, Matt went upstairs to find Andrea beaming at her phone like a smitten teenager, oblivious to her surroundings. When she finally noticed him standing there, she jumped and tucked her hands behind her back.

"What's going on?" Matt asked.

"No one! Uh—nothing!" Andrea yelped. "It's nothing."

She blinked at him silently with a tortured look on her face, as if she was waiting for him to say something more. Then she burst into tears and confessed to having an affair.

A Crisis of Faith

Matt took a break from QAnon.

He was too depressed to do anything. Most days, that included getting out of bed. The thought of Andrea's betrayal—of her with the man who'd made her smile like that—was excruciating. He asked God for strength. This had to be part of His plan.

One of the first people Matt told was Joseph, his boss, who'd started asking questions when he requested the entire week off work without advance notice. After he shared what had happened, Joseph expressed his condolences, then reminded him in the same breath that if he and Andrea were to get divorced, they would be handing their kids over to Satan.

Matt moped around the house in a heartsick stupor, unshaven and unshowered in the same plaid pajama pants and gray PlayStation T-shirt day after day. He forced a smile only when Abby and Hayden were present, and said nothing to his wife, ignoring her sobbing pleas to "just talk" after the kids went to sleep each night. The blue eyes that could once convince him to do anything had lost what was left of their power over him.

Just the sight of Andrea texting on her phone was so triggering it could send Matt from breakfast back to bed for the rest of the day. For three months, she tried to explain again and again that she had cheated only because she felt like Matt had completely lost interest in her, and she was desperate for some morsel of validation. The affair meant nothing, she insisted.

Then, out of nowhere, came Covid-19.

For their marriage, it was a twisted blessing, at first: There was no way for them *not* to talk. Everything was just too shocking. In a single day, the World Health Organization declared a global pandemic, the stock market crashed, the United States banned all travel from Europe, Tom Hanks said he had contracted the disease, and the NBA shut down for the season. Matt, Andrea, and the kids sat in front of the TV together every day for the first couple weeks, stunned by each new development. The raw pain of the infidelity was quietly blending away into the daily chaos of the lockdowns without Matt even noticing. Abby and Hayden were attending virtual school classes in their bedrooms, Andrea was working from a laptop propped atop a stack of books in the living room, and Matt was still down in the basement doing news programming for the radio station.

He was also diving back into his QAnon research.

The vortex of information about the lies and corruption surrounding the pandemic was staggering. The Deep State had all hands on deck: The Democrats were wildly overexaggerating the threat of Covid, the mainstream media was parroting their narrative in a circus of hysteria, Big Tech platforms were suppressing any and all counterspeech, the CDC was hyperinflating the death tolls by attributing unrelated fatalities to the virus, and Big Pharma was rubbing its hands together.

Trump seemed to be saying much of the same. He suggested that Covid was no more dangerous than the flu and that it would disappear with warmer weather, leading to "packed churches" by Easter. Meanwhile, the Left, he said, was overhyping the outbreak to hurt him politically—a claim echoed emphatically by Q and Praying Medic, and accepted unquestioningly by Matt.

> Why do they want you locked inside?
> Why do they want you to panic?
> WHY DO THEY WANT YOU TO LIVE IN FEAR?
> Why is the media banning anyone who challenges the
> COVID-19 narrative?
> THIS HAS EVERYTHING TO DO WITH THE P_ELECTION.
> WHO BENEFITS THE MOST? . . .
> Q

Matt's work as a digital soldier suddenly felt more urgent than ever. The fearmongering was ubiquitous; it was impossible to turn on the TV or open Facebook without seeing sob stories about people suffering and dying at scale, but he knew better: In his QAnon feeds, individuals identifying themselves as whistleblowing doctors and nurses described emergency room photo ops staged to make hospitals look far busier than they actually were. The hashtag #FilmYourHospital soon trended on Twitter as vigilantes encouraged each other to expose the media's lies. Even Fox News was airing suspicions.

Anons were convinced that crisis actors were posing as grieving loved ones in front of news cameras and that doctors were being paid off to stay silent about the truth or to spout lies to the press. But in the late spring, for Matt, something changed.

He got a call to help Mr. Jackson, the owner of a local auto repair shop, who was having an issue with his security camera. Matt had been doing some on-call tech support work as a side gig since mid-2019, after he secretly took out the $35,000 home equity line of credit to spend on silver and gold coins.

Mr. Jackson was a gruff, snappy, intimidating guy in his midsixties who looked like a white-haired Ron Swanson from *Parks and Recreation*. During a previous visit to the shop, Matt had watched him lay into his employees in a red-faced tirade. (For what, Matt wasn't sure; he just knew that he never wanted to piss the man off himself.) He'd also done a job at Mr. Jackson's home back in the fall, when his wife, a delightful little woman with bottle-blond hair, heavy makeup, and a sweet smile, had needed assistance with a simple but time-consuming data transfer. She'd sat by Matt's side the entire time, asking all about his life while her three fluffy cats swirled by his feet. After he finished, she brought him into the kitchen for homemade potato soup and cornbread.

When Matt returned to the shop in 2020, Mr. Jackson looked as if he hadn't slept in days. His eyes were vacant and sunken, his head was hanging, and his broad shoulders were slumped forward, as if he might just tumble over with the slightest tap. He wasn't a particularly chatty guy at the best of times—when he wasn't barking at people—but his radio silence was unnerving, as was his hovering, empty gaze into space while Matt tinkered with the camera. He seemed smaller, somehow. Broken.

"So, uh . . . how's Mrs. Jackson been doing, Mr. Jackson?" Matt asked.

Mr. Jackson turned his head to look at him blankly.

"Wha—what?"

"I was just asking how Mrs. Jackson's doing. Is she doing well?"

Mr. Jackson squeezed his eyes shut and clutched his face, running his hand down slowly. He took a loud, deep breath and shook his head.

"I almost lost her . . ." he mumbled, his mouth quivering.

Tears pooled in his eyes as his gravelly voice hushed to a whisper. His wife, who'd been in great health, had just spent a month fighting to survive in the hospital with Covid-19. At one point, her condition was so dire that the doctors had asked for his permission to take her off life support.

Matt stared at him.

"Covid?" he asked.

Mr. Jackson nodded. The pain in his face was real.

Back in his car in the parking lot, Matt gazed into space himself. He was shaken. Had he heard about Mrs. Jackson's infection over the phone or some other way, he wouldn't have believed it. But seeing Mr. Jackson like that, watching him tremble to keep from crying, Matt knew that he was hearing the truth. Mr. Jackson wasn't someone who could be bullshitted; if there was something shady going on at the hospital, or some kind of danger to his wife, he would have had people up by their necks against the wall.

A moment of raw human connection had just accomplished for Matt what no amount of fact-checking or debunking ever could: It started to shake his faith in the lies he'd been sold.

After his encounter with Mr. Jackson, Matt's blind faith in Trump and in QAnon figures became a little less blind. Factual inconsistencies, illogical claims, and conflicting information that he would have previously looked past without a second thought were starting to linger uncomfortably in his mind. The president's efforts to downplay the severity of Covid, in particular, grated on him. His hero, it seemed, was more concerned about his own political prospects than human lives. Matt also saw online that multiple anti–child trafficking organizations had put out statements denouncing QAnon, warning that its viral "conspiracy theories" had caused their tip lines to be flooded with nonsense, detracting from their ability to help kids in real danger. Decoders brushed such criticisms aside. They claimed that those groups were in fact complicit in *abusing* children, not saving them. But they didn't provide any evidence—and this time, Matt wanted it.

As he struggled in his beliefs, Matt felt rudderless. He missed his family and the life they used to have. He wasn't ready to forgive Andrea, and didn't know when or if he would be, but it had been six months since the affair, and his anger had dissipated. She wasn't entirely at fault, he knew. He had broken their marriage too. Maybe it was time to let her back in.

But Andrea wanted out.

Matt was in his office one day toward the end of summer when she burst down the stairs, wide-eyed and disheveled. He stood up to speak but before he could get a word out, she told him that she'd been seeing another guy whose wife had just caught them together. Matt collapsed back into his chair.

The other guy turned out to be one of Abby's teachers. Andrea had gotten to know him through an online parent-teacher messaging system that the school had set up when the lockdowns began. He was going to leave his wife for her, she told Matt, and they were going to be together. She was taking the kids.

. . .

For the first time, Matt was angry with God.

Had he not suffered enough already? Was there some grand lesson he'd failed to grasp the last time his wife had shattered him into pieces? And did it have to be their daughter's fucking teacher?

Matt couldn't fathom how *this* could possibly serve God's plan for his life. It just felt cruel. But he needed God now more than he ever had.

Remembering what Joseph had said about divorce, Matt decided that it was out of the question. His marriage was dead, but it wasn't over. He spent the next few months furiously and miserably guilting Andrea into staying, echoing Joseph's warning and telling her how horrendously selfish she was being. Things weren't going as smoothly on the other end either; Abby's teacher wasn't able to break away from his marriage as easily as he and Andrea had planned. She ended up breaking things off with him and recommitted to Bible study to seek God's forgiveness.

As Matt's home life crumbled, so did the Plan. Trump wasn't supposed to lose. Decoders kicked the can down the road yet again: The Great Awakening was instead going to happen on January 20, 2021, the date of Joe Biden's planned inauguration, they assured their followers. The military would swoop in and round up members of the Deep State in the streets to haul off to Gitmo. Mark their words.

But eleven weeks and one insurrection later, on the steps of the recently desecrated Capitol Building, a grinning Biden placed his hand down on a Bible and was sworn in as the forty-sixth president of the United States.

Q and Praying Medic went dark. Trump was impeached. And in March, Andrea came to Matt once more to tell him that she no longer loved him.

She was having another affair.

The next day, Matt lay in bed in an empty house, thinking about his life. What he was feeling transcended pain. He wasn't sad or angry. He was in existential freefall. At long last, his Awakening had come and revealed the truth: He'd been living a delusion. He wasn't loved by God, nor was he serving a higher purpose. There was no Plan. He was a guy whose life had fallen apart while he was busy worshipping a figment in the sky, a demagogue in the White House, and a troll on the internet.

Matt glanced over at his nightstand. Next to his phone was a small orange bottle full of little round pills. He got up, went to the kitchen, and cracked open a beer, taking a long, slow sip. He savored the taste as the cold amber suds washed over his tongue. It was light and subtly sweet with a hint of caramel malt. Then he went back into the bedroom, called his wife, and told her goodbye.

PART III

ESCAPE

TWO STEPS FORWARD

—Alice—

"I hate you! I want to live with my dad!"

Alice heard those words every single day. It was 2008, six months since she'd renegotiated her custody arrangement with her ex-husband. Their ten-year-old son, Dawson, had spent the first few years of his life going back and forth between his parents and the next several living with his father's new family, plunging his single mother into a long, dark depression. Now she had her baby back for part of each week—and he was fighting to get away. Trying to reason with him got her nowhere, as did begging him to stop. It always ended with those same shattering words screamed back in her face.

Alice knew her son didn't really hate her. While dealing with his outbursts, she'd been learning about compassionate communication, the conflict resolution strategy centered on people's psychological and spiritual needs—those nourishing the heart, mind, and soul, like the need to feel understood or to belong. Its philosophy was straightforward: Behind every behavior there was an emotion. Behind every emotion there was a need. So in order to change someone's behavior, their need had to be met. It was about focusing on the cause, not the symptom.

If Alice could figure out which of her son's needs were unmet, hidden behind his anger, maybe the two of them could come up with ways to meet those needs here in his new environment. She just had to get through to him.

One evening, after another meltdown, Alice tried a new strategy. She asked Dawson if he wanted to play a little game. He could win points, she offered, and if he earned enough over time, she would buy him the video game of his choice.

His big brown eyes lit up.

"Okay," he agreed. "I'll play."

Alice pulled out two decks of handmade cards. Written on each one in the first deck was an emotion.

"This part is easy," she explained. "I'm going to guess how you're feeling, and to get a point, you just tell me if I've got it right."

She placed two cards in front of him: "SAD." "FRUSTRATED."

Dawson nodded, then studied the deck and selected two more: "LONELY." "BORED."

Belying her pain upon reading those words, Alice smiled softly at her son.

"Thank you for sharing that," she said. "Now, for more points, here's the harder part."

She fanned out the second deck of cards, each displaying a psychological need, and told Dawson to choose the ones that best explained the emotions they had picked out.

"Ask yourself why you feel the way that you do," she encouraged. "Think about what it is that you're missing."

After a couple minutes of rapt deliberation, he settled on just three: "FREEDOM." "COMMUNITY." "FUN."

Alice felt like she'd had a breakthrough. She and Dawson sat down and brainstormed what changes they could make to give him what he needed. To start, they agreed, he would be allowed to have his friends over after school more often, provided that he did his homework, and she would find more time to take him to the park to play wall-ball. Before long, the outbursts stopped.

It was incredible. Blown away by how something so simple could have such an impact, Alice felt compelled to share her new skills with others. She pursued a career in compassionate communication, helping her clients peel back the layers of the behaviors harming their lives and relationships to root out the underlying issues—their unmet needs—and address them.

But when it came to her own behavior, Alice had a blind spot. She couldn't see that her sudden obsession with QAnon in 2020 was a symptom of something deeper. It was her loved ones who put the pieces together and, using techniques they'd learned from her, tried to meet her needs.

Peace, Love, and QAnon

After a long, dusty drive over from the Bay Area, Alice and Christopher arrived in Sedona at the beginning of August. Their temporary new home was a single-story brown stucco townhouse with high ceilings and big windows on a sleepy cul-de-sac. It was a charming little getaway; out back, poking above the trees and lilac bushes in the courtyard, was the rounded red peak of Thunder Mountain. But the purpose of their visit wasn't leisure—it was refuge.

Christopher had rented the place just days ago, caving to Alice's unrelenting demands that they flee California. She was terrified that the Deep State would set the West Coast ablaze using space lasers financed by the Rothschilds, a wealthy Jewish banking family viewed within QAnon as the pinnacle of evil. The plan was to stay for three months. Neither of them knew if they would end up leaving together or as exes.

Their five-year relationship was hanging by a thread. In his desperate attempt to save it, Christopher had promised to be accepting of Alice's new beliefs. It was a commitment he knew he couldn't keep for long. Of his three decades in the life sciences industry, fifteen had been spent in neurology; listening to his fiancée talk about how Covid vaccines would be used to implant microchips that would somehow migrate to the brain and create new neural pathways made every hair on Christopher's body stand up. So did her insistence that the death tolls were being hugely exaggerated. The firm he helped lead had worked with a network of ambulance providers in various states to rush eight crews up from southern Florida to New York City, where people were dying at such a scale that bodies were being ferried to a mass grave site on an island off the Bronx.

Christopher and Alice got through nine days in Sedona before he reached his limit, yelling that she was deluded and brainwashed. It became a dismal cycle: As soon as Christopher finished work, Alice—whose clientele base had shrunk amid the pandemic, giving her ample free time for "research"—would barrage him with conspiracy theory content that she'd spent the day excitedly discussing with her new online network of QAnon friends. He'd hold his tongue until he couldn't anymore: sometimes days, sometimes less. Then he'd storm into his makeshift office, and she'd wander off into the desert for long solo walks with her headphones in.

As she'd make her way through tranquil scenes of jagged red rocks and flowering cacti jostling in the hot, dry breeze, occasionally crossing paths with little garter snakes or horned lizards basking in the sunshine, QAnon influencers would hyperventilate in her ear about the ghastly depravity that Trump was battling behind closed doors in his quest to save humanity. Sometimes she'd stop in Peace Park at the base of the mountain to visit the Amitabha Stupa, a thirty-six-foot dome-shaped Buddhist monument with a delicate lotus blossom at the top, symbolizing enlightenment. She wished Christopher would try to understand.

Christopher wanted to; he just couldn't. It made no sense to him. Nearing his wits' end, he called one of the only people who knew her better than he did: her father.

Down in the tropics with his wife, on their little pin-shaped island with turquoise waters, white-sand beaches, and gently swaying palm trees, Ted was happily sequestered from the rest of the world and its woes. He could typically be found in an untucked linen shirt—often a Hawaiian tee—and *always* with a smile on his face. Life was best lived that way, he believed; too much stress was bad for the soul.

Christopher had plenty for him.

Over a cluster of panicked, cross-border phone calls, his voice breaking, he explained to Ted that Alice appeared to be losing her mind, in a cult-like trance, or both. He was trying to snap her out of it, he said. But he couldn't do it alone. He felt like he was losing his mind too. Ted seemed to understand. His would-be son-in-law was a proud and ever-composed man; hearing him in such distress was unnerving. And when it came to Alice, Ted would do anything. So, united in their love for her, with a couple thousand miles between them, they worked in tandem to try to bring her back.

Ted liked to say that Alice was his "flower child." She was caring to a fault: While he could live cocooned in his bliss, untroubled by the chaos beyond his shores, for Alice, to learn of others' pain was to suffer it herself. In her four and a half decades, Ted had known her to be an unapologetic proponent of peace and love. And now . . . of QAnon.

What his sweet, softhearted daughter saw in the Far Right movement that appealed to her, he couldn't fathom. The more he learned about it, the more it repulsed him. But he was willing to listen when no one else would.

Ted's approach, to start, was simple: Before making any effort to deprogram her, he sought to understand her. He welcomed her to send him whatever she wished to discuss. She eagerly obliged, peppering him with a daily blitz of content, from YouTube rants purporting to expose Jewish billionaire George Soros as a puppet master controlling the media, to detailed charts revealing code words used by Deep State pedophiles while purchasing their victims, like "cheese pizza" for "little girl." It was the most stomach-turning homework he'd ever been assigned. He waded through it all on his iPad from the patterned teal couch in his also-teal living room, longing every time to go out into the beautiful weather calling to him through the window at his back, like a schoolboy stuck in detention. It was exhausting, mentally and emotionally. Sometimes he would have to meditate afterward just to get back into a better frame of mind. But he felt it was necessary to do.

He wanted to give Alice a safe space to share her theories. Christopher had told him about the many dear friendships she had already destroyed while doubling down on false and disturbing narratives on Facebook, unleashing a cascade of accusations that she was stupid, crazy, and worse. There weren't many other people left who she could talk to about these things. She FaceTimed with Dawson but kept her beliefs from him out of a motherly compulsion to protect her son; he didn't need to know about the atrocities going down in the shadows. A quiet part of her was also afraid of what he might think, given the reactions she'd gotten so far. He was the most important part of her life. She couldn't risk losing him.

Ted worried that if Alice's QAnon community was the only place where she could freely and consistently speak her mind, without judgment, she might disappear into it for good. They talked via FaceTime and text, in mostly one-sided conversations. Having someone so important to her show an interest in something she cared about so deeply meant the world to her, even knowing that he didn't agree with much of it. What quickly became apparent to Ted was that QAnon, for his daughter, was less a hobby than a religion. It seemed to have already woven itself into the very fibers of her identity. When she spoke of the vast human suffering wrought by the Deep State, and the coming Great Awakening that would bring an end to it all, she often did so in tears. Being part of the movement, she'd say, meant being part of the change.

Ted knew that trying to persuade her out of such intimately held beliefs would be futile, or worse, counterproductive—a phenomenon aptly called the "backfire effect." Whether they made sense to him or not, her QAnon-related fears, anxieties, and hopes were entirely real to her. So whenever she asked for his opinion on the things she'd sent him, he would give it to her, gently but honestly, without challenging hers.

No, he didn't believe that kids were being trafficked in tunnels beneath the White House, he'd say, and *No*, he didn't think that they were being shipped out in Wayfair storage cabinets either. But he could understand her concern for the welfare of children, he'd add, and he admired it.

His goal wasn't to change her mind—not yet. He adopted an approach known as "motivational interviewing." Rather than trying to convince her of the true or the false in her theories, his goal would be to get her to consider the *harm* in them: to help her step back and recognize the objective damage they were causing to her life, like endless stress and broken relationships, and to gradually help her see that QAnon didn't truly align with her values of peace and love. The hope was that, in the process, she would find the personal motivation to make a change on her own. It would take time, Ted knew, and lots of empathy.

"I love you unconditionally, Honey, and I'm going to support you through this whole journey and just see where it goes," he told her. "You can count on me to be there for you in any way possible."

Lines in the Sand

From his front-row seat to Alice's unraveling, Christopher didn't have the patience to indulge her delusions. He believed that she urgently needed intervention, not encouragement. The views she was espousing were often dangerous and, at times, he thought, reprehensible.

After she parroted Trump's birther theory about Kamala Harris, inaccurately implying that she wasn't eligible to serve as vice president because of her parents' immigration status at the time of her birth, he was so disgusted he called her "racist" and nearly walked out the door. That wasn't the Alice he knew, and that wasn't the Alice he was going to accept. But coming to her with facts and evidence was like bringing a slingshot to a gunfight. By the time he loaded up with well-sourced information, which usually just bounced right off her with little to no impact, she had already fired off another round of blog posts and videos for him to waste his time debunking. He needed a new strategy. So he turned to a professional.

Christopher had been seeing his therapist, Dr. Handley, since just after his divorce. He was a fatherly man in his midsixties who wore cardigans and glasses and specialized in "men's issues," including anger management. Counseling partners of QAnon believers was by no means his forte, but he had worked with clients who espoused conspiracy theories themselves.

His first question to Christopher was a two-parter.

"Is this a relationship you want to fight for?" he asked. "And if so, are you willing to stay with her if she never comes back from QAnon?"

"Yes," Christopher replied with confidence. Then, with less, "And, honestly . . . I don't know."

Most of the people Christopher had looked to for guidance—including friends he shared with Alice—had told him to break off the engagement and run. They couldn't imagine what kind of a future he could see with a woman who now believed that John F. Kennedy, Jr., had faked his own death and would soon emerge as Trump's running mate. But Christopher wasn't ready to let go. Alice was still in there, and he was still in love with her.

He had given himself a year-end deadline to decide if he could make things work with his "beloved," as he and Alice used to call each other. It wasn't a name that either of them had pulled out much since QAnon had come into the picture as an unwelcome third party in their life together. But if they could find happiness across separate realities, Christopher thought, then maybe they could still have a successful marriage. It was a big "if."

Dr. Handley advised the "Socratic questioning" method, named for the legendary philosopher. Socrates asked strategic, open-ended questions to encourage his students to think through and examine the validity of their own ideas, while carefully challenging their biases, assumptions, and blind spots—all from a place of curiosity, not criticism.

That last part was the key, Dr. Handley said. If Christopher continued to criticize Alice and her beliefs, reinforcing the notion that she was wrong and bad, it would only back her further onto the defensive, where logic stood little chance against anger. Unless he allowed her to keep her dignity, showing her that she could emerge from QAnon still feeling loved, appreciated, and respected, then why would she ever come out? Inside its walls, she belonged to a community that valued her deeply.

By instead exhibiting an almost childlike curiosity—a genuine desire to learn about the things she brought to him, as ludicrous as they might be—he could open her up to a dialogue, not a shouting match or an attempted conversion. That was half the battle: shifting her mindset into a place of exploring and probing ideas *with* Christopher, instead of trying to force them on him. If she viewed him as an ally in finding the truth, even one with a different perspective, she would be more receptive to his mindfully phrased questions about factual inconsistencies and contradictions in the content they inspected together.

Dr. Handley assured Christopher that he didn't have to agree with things he knew to be false. He just needed to consider and patiently inquire about them in good faith, and to vocally celebrate any common ground unearthed in the process, no matter how seemingly insignificant. In time, this could open Alice's mind enough to allow doubt to seep in.

It was a hell of a lot to ask.

Christopher was standing out in front of the Airbnb on the phone, gazing into the mountains, wondering how he could possibly muster the energy to sit through Alice's avalanche of "research" with a smile on his face. The sheer volume of content was overwhelming, to say nothing of its often-gruesome insanity. She could spend half a day just watching YouTube videos. On top of his full-time job, Christopher didn't have it in him. So Dr. Handley offered one more piece of advice. To both of their surprise, it would end up making the biggest difference in pulling her back toward reality.

Set boundaries, he said.

Christopher was to block off one evening per week to give Alice his full, undivided attention to discuss, watch, or read whatever she wanted. On other days, he needed to remain firm in keeping such conversations off-limits, and to try to re-engage her in activities that they used to enjoy doing as a couple, pandemic permitting.

He laid out his rules the next day.

· · ·

At first, Alice bristled at Christopher's insistence that they talk about "politics"—his stand-in word for all things QAnon—only on a strictly limited schedule. It didn't seem fair; she would never restrict *him* from discussing the things he cared about. But after their first conversation, she realized that having his inquisitive focus for a few uninterrupted hours a week was infinitely better than talking *at* him on a daily basis while he either tuned her out or looked like he was in physical pain.

She chose to focus on a topic that would directly affect their lives: the vaccine. Christopher was planning to get it; she refused. She sat him down in the courtyard and restated her fear that it would be dangerous, even deadly. Much of her reasoning had to do with Bill Gates, who was spending hundreds of millions of dollars developing it. The notion that his longtime interest in public health was in any way philanthropic was laughable, Alice said: She'd seen a CNBC interview from 2019 in which he openly admitted to earning a "twenty-to-one" return on his foundation's $10 billion investment into vaccines globally. This time, he wouldn't get away with it. QAnon was going to bring him to justice, and the world would be safe from the evils he was plotting.

Christopher knew which interview she was talking about. He'd seen her posting about it on Facebook, which had prompted him to look into it himself. She was dead wrong. His first inclination was to tell her exactly that. But leaning into Dr. Handley's guidance, he chose to lead with empathy and to create a path for them to work together, not against each other.

"Look, first of all, I get why you're worried about this. You want us to be safe from harm. So do I," he said, intentionally echoing her concern to show her that he understood where she was coming from.

"And I hear what you're saying about Bill Gates: You don't trust him. He's an extremely powerful person, and it's good to be skeptical. So let's make sure we've got our facts straight here, okay? In that CNBC report, I thought he was saying that his investment into vaccines had a twenty-to-one return in economic benefits for the *world*—not that he was profiting himself. Maybe I misunderstood, though. Can we double-check?"

Alice nodded, already excited by Christopher's level of engagement. *At last,* it seemed, he was really hearing her.

They found the full exchange with Gates on YouTube. Alice's excitement faded. It was immediately clear to her that the clip she'd watched earlier had been cut out of context.

"Okay, fine. I was wrong about *that*. I'm not wrong about *him*," she argued, anticipating an "I told you so" that didn't come. "The man is still a monster. He's still planning to microchip people."

Christopher sighed. *Not the damn microchip again.* They had been through this so many times, and he had explained to her until he was blue in the face that what she was describing was physically and biologically impossible. Yet she was still choosing to believe nonsense on the internet over her fiancé's own expertise.

He said nothing. There was no point in trying to break down the science for her again; it was like speaking two different languages.

Alice played a couple videos on her phone, each purporting to "expose" Gates's diabolical plans. One warned that he was trying to depopulate the earth, while the other said that he was trying to track people so he could continue making money off them. Christopher stayed silent until the end, then asked Alice what she thought about the discrepancy there. She didn't have an answer. Sticking with the curiosity that Dr. Handley had encouraged, he posed a handful of other questions thoughtfully prodding at some of the videos' claims about Gates, avoiding for his own sake the topic of the microchips. When she pushed things back in that direction, he did his best to keep his cool. He asked her something simple.

"How sure are you that this is true? This vaccine microchip stuff—on a scale of 1 to 10, how confident would you say you are?"

There was a brilliance to that question, whether Christopher saw it or not. It prompted Alice to hold her own belief up to the light, critically assess it, and acknowledge her doubt in it.

She paused.

"Um . . . a 9, I guess. No, a 9.5."

"Okay," he said, perking up. "I'm curious: What's holding you back from a 10?"

"I mean, I've seen a ton of evidence. A *ton*. Bill Gates is shady as hell," Alice said quickly, with a touch of defensiveness in her tone.

"But . . . I don't know *for sure*," she ceded, thinking momentarily of the CNBC clip. "I guess it's possible that some of the things I've seen about him aren't 100 percent true."

Christopher saw an opening. As casually as he could, he took it.

"That makes sense. There's a lot of conflicting information about him out there right now, especially on vaccines. But I did read that he's invested really heavily into climate tech."

Trying to appeal to the environmentalist in her, Christopher added, "He's put around $2 billion into clean energy solutions. Did you know that?"

Alice did. She'd just been subconsciously putting it out of her mind to square Gates as the bad guy that QAnon made him out to be. A year earlier, she'd watched the Netflix special *Inside Bill's Brain: Decoding Bill Gates*. She remembered how impressed she'd been with his innovative plan of action for tackling the climate crisis, and how angry she'd felt upon learning in the film that Trump had squashed it for political reasons.

She sat uncomfortably in her cognitive dissonance for a moment as the sun slipped away, leaving behind a pink and orange cotton-candy sky. Then she turned back to Christopher.

"What about you?" she asked. "How sure are you that Bill Gates *isn't* up to something malicious with the vaccines?"

The honest answer, Christopher supposed, was a 9.999. In a Socratic spirit, he recognized that the only thing he could know with absolute certainty was that he knew nothing with absolute certainty.

"Also close to a 10," he replied. "I'll accept that it's possible I could be wrong."

Alice smiled. She felt closer to her beloved than she had in a long time. It was clear to her that he was at least trying to see things from her point of view, even though he hadn't come around yet. She wished she didn't have to wait another whole week to talk "politics" with him again. Even her dad had asked her to dial back the amount of content she shared with him.

Given these limits, Alice became highly selective of the items she chose to present to them—especially Christopher—prioritizing ideas on the more digestible end of the spectrum, as opposed to clones and cannibalism. She started compiling links to videos, articles, and blog posts into categories using the Notes app on her iPhone. One was called "Trump is not a racist"; another was "Masks do not work." Once Christopher was ready, she'd bring out the "Red Pill" content, a collection that would surely tip him all the way into QAnon.

Knowing that he might suggest they try to debunk her content to ensure it was trustworthy, Alice started prebunking it herself. She attempted to verify the foundational layers of information she got from QAnon influencers, so there wouldn't be any more setbacks like the Gates clip. To her surprise, she was often unable to do so.

In one case, in late September, Alice was sitting in the living room, watching a shaky, close-up video of Pope Francis. It was an informal setting; he was alone on a green couch in a cramped space, and he looked serious.

"Dear brothers and sisters, excuse me because I speak in Italian," he said in English, before switching languages. Subtitles popped up to translate the rest of his speech.

"Just like the sky and whether you believe it or not, the truth is, it is blue," they read. "I am ashamed to tell you this, but I have [a] secret agenda to deceive you."

Alice gasped as the pope confessed to orchestrating a one-religion New World Order. Christopher had been raised Catholic. He *needed* to see this. But she caught herself, remembering her need to double-check things before he had them do it together. She scrolled to the comments section to see if anyone had raised concerns about the video, and noticed several Italian people explaining that the translation was false. The pope had been talking about uniting Christians.

It was deeply embarrassing. Alice realized she had reacted out of emotion, not logic, swept up in the shock value. She wondered how many times she'd done that before.

As time went on, Alice's convictions were ever-so-slowly softening. Her efforts to maximize her exchanges with Christopher and Ted were inadvertently restimulating her critical thinking skills and chipping away at her confidence in her trusted cadre of decoders. She was also putting much less energy into researching QAnon's most fringe conspiracy theories. But she was committed to the process. Christopher's approval, and her dad's, meant more to her than most anyone else's. Getting them to accept her new worldview would be profoundly validating.

Mostly, though, she wanted them to share in the pure joy and relief that came with knowing that they were on the cusp of the Great Awakening. With the Deep State no longer at the helm of all systems of power, and democracy no longer held hostage by corporate greed, they wouldn't have to live in existential fear of the next climate travesty or financial crash or manufactured crisis . . . *everything* would be better.

Christopher's thoughts were softening too.

In speaking to Alice with a mindset of cooperation—not conflict—and actively listening to the concerns behind her doomsday conspiracy theories, he was coming to understand *why* she believed them, and his frustration with her was melting into sympathy. QAnon was poisoning her already-frightened mind with crackpot paranoia and then dangling silver-platter solutions before her eyes. Watching her light up as she spoke passionately of the brighter days ahead, he was reminded that she used to talk about the Bernie Revolution in the same way: It gave her hope in the face of a scary, unknown future. Her attraction to QAnon, he was realizing, wasn't a matter of losing her mind or falling prey to a cult. It was an attempt to meet a need.

Behind her fear and anxiety, like so many other people, Alice longed for certainty: a need to feel safe, secure, and in control. She just wanted to know that everything would be all right, and QAnon promised her it would be. The Great Awakening was her beautiful mirage; it was as real to her as water on the desert horizon to a thirsty traveler.

How could he take that away from her?

"Cultivate Your Garden"

Growing up as a Jewish boy in America, Ted was reminded often that he was lucky to have been born.

His mother would tell him of the terrors that his grandparents and other relatives had survived while living in shtetls, small villages, in Czarist Russia. It was before the Holocaust, at a time when Jews were being brutalized and mass-murdered in pogroms for the crime of their ethnicity. Her parents had escaped by hiding inside wine barrels on a cargo ship to New York City, where they found work in airless tenement sweatshops on the Lower East Side. That was where the luck began, she explained: Had they been discovered, they could have suffered the same fate as other Jewish stowaways, thrown overboard like trash and left to drown at sea.

At first, Ted didn't understand. *How could people be so hateful?*

His mother's answer disturbed him.

They were brainwashed, she said: fed such powerful, blinding lies that many came to view Jews as blood-drinking, child-abusing monsters hell-bent on taking over the world and spreading their evil.

That idea—that people could be convinced en masse of such heinous, illogical things by appealing to their fear—stayed with Ted. It haunted him. As he got older, still seeking to understand it, he spent years re-searching the persuasive power of antisemitic propaganda and false nar-ratives in Nazi Germany and beyond. So, decades later, when his daughter texted him on an October afternoon with a pair of videos about adreno-chrome harvesting, Ted panicked. The echoes of blood libel were chilling.

Alice knew that Ted used to volunteer for an anti–child trafficking organization; she figured that he'd be horrified to hear about little kids being tortured, raped, and drained of their blood in satanic rituals. And he was.

This was the opportunity he'd been waiting for.

"Sweetie, the whole Adrenochrome thing is way over the top for me," he wrote back, starting gently. "This dark blood libel stuff has been circu-lating around Europe for centuries. It stirred up virulent anti-semitism with horrible consequences."

"I believe this is absolutely real," Alice replied, recalling a video she'd watched describing babies being beheaded with a cleaver over a bowl to catch their blood. "We didn't want to believe that Catholic clergy were raping children, but now we can't deny it."

Ted asked her to look into *The Protocols of the Elders of Zion*, the most influential antisemitic text of all time, which detailed a fictionalized Jew-ish plot for global domination presented as fact. It had been used repeat-edly throughout the twentieth century to incite violent hatred against Jews, he told her—including her own ancestors. He reminded her in pain-ful detail of the atrocities they had suffered, and asked her to keep them in mind while reading.

Ted knew that Alice's interest in QAnon came from a good place. He needed her to see that it wasn't the peaceful, loving movement she be-lieved it to be.

Alice agreed to his request. She did a Google search and visited a page from the United States Holocaust Memorial Museum's website. What she found led her down an entirely different kind of rabbit hole.

The parallels between QAnon lore and *The Protocols*—which fabricated a secret scheme by a cabal of wealthy Jewish elites "to rule the world by manipulating the economy, controlling the media, and fostering religious conflict," according to the site—were undeniable. Alice's heart started racing. She clicked another page about blood libel, and another about Nazis' propaganda techniques, and another, and another, and another . . . It was all the same . . . from the gory, specific details, like the ritualistic consumption of children's blood, to the broader themes, like a singular enemy group standing between the people and prosperity, and the promise of a just and unified society once it was exterminated . . .

Alice stepped outside for air in a daze. She felt sick to her soul.

Was it all a fucking lie?

It couldn't be, she decided. Not all of it. There was too much proof, too much evidence. Too much sacrificed on her part. In her head, all the friends she'd scared away were supposed to come back after the Great Awakening—after she was vindicated. Accepting that QAnon was a lie meant accepting that there would be no Great Awakening at all, and that the damage she'd done to her life could be permanent.

The extent of that damage was, in fact, even worse than Alice had realized. She soon learned that she and Christopher weren't invited to her paternal cousins' Thanksgiving celebration. She had assumed it was because of her lax attitude about Covid, but her dad told her otherwise: They had seen her QAnon content on Facebook, he said, despite Christopher's best efforts to dissuade her from posting publicly, and they had no interest in speaking to her again.

Alice's heart was torn in two. Her own family members thought she was a bad person—even irredeemably so. She thought that by being in QAnon, she'd been standing up for what was right. She turned back to her dad for solace. He had two earnest questions for her.

"With this QAnon stuff . . . Why do you care? And is it worth it?"

He truly wanted to know. Even if there really was a demonic cabal of elites secretly controlling the world, what could she meaningfully do about it? What did her "research" or Facebook posts really accomplish at the end of the day? This wasn't an election; her "activism" wouldn't help win votes for the good guy. Wrapping herself up in these things, be they true or false, added no net benefit to her life. The destruction it caused, however, was staggering: Beyond the relationships she'd lost and the emotional strife she'd suffered, she was actively demolishing her reputation as the kind, compassionate human he knew her to be. How much more was she willing to wager on a dream that might never come true?

Ted could only hope that his daughter would take this moment of inner turmoil to rethink the path she was on. Though he and Christopher didn't realize it, they'd been using complementary approaches to get her to this stage. While Christopher had helped her start to question her conspiracy theories, Ted had helped her see the big picture of how they served—or disserved—her life. But no one could force her to let go of them. That decision was hers.

Alice was at a crossroads. She had known it was coming; she couldn't straddle two realities forever. Inside one was her hope for the future. Inside the other were the people she cared about most. No matter what, she felt like she'd be breaking herself apart.

She thought about Dawson. Though she still hadn't told him about QAnon, he was her biggest reason for believing: She wanted the best possible life for him. But now this precious vision she had was in doubt, and the longer she tried to cling to it, the more she risked alienating herself from the rest of their family forever. That could only end up hurting him.

Unlike her entry to QAnon, Alice's exit happened slowly.

She called her dad and told him that she wanted to take a step back, but she didn't know how. It wasn't in her nature to sit idly by as the world burned.

His advice to her was simple: "Cultivate your garden."

It was a reference to *Candide,* a novel written by the French philosopher Voltaire, who warned of the perils of worrying about things beyond one's control. Rather than fret over the state of the world and the many issues plaguing mankind, which would only lead to endless despair, Voltaire argued, people ought to focus on their own lives, or tend to their own gardens. That was the way to find true peace of mind.

Wanting to meet Alice where she was—on YouTube—Ted sent her a video of a talk by spiritual practitioner and clinical psychologist Jack Kornfield, a sweet-faced man with a salt-and-pepper mustache and tufts of gray hair on either side of his head. Kornfield began the video by speaking about his time studying as a Buddhist monk in the forests of Thailand, near the borders of war-torn Laos and Cambodia. From their monastery, he and his fellow monks could hear bombers zooming overhead and see explosions lighting up the sky in the distance. They had no idea what would happen next or when the violence would end. When they looked to their teacher for comfort and answers, he would simply smile and say, "It's uncertain, isn't it?"

Alice understood the message her father was trying to convey: Her need for certainty in an uncertain world could *never* be met. Instead of trying to comfort herself with QAnon, it was time to let that need go. She considered her options. If the Great Awakening *was* coming, she reasoned, it would come with or without her involvement in the movement. But if it *wasn't* . . . she had to prepare to live with uncertainty forever—an existentially terrifying prospect. Her garden seemed like a good place to start.

Just before sundown, Alice went to Sedona's Cathedral Rock Trailhead, a red-bed geological formation known for its mesmerizing, otherworldly views. In denim flare jeans, a white turtleneck, and a knit hat with cat ears and big dangling pom-poms, she danced barefoot beneath a cloudless sky, letting her body guide her this way and that. Her hips swayed and dipped. Her arms twirled like ribbons in the wind as her curls bounced over her shoulders. She savored the warm sun on her cheeks, the cool air in her lungs, and the smooth-but-scratchy texture of the sandstone against the soles of her feet and each of her toes. Gazing out at the ethereal grandeur of the horizon before her, where red touched blue in a spectacle so dazzling she could cry, she felt tiny and insignificant. Powerless. It was a curiously calming, freeing sensation. She returned to her dancing.

Over the weeks to follow, after Alice and Christopher returned home to the Bay Area, Trump lost the election and JFK, Jr., failed to reveal himself. The Great Awakening didn't happen.

At the back of her mind, Alice still hoped that one day it would. As she committed to disentangling herself from QAnon and politics at large, true versus false mattered less and less to her. The world was full of conspiracies—some real, many fake—and that was a scary thing. But it was out of her hands.

Her calmed outlook on life was fostered not only by her father but by her beloved. While Christopher couldn't guarantee her a utopic future, as QAnon had, there were things within his control that he *could* promise her. He went through each of her worst-case-scenario fears and created a game plan with her to address them. In the unlikely event that harmful vaccines were being forced on people, he promised, they would get Dawson and leave the country. Hearing these reassurances put Alice's mind at ease tremendously.

For the next year, she continued to actively turn her attention inward, meditating daily, minimizing her social media use and news consumption, getting back into her workout routine, and taking up painting. She even grew a literal garden in her backyard with plump red tomatoes and strawberries. Where paranoia and anxiety had reigned, Alice's life was gradually filling back up with joy. She came to think of herself as the eponymous protagonist in *Alice in Wonderland*: After tumbling down the rabbit hole, she had eventually realized that she was embedded in a delusion, and had escaped.

She and Christopher eloped in late 2021, vowing under the Maui sun to love each other unconditionally for the rest of their days. It felt like a fairytale ending to a nightmare.

Too good to be true.

13

DEAD TO ME

—Emily—

Adam's message hit like a heart attack.

I know my destiny well by now . . .
Be well mom, I'm sorry.

Emily had received that kind of note before, left behind by her husband for her to find once it was already too late. Now their son was saying his final farewell.

Her calls went straight to Adam's voicemail.

She tried Leah.

And Jessica.

All three of her children had blocked her number.

The deeper Emily had barreled into QAnon, the tinier her already-small offline community had become. So in her desperation, she turned to someone who had always been willing to lend an ear: her hairdresser.

Dell was a proud southerner in her midforties who had a wispy bob cut, wide-set brown eyes, and a saccharine voice. She owned a strip-mall salon in a nearby town, but over the pandemic, she'd started visiting Emily at home to maintain her honey-blond dye job. Few people ever saw it; even before the crisis, Emily rarely had visitors. She kept Dell coming back often, though, at the earliest sight of gray, eager to chat—and to vent.

Despite the nearly twenty years between them, the two women had a fair bit in common: Dell was a mother, an animal lover, and a Trump supporter who was suspicious of the official Covid narrative and would post things on social media like "I identify as a conspiracy theorist, my pronouns are . . . Told/You/So." Still, even she was startled by some of

Emily's beliefs. Every time she went over to Emily's farmhouse to dab at her barely-there roots, she'd end up listening in troubled silence to blood-lusting diatribes about treasonous politicians and sad rants about her newly estranged kids who refused to "wake up." It was obvious how deeply Emily missed them. Dell wondered why she'd let such nonsense get between them, but it was best to keep quiet and just nod along. It wasn't her place to butt in. One day, though, when Emily contacted her in a panic and shared a screenshot of Adam's message telling her to "be well," Dell knew she had to get involved. She had experienced the torment of losing a loved one to suicide herself, and she couldn't bear to even imagine receiving a text like that from her own son. So she offered to contact Emily's children on her behalf.

In texts to Leah, Dell explained Emily's concern and acknowledged that she'd gotten "sunk in" to politics and conspiracy theories. She asked if Adam was all right.

"He's not ok and she is a large part of why he is not ok," Leah replied. "She has done and is continuing to do way more emotional damage to all 3 of us than our father did with his suicide. She's consciously choosing this extremist garbage over relationships with her children."

"This year has done a number on alot of peoples mental state," Dell wrote back. "The void of [you guys] has been her topic lately . . ."

Facing the Past

As soon as Leah and Jessica found out that Adam had failed the California bar, on January 8, they called the police. He had sent them a blunt text with the news and then immediately turned off his phone. They knew their little brother. They knew the hell he'd been going through with Emily, and the wicked things she'd said to him in a pair of emails just a couple weeks earlier. They feared he was a danger to himself.

They were right.

A pair of deputy sheriffs arrived just after dark to perform a welfare check at the San Francisco address Jessica had provided, an eighteenth-floor unit of an upscale apartment building downtown. They knocked three times.

"San Francisco Sheriff's Department," one announced.

He knocked again.

"Hello? San Francisco Sher—"

The door cracked open. Peering out, red-eyed, was Adam.

"Are you Adam Porter?" the other deputy asked.

"What the fuck do you want?" Adam hissed.

"Adam, do you know why we're here? Have you been talking to any-body, Adam?"

"I'm fine. Please, just leave."

"Adam, we're just trying to get a sense—"

"I said I'm fucking fine! I'd like you to leave. *Now.*"

He slammed the door shut, and the deputies left.

Adam was not fine. He was suicidal. He had spent the last year trying agonizingly, in vain, to wrest his mother from QAnon. In the process, he had pushed her further away and alienated himself from just about every-one else he cared about, while gambling his way into a dark and terrifying place. And now, barely hanging on, he had failed his exam. Practically, having passed the Illinois bar years earlier, he could continue to practice law in California on a restricted basis; it just meant that his firm would have to keep paying a higher liability premium in the meantime. But to Adam, it meant that he was an irredeemable failure. He had failed his mother, he had failed his employer, and he had failed himself.

If there was a light at the end of the tunnel, he couldn't see it. Waiting endlessly for things to get better wasn't a life he wanted to live any longer. He set a deadline: Unless, somehow, the future was looking less bleak by March 1, he would kill himself. It was the anniversary of his father's death, which seemed fitting, in a way. The absence of his dad was the backdrop to every moment of his life, dulling the joy of each triumph and intensi-fying the pain of each hardship. And right now, he didn't know how much more pain he could take.

It was coming up on twenty-one years since that tragic night back in Tennessee, yet it still felt so raw that talking about it could reduce Adam to tears. So he rarely did. The last time he'd discussed it in any great detail was right after it happened, when he was a little boy. Emily had enrolled him and his sisters in weekly bereavement classes inside a community center in Nashville, where, in a circle of squeaky plastic chairs, they sat around and talked about their feelings with other kids who'd lost loved ones. Parents were welcome, though Emily never stayed. She'd take off to do errands or just sit in the car and wait.

The siblings also met with specialized therapists and psychiatrists, learning how to progress away from a place of denial and despair toward one of acceptance and healing. That was especially difficult for Adam. For a long time after Dan died, he woke up each morning with a morsel of hope: *Maybe it had all been a nightmare. Maybe, if he just wished hard enough . . .*

That lingering *maybe* was an anchor, and that was why Adam had clung to it so tightly as a child. He wasn't ready to move forward. Even after coming to accept with age that his dad was never coming back, he couldn't bring himself to work through his trauma. While Leah and Jessica carried on with therapy into adulthood, battling through eating disorders and self-harm arising from their grief on their paths to healing, he resisted help.

So did their mother.

Overnight, with the pull of a trigger, Emily had become a young widow left to raise her children alone. Where they felt loss, she grappled with an added layer of resentment. Dan had betrayed and abandoned her. She kept herself too distracted to stew in her emotions: Being a single mom of three, going to law school, and launching a career as an attorney didn't leave much time for things like therapy.

Once life slowed down, Emily and Adam leaned on each other as crutches. With the girls off at college, they immersed themselves in the new intimacy of their mother-son relationship, tending to the farm animals together, going out to fancy restaurants on their "little food journeys," and loving one another through their pain without ever confronting it. Then Adam left too, leaving Emily alone once more.

Leah and Jessica had watched both of them spiral in the time since. Adam turned to online gambling to keep the past at bay, while Emily veered toward radicalization by way of Fox News and Trumpism, eventually finding in QAnon an outlet for the resentment she'd kept bottled inside for so long. Her recent tweets made no secret of the pleasure she derived from raging against her bevy of "Deep State" enemies, or from interacting with a community of others who seemed to feel just as personally aggrieved as she did. But lately, her biggest target had been Adam. And now, after pushing him right to the edge, she was pleading for forgiveness.

With help from Dell, after Adam's suicide scare, Emily had gotten in touch with Jessica for the first time in months. Her daughter wouldn't speak to her over the phone, so they conversed via email.

The difference in Emily's tone was striking. The rising anger and hostility she'd been spewing for years—catalyzed by QAnon—had crumbled into a mess of panic and fear. She said that she was sorry. That she loved her children. That she'd do anything to come back together as a family.

She was petrified of losing Adam, that was clear. But it was disorienting trying to square these words of sudden contrition and affection with those she'd sent to him just before Christmas, when in response to his breaking-point declaration that he wanted "absolutely nothing" to do with her anymore, she'd called him a "huge disappointment" and told him to shed her DNA.

As her tirades had grown increasingly personal and unhinged, Leah and Jessica had pieced together a theory as to why she was so atrociously hurtful to their brother in particular—who, in an attempt to deradicalize her, had remained by her side far longer than they had. It had nothing to do with his politics or beliefs, or hers. Simply: He reminded her of their father, the person who'd hurt her the most.

Adam had Dan's effortless brilliance and Dan's haunting vices, and was around the same age Dan was when Emily married him. But Adam hadn't betrayed her. His big crime, it seemed, was denying her delusions.

That kind of damage—the kind that leads a mother to disown her child over a bunch of conspiracy theories—couldn't be debunked away with facts and evidence. QAnon, for Emily, wasn't really about the claims themselves, her daughters had realized, even if she *had* come to genuinely believe them. It was a Band-Aid on a wound that had been festering for more than two decades. Worse, it was a drug numbing her pain while satisfying her human desire to hurt others as she had been hurt, and she was addicted. She needed professional intervention.

Jessica wrote back to her.

> *You ask what you can do. . . . Get psychological help and continue with it for the foreseeable future. That's the ONLY way any of us will even consider having a relationship with you ever again. Commit to seeing a therapist/psychologist/ psychiatrist. You've done far too much damage for words ("i'm sorry, I love you") to make a bit of difference. . . .*

*Read and re-read my words and look inward if you truly
have any love left for us (as opposed to just loneliness) because your actions have demonstrated otherwise.*

Until Emily faced her trauma head-on and put in the work to heal
from it, Jessica believed, she would only continue to harm those around
her. This was her chance to prove that her remorse was real. Her chance,
at sixty-two, to rise up and be the mother her daughters missed and her
son needed.

She didn't take it.

Instead, she retreated into the safety of her anger, like a beaten dog
baring its teeth at anyone who tried to help. She didn't need to be depro-
grammed, she fumed. Jessica promptly reblocked her.

No More Maybes

For weeks after failing the bar, Adam got high and gambled daily, even
while on the clock. It was a line that he had rarely crossed before. Still
working remotely under California's extended lockdown orders, he was
betting on sports games all over the world, winning a little, losing a lot,
and caring less and less. Senior associates at his firm had started stepping
in to pick up his slack. They never said anything to him directly, but he
was certain that they felt, as he did, that he didn't deserve to be there.

He was still closely monitoring his mother online. Her Twitter account was among the tens of thousands that had been purged amid the
platform's post-insurrection QAnon crackdown, but she was still hyper-
active on Telegram. Consequently, so was he. Despite blocking her number and email to try to keep his distance, he had continued miserably
clinging to hope: *Maybe, with Trump now out of office, she would eventually log off and begin to peel away from her conspiracy theories.*

The greater Adam's disappointment, the more he dissociated from the
demands of his own life. He was mentally drifting away. But in late February, he received an email that abruptly grounded him. It was about an
empty box.

He still got UPS alerts about deliveries to his old home, where Emily
had been living by herself since he moved out. DISH Network, their longtime family TV provider, had mailed her packaging with which to return

her satellite equipment. He knew immediately what was going on. One of QAnon believers' many mottos was a string of five words that he'd been seeing all over Far Right Telegram channels lately: *We Are the News Now.* Rioters had shouted it on the Capitol grounds after gleefully destroying film gear belonging to Associated Press journalists and fashioning a noose out of the cords. It was a message of pitchfork populism and a call to action: Boycott the establishment media in favor of QAnon's independent online "citizen journalists."

Adam was numb. All alone in rural Tennessee, Emily was surrounded by nothing but farmland with little to no remaining real-world interaction. And after watching her cover her professional Facebook page in QAnon content about child sacrifice, he doubted that she even had many legal clients left. Now she was locking herself inside her conspiracy theory echo chamber and throwing away the key.

She was gone. *Forever.* It was time to accept that.

Adam thought back to the hope that had kept him anchored in stagnant grief as a little kid. This was no different: Until he let go of that lingering *maybe—maybe, one day, she'll come back—*he would be stuck. Cutting off contact with her wasn't enough; he needed to mourn and move on. To view her as dead.

He didn't know how he felt, or how he was supposed to feel. What emotions were appropriate upon privately declaring one's own parent symbolically deceased? There were tears, but they didn't come out; they stung Adam's eyes and nose without wetting his face. Everything and nothing was different: The biggest person in his life was no longer there, yet there would be no funeral, no condolences, and no bereavement leave—no transition period or acknowledgment of any kind. Just him and his unspoken sorrow.

In a grim sense, Adam was—relatively—fortunate. He'd recently discovered r/QAnonCasualties, a rapidly growing subreddit that served as a support group for loved ones of QAnon believers. It helped him put things into perspective. He read stories from people who were dependent on the Emily in their life and therefore had no option but to maintain a relationship with them—often at the severe expense of their own mental well-being. There were teens and kids who lived at home with their conspiracy theorist parents, disabled folks relying on their conspiracy theorist caretakers, parents who feared getting into custody battles with their conspiracy theorist spouses, and elderly individuals who couldn't imagine starting over without their conspiracy theorist partners at such an advanced age. Adam, at least, had the freedom to walk away for good.

The first time he lost a parent, he had the other one to help him get through it. This time he was on his own, leaps and bounds behind his sisters in the mourning process. But he was a grown man now—not the eight-year-old boy who'd suddenly had his daddy ripped away from him. If ever in his life there was an occasion when he needed to lift himself up and put himself first, this was it. He was done fighting for Emily. It was time to fight for Adam.

Another remotely conducted bar exam was due to take place at the end of July. The common understanding was that it took four hundred hours of studying, at a minimum, to pass. Before Adam's first attempt early last fall, most of that time had been sidetracked by QAnon research and fruitless fact-checking battles with Emily. This year, he'd be ready. He had just under six months to go, but with a full-time job to work around, it would be tight. That was something of a blessing: Adam sorely needed a distraction to keep his mind away from his grief and the urge to gamble. Idle nights alone with his thoughts never ended well anymore.

He hit the books hard, whipping together little paper flashcards and purchasing pricey commercial guides. He also got his hands on some Adderall, determined to maximize his grind time by whatever means necessary. If his life were a movie, this would be the time-lapse scene showing him shuffling around his couch with his laptop, notebooks, and scattered piles of takeout containers as the sun bobbed outside his windows. Indeed, if his life were a movie, he would emerge fully prepared to crush the bar and leave his mom in the past, closing this God-awful saga with a Hollywood happy ending. If only.

The problem with mourning the living, Adam very quickly learned, was that they had a tendency to pop back up when and where they pleased.

On his thirtieth birthday, an Amazon package arrived in his mailbox. It was a book. He had no doubt as to who it was from. Despite the old adage, the cover told him everything he needed to know about its contents: It featured a hand clutching a glowing portal displaying a colorful collage of aliens, chemtrails, the antifa logo, a human skull, and a pyramid with a flaming red eyeball.

"ALL THAT IS HIDDEN WILL BE REVEALED," its back panel promised.

Already, from beyond the figurative grave, Emily had managed to make her son's birthday about her delusions, knowing full well how acutely distressing they were to him. It seemed more like a taunt than a gesture of love—as if she could sense that Adam had finally committed himself to pulling away from her, so she was trying to lure him back in. He wasn't taking the bait. But it still set him backward: He tossed her farce of a gift on top of his bookshelf, unable to throw it out, and opened his betting app on his phone.

Those sorts of setbacks happened intermittently, though they weren't always Emily's direct doing. After the many months Adam had spent chasing her down the rabbit hole and lurking in the QAnon forums she frequented, he couldn't help himself from going back whenever there was a major breaking news event. He hated that he could almost always predict how the facts would be twisted. In April, when a Capitol Police officer was mowed down by a man in a car, conspiracy theorists scavenged for dirt on the slain officer, a father of two, and concluded that he was a hired actor. In June, when ninety-eight people were killed in the collapse of a condo in Miami with long-neglected structural issues, QAnon influencers spread the rumor that it had been demolished as part of a targeted assassination.

As badly as he wanted to, Adam wasn't able to ignore them. These same opportunists who had poisoned Emily's mind—effectively killing the mother he knew and loved—weren't just going about their lives scot-free . . . they were still actively causing harm. And they were *thriving*. Their well-trodden path to prosperity via tribalist lies and fearmongering cut directly across his road to recovery. He had never learned to properly grieve, if such a skill even existed; he just craved closure, in some way, shape, or form. But in this broader system of conspiracy theory capitalism, it felt like a fool's fantasy—like losing a loved one to cancer and then trying to find peace in a society where carcinogen dealing was a booming, normalized profession and business model.

In a moment of weakness, Adam texted his mother. She was still blocked; as far as he knew, that meant his messages wouldn't actually reach her. It was purely cathartic, as if he were crying into the abyss or leaving letters at a grave site. He told her that he would always love and miss her, and that he would always wish he didn't—unaware that messages to blocked recipients could, in fact, go through; they just couldn't be replied to. Then he disconnected his phone number.

When the day of the bar arrived, Adam popped more Adderall and tried to ignore the screeching voice of self-doubt in his head. The past year had decimated his confidence, and California's exam was notoriously grueling. A full third of his fellow examinees had failed at least once before, like him. Of that group, 81 percent would do so again.

Adam was bracing for the worst while knowing that he *had* to pass: A lot more than his career was riding on it. Since he was a little kid, he'd been the brainiac who could ace any test, just like his dad. He desperately wanted to be that person again. To feel like himself again. Five essays, a performance test, and two hundred multiple-choice questions had the power to make or completely break him—there would be no coming back from failing twice.

Chasing Closure

For months, Leah and Jessica had been trying relentlessly to get in touch with Adam. The last time he'd spoken to them was the night they sent the police to his door. They'd even gotten a cousin and an ex-girlfriend to reach out on their behalf, but he'd ignored them at every turn. Not only had QAnon driven a wedge between him and Emily, it had indirectly hurt his relationships with his sisters as well. At first, he'd resented them for giving up on Emily as early as they did. Now he envied them. From his vantage point, it seemed like they both had gotten by relatively unscathed, while he had come undone.

Theirs was a plight familiar to myriad others, like the then two hundred thousand members of r/QAnonCasualties, whose loved ones had become a toxic influence on their lives after sliding too far into conspiracy theories, hyperpartisan politics, religious extremism, cult worship, or other identity-warping fixations. Each of the Porter siblings was mourning their mother in their own way, with varying degrees of success, like a private case study of what tends to work and what doesn't.

Adam was trying to will himself to "get over" Emily cold turkey, a lonely and emotionally draining strategy that he was doing his best to figure out as he went. Whenever he missed her too much, he'd think about all the awful things she'd said and done, or reread the devastating emails she'd sent him. It reliably dissuaded him from making contact but still left him feeling worse than he had before, clouding out his sadness with indignation. Hating her was easier than missing her.

Over in Arkansas, Leah was also attempting to move on from Emily. It was less challenging for her to do, at least temporarily. As a doctor in the trenches of a Covid hotspot in the state, she barely had a chance to sleep or eat. She certainly didn't have time to sit around grieving her mom, or to commit to the kind of long-term counseling that had helped her grieve her dad. She just put it out of her mind and focused on the emergency unfolding right before her eyes. Not thinking about Emily didn't truly resolve anything, to be sure. Leah was still distraught that her mother had chosen conspiracy theories over her own flesh and blood, but for now she could set her feelings to the side.

Jessica was the only one to seek professional help. Like Adam, she was in search of closure. But her longtime therapist, Nita, a warm and gentle Native American woman who was also in her midthirties, encouraged her to think deeply about what that would actually look like. Jessica decided that real closure would require accountability—from both Emily and those who had taken advantage of her. Saying this out loud, having to resist the impulse to laugh or cry, made it glaringly obvious that these things were almost certainly never going to happen. Much like holding onto anger or hope, Nita said, chasing the idea of closure was counterproductive. It would only set her up to fail.

There were two Emilys now: the current one, who couldn't be expected to ever change, and the old one, who was already gone but had yet to be properly memorialized. Jessica needed to let go of both. Nita had her write a goodbye letter to the old Emily, expressing thanks. It was a tall order. Jessica was feeling many things; gratitude wasn't one of them. But two days after her therapy session, she took out a pad of paper and inked the letter by hand. She thanked Emily for teaching her to be ambitious and brave, for inspiring her to be strong, and for including her in her passion for animals. She still treasured her childhood memories around the barn helping out with feedings and groomings.

Once, when Jessica was seven or eight, Emily woke her at 1 a.m. to witness the birth of a calf. She sat cross-legged in the shavings as the mama cow, chestnut brown with a white stripe down her nose, lay on her side, breathing heavily. Emily coaxed her along, stroking her neck and whispering into her ear. The baby, a female, entered the world slowly and quietly—enough to hear the buzz of the fluorescent lights overhead. Within minutes, she was trembling into a standing position, her scrawny legs trying not to buckle. Then she wobbled over to her mom and they nuzzled silently in the hay. It would remain the most serene and tender experience of Jessica's life: mother and daughter watching mother and daughter in the dead of night. Emily was her purest self with her animals: fearless, nurturing, at peace. That was how Jessica wanted to remember her. She finished her letter, read it aloud, then ripped it up and threw it away.

It was one of many exercises that Nita, a trauma specialist, had created for Jessica, in addition to setting firm boundaries to keep her distance from the current, QAnon-obsessed Emily. That included blocking her and, when Jessica was ready, letting people know that she no longer had a relationship with her or wished to be reminded of her.

But sometimes, as Adam had learned soon after declaring Emily dead, reminders were impossible to avoid—like when Jessica found out that Emily might really be dying.

In November, Jessica and Leah found themselves frantically going back and forth with Dell, the hairdresser, who had reached out again—this time without Emily knowing—to inform them that she was extremely ill. She said Emily had been self-medicating with ivermectin, an antiparasitic agent that was being widely touted in right-wing circles as a way to treat or prevent Covid. Because of a lack of scientific evidence supporting such claims, prescriptions were hard to come by, stirring conspiracy theories that elites were withholding the drug from the public. But as many thousands of Americans had discovered, they could easily purchase ivermectin produced as a dewormer for livestock, in the form of a horse paste or bovine injectable. Emily got hers at Tractor Supply.

The last time Dell had seen her, Emily was alarmingly pallid, frail, and disoriented. Dell told the sisters that she suspected the ivermectin was to blame, though she couldn't be certain. It wouldn't have been an isolated case: The CDC had already reported a wave of calls to poison control centers from people taking the medication unprescribed. The side effects of overdosing could be severe, even deadly.

Dell had started bringing Emily meal replacement drinks, she said, as she was so weak she could barely stand. Leah wasn't taking any chances.

As a doctor, she knew how rapidly patients' health could deteriorate. So after talking it over with Jessica, she called an ambulance to take Emily to the ER, where she received immediate care from a team of physicians. It was at that point that Jessica decided she no longer needed to peripherally involve herself in the situation. Her mind didn't change when she learned that Emily had requested to sign a do-not-resuscitate order, seemingly aware of how dire her condition was. In Jessica's view, no good could come from reaching out to her, even if it was to say goodbye. She had already done that.

Emily's life-threatening health scare, from which she eventually recovered, was, for Jessica, like a test. She could have abandoned the boundaries she'd set, risking a reversal of all her progress toward healing. But she didn't. She attributed her ability to stand firm, in large part, to her therapy—something she knew she was fortunate to have access to. It provided her with continued emotional support, personalized coping strategies, and an inexhaustible outlet through which to vent whenever she needed it. On hard days, she reached out to Nita, who would remind her that she was only human, and that her feelings of sadness and confusion were entirely normal. They processed them together, revisiting the reasons why she had let go of her mother in the first place. None of them had changed.

With time, Jessica stopped worrying as much about Emily. Days went by—then weeks—when she hardly thought about her at all. Still, she worried for her siblings. Leah was in limbo, held there for now by circumstances beyond her control as the pandemic dragged toward its third year. But Adam, Jessica feared, was spiraling down the same lonesome path he'd taken after their dad died, trying again to outrun his trauma instead of seeking help.

Across the country, still out of touch with his family, Adam had spent the months following the bar exam continuing to gamble and smoke as he awaited his results. But with California gradually reopening, he was also working out in the gym again and visiting his favorite coffee shop, taking baby steps back into the world from which he'd been hiding. He got a new phone number and reached out to three of his buddies from college to invite them to the Golden State Warriors game on November 12, the evening that the results were scheduled to drop. He'd gotten free tickets from work, and the last place he wanted to be at that time was alone in his apartment. It would be his first social outing since Covid—and QAnon—had turned his life upside down.

When the date came, Adam was a wreck. He tried to focus on his excitement for the game as the workday crawled by. The seats were in the second row off the court, close enough to hear the ball swish through the net. It would probably be best for him to hold off on looking at his results, which were set to come out at 6 p.m., until after he got home that night, he figured. But he couldn't trust himself to make it through all four quarters without checking, and he didn't want his reaction—be it joyous or devastating—to wind up on ESPN.

Deep, deep down, beneath all the unshakable anxiety and pessimism, part of Adam was expecting good news. He could hardly admit it to himself; hope felt like the most dangerous thing in the world to him. He was at the Embarcadero BART station en route to the Chase Center when 6 p.m. struck. It had been precisely 107 days; he couldn't wait another minute. Clenching his jaw in anticipation, he entered his login information into the "CalBar" portal system. There it was, waiting for him.

> The Committee of Bar Examiners of the State Bar of California is pleased to report that you achieved a passing score on the July 2021 California Bar Examination. Congratulations; you may be justly proud of your achievement.

Adam collapsed into tears on the platform. As concerned passengers looked on, he gasped the first real breath he'd taken in over a year. His emotions were bursting from every pore on his body: Elation. Relief. Pride. And an aching, familiar sadness.

He remembered the day he'd gotten his acceptance letter to law school. As soon as his eyes had jumped to the word "congratulations," he had leapt to call Emily, who was so proud of him she sobbed on the spot.

Now she was gone.

Adam had suffered this pain countless times before, with every piece of good news that he'd wished he could share with his dad. But even without parents, he wasn't alone. He texted Leah and Jessica from the subway, then raced out through clusters of blue-and-gold-jerseyed passersby to find his friends to celebrate. His smile didn't leave his face for the entire game, which ended in a Warriors victory. The natural high he was feeling made it seem as if all of his problems had evaporated. *This* had to be the closure he'd been seeking, he told himself: a full-circle end to the domino chain of destruction that QAnon had wrought on his life. After falling into a debilitating pit of depression while trying to save his mother—which had more than contributed to his failing the bar—he had written her off and passed his exam. Surely, now, he could move on.

The next morning, still buzzing, Adam opened Instagram. His profile was empty; he wasn't one to upload much personal content online. But on this day, he had something to say. He drafted a post with a lengthy caption airing out many of the things he'd been keeping to himself. He shared that his mother, once his hero, was now a stranger with whom he'd likely never speak again. He wrote about her QAnon addiction and the brutal toll it had taken on him behind the scenes. And he explained that his radio-silent disappearance from public life had been spent in a tailspin that, for some time, he didn't think he'd make it out of.

It was one of the most frighteningly honest things Adam had ever written, but getting the words out left him feeling a little lighter. He typed out the final two lines of his caption, which accompanied a screenshot of his passing bar results, and clicked "Share."

> *Nobody is owed anything in life, especially not a shot at re-demption, but it's hard to view this as anything otherwise.*
> *I sure as hell won't waste it.*

Adam wasn't looking for pity or praise; he just wanted to reemerge with his head held high, leaving himself no path back toward hiding in shame. But the outpouring of responses floored him. Messages streamed in from old friends, several of whom remembered Emily as "Mrs. P." from when they were growing up. They seemed sincerely heartbroken for him—and for her—expressing their profound shock that someone so very intelligent and sweet could ever pivot to QAnon. Adam was touched by how fondly they all remembered her. He wondered how it would make her feel to learn that so many people still missed and cared for the woman she used to be.

His mind slipped into a familiar trap: *Maybe, if she knew . . .*

14

EVER AFTER

—Doris—

Once upon a time, Dale and Doris were celebrating their forty-fifth wedding anniversary. The year was 2015 and the scene was Tony's, the little Italian joint with flocked gold wallpaper, argyle tablecloths, and sepia-tone photographs of American musical legends, where they'd gone on their very first date. The decor, now vintage, was still the same all this time later, and so was their order: classic spaghetti and meatballs for him, cheesy lasagna al forno for her. Even the recipes were untouched.

To dine there, as Dale and Doris did every year on December 6, was to visit a place where time stood still. The ambience and the rich, zesty-sweet flavors whisked them right back to that romantic evening so very long ago, like a living memory that was always there waiting for them. But Dale was no longer shooting bashful glances across the table at a daunting southern belle, racking his smitten brain for ways to impress her; he was gazing deep into a pair of wise, soulful eyes that felt like home. They saw him for exactly who he was, at his best, his worst, and every state in between. That was among the sweetest blisses of having loved each other for nearly two-thirds of their lives: feeling wholly seen and wholly accepted.

People sometimes asked if there was a secret to staying happily married for as long as they had, or if it was merely a matter of luck. Dale didn't think so. The only role luck had played was his being in the right place at the right time when he and Doris met at a literary event in their twenties back in New Orleans, and his only secret for a successful marriage was hardly a secret at all. Plain and simple, it came down to being there for each other—always and no matter what.

Their wedding vows weren't sweet nothings recited for a crowd, they were sacrosanct commitments that demanded an unending willingness to adapt individually and as a couple. As their lives had evolved, with new jobs, new cities, new opportunities, and new challenges, so had the world around them, with new culture and new technology. They navigated it all arm in arm, embracing one another's shifting passions and accommodating each other's emerging limitations. Now in their golden years, it was mostly the latter.

While they had once found joy going for moonlit bicycle rides under starry skies, spending late nights out on the town with their friends, and dancing their hearts out at rock 'n' roll concerts, they had come to prefer taking short, sauntering strolls through nature and hosting the occasional early-evening get-together from the comfort of their home in Tuscaloosa, Alabama. Dale still exercised daily, but Doris's mobility issues made it difficult for her to be on her feet for long. Quieter and slower was better these days. At the last concert they'd attended, to see Bob Dylan, they had to stick cut up sponges in their ears just to get through the show. Even long-term rituals had changed. Their annual visits to Tony's were now for lunch instead of dinner, to avoid the eye strain of night driving when returning to their hotel after eating.

With age had come many adjustments for Dale and Doris, including spending more and more downtime with only each other for company. They didn't mind. As a couple without children of their own, he was all hers and she, all his. It had always been that way. They could still pass hours thoughtfully discussing politics and current affairs over a pot of coffee, chatting about their favorite novels old and new, and excitedly looking for clues in murder-mystery dramas on TV, like a pair of amateur detectives. But holding onto happiness in retirement, they had found, meant enjoying the silence too. It was the sound of profound comfort and unspoken understanding that came with knowing someone as intimately as they could be known. They were content reading side by side on the living room couch, quietly sitting out on their patio in the warmth of the morning sun, birdwatching at the lake near their townhouse, and, simply, being together.

Dale reached over the restaurant table and clasped his wife's small hands. They were weathered with age spots and wrinkles, a testament to all they'd done over the decades: all the food they'd cooked for private meals and rousing dinner parties, all the rooms they'd carefully decorated and redecorated from house to house and city to city, all the times they'd laced snugly into Dale's own. It had been forty-five years—*forty-five years*—and he and Doris were still coming back to the place where it had all begun, still in love.

How very special it would be, they exclaimed over tiramisu, when they made it to fifty.

In Sickness and in Health

By December 6, 2020, the silence sounded different.

Tony's was operating under strict capacity limitations, but even if it had been open for business as usual, Dale and Doris weren't in the mood to celebrate. After exchanging strained anniversary wishes in the morning, they parted ways. She strode off to the study to warn the world—one Facebook post at a time—about the Deep State oligarchs who secretly controlled all levers of power in society. He fled to the recreation center at the University of Alabama to do socially distanced water aerobics, then retreated home into the bedroom with his books to get through the rest of the day. It had been like that for months.

In 2021, things got worse. And then, toward year's end, much, *much* worse. The deeper Doris traveled down the rabbit hole, the more skeptically she seemed to view her husband. For a retired college professor—"an intellectual"—she'd remark, he was curiously dismissive of her research. He was one of *them:* the kind of people who were abhorred inside her online communities for using labels like "conspiracy theory" to swat down any idea that deviated from the official narrative.

Dale's playful, discerning, timid-but-charming wife of half a century, whose coy smile never failed to bring out his own, had gone cold. In public, to his private humiliation, Doris treated requests to wear a face mask as grave personal insults. Online, she came off as smug and overbearing, screaming from the digital rooftops about a plot by Bill Gates to cull the global population with fatal injections. She was following the commands of her trusted internet "truth-tellers," like antivax kingpin Del Bigtree, to resist public safety orders and "awaken" the masses, as if it were her sworn duty to do so. Those who expressed doubt or criticism of her claims, close friends included, were met with snide pity. She felt sorry for them, she'd retort, because they were too brainwashed by the "corporate media" to think for themselves. Her and Dale's social life was suffering immeasurably as a result.

So was their home life. The silent comfort and understanding between them had transformed into a droning, palpable discord. Engaging in conversation was like maneuvering a minefield. Dale's past attempts to debunk the wild falsehoods that Doris clung to as gospel had gone horribly awry. Not knowing what else he could do for her, he was keeping his distance—as much as was possible within 1,200 square feet. Giving her space, he hoped, would ease the tension and create an opportunity to come back together.

Yet as the seasons rolled by, Doris's mood only soured. She was irritable and seemed acutely stressed. It wasn't surprising, given her stated belief that a global genocide was under way. But Dale could tell that something else was troubling her. There were days when he'd get back from the pool to find her still in bed. Whenever he'd ask if she was all right, she'd say she was just tired. It wasn't until the late fall that he learned what was really going on.

Upon returning home from his water aerobics meet-up one brisk November morning, Dale walked into the living room and was startled to encounter Doris sitting quietly on the couch. When she wasn't sleeping, she was almost always in the study on the computer, too engrossed to pay him much notice. But here she was in front of him, with a broken, exhausted look on her face.

"I just can't take it anymore," she moaned, almost to herself.

Dale froze. The last time Doris had confronted him like this, she had blindsided him with a shattering accusation of being "verbally abusive" for trying to disprove her beliefs, and had implied that if he didn't stop, she would leave him.

"Can't take what?" he asked nervously.

Doris grimaced and looked down.

"My arm."

Dale felt the briefest moment of relief, until he realized what she was talking about. In the spring, she had complained of an inflamed red rash on her left arm below her shoulder, an area that was always concealed by her linen tops and dresses. She had thought at the time that it might be a spider bite or, worse, a reaction from being in the vicinity of people who'd just gotten "the jab." In the immediate aftermath of their shots, they could "shed" toxins onto those around them, she believed, causing yet-unknown side effects.

Dale hadn't dared press Doris to see a doctor; that would have only provoked an argument. Her distrust of the medical system, sparked by her cancer misdiagnosis in 2016, was what had steered her toward conspiracy theories in the first place, by way of alternative medicine groups on Facebook. That was precisely where she had turned earlier this year for guidance on how to treat her rash. People there had all kinds of advice for her—anything but going to a qualified medical professional, apparently. Their fear, as Dale understood it, was that many "establishment" doctors were in the pocket of Big Pharma and were ordered to keep their patients sick in order to profit endlessly off their treatments. He knew that kind of paranoid thinking was what led the vulnerable and desperate right into the wide-open arms of grifters, cranks, and pseudoscientific "healers"— like Louise.

Doris found Louise, a loquacious young woman living out west, after her initial course of internet-prescribed essential oils, botanical ointments, and concoctions shipped from overseas had failed to produce any results. Louise was a longtime practitioner of homeopathy, the unscientific system of therapeutics involving the dilution of minerals, herbs, and other substances to create biochemically inert "remedies" (a process condemned within the medical community as a scam). Her services weren't covered by insurance. In fact, a state consumer protection act required her to instruct her clients to consult with a primary care physician prior to acting on her advice, as she was not licensed to prescribe treatment for any kind of condition. But she touted her skills in vague yet compelling terms: They were invaluable in addressing "imbalances of all types," she said, like throwing "a pebble" into the center of "your pond" to send "healing ripples to every part of you."

After an initial $350 video consultation, Louise mailed Doris a package of little white pellets. Each contained less than half a milligram of sulfur, the active ingredient. Doris dissolved them under her tongue every day and waited to get better.

And waited.

And waited.

In her intake forms, Louise had cautioned that her remedies could be "inactivated" by influences including "emotional upset"; Doris needed to stay positive. But sitting in the living room before her husband, more than half a year since the issue had first emerged, she appeared distraught. Desperate.

"My gosh, Doris. You still have that rash?" Dale asked her.

Doris shook her bowed head. Then she unbuttoned her blouse over her camisole, slipped off the right sleeve and, ever so slowly and carefully, the left.

Dale let out a loud, horrified gasp and looked away. His stomach lurched. He felt like he might be sick. Glancing up at Doris's face in shock, he could see how scared she was.

She began to cry.

"Doris . . ." he stammered, lowering his hand from his mouth. Asking if she was okay seemed senseless.

"I don't understand . . . how could you keep this from me?"

He stared down once more. The rash was long gone. In its place, surrounded by scabby pink tissue, she had developed a deep, raw, festering open sore. It was the size of a credit card.

"What do we do?" Doris whimpered.

Dale didn't know what to say. He couldn't muster any empty words of reassurance. His wife's conspiracy theories, he feared, would end up costing her an arm.

Till Death Do Us Part

The older Dale got, the more he thought about death.

Doing so was only natural, he figured. One way or another, it was coming. At nearly eighty-two years old, he could have a decade or he could have a day. That didn't worry him. It made him grateful: He still had his health, his mental faculties, and his mobility. Every morning that he opened his eyes truly was a gift.

He had imagined spending this final chapter of his life doing the things he loved most: laughing with dear friends over good wine and great food; savoring the dreamy pastel sunsets at the lake; taking in the fragrant magnolia and holly blossoms decorating the UA grounds in the spring and summer; walking beneath the harvest-hued sugar maples lining the Tuscaloosa Riverwalk in the fall; and, on rare winter snow days, touring the campus's frosted, glittering wonderland. All, of course, with Doris. She made the flavors richer and the colors brighter.

Doris thought often about death too. Every time she and Dale got word that someone they knew had died, which wasn't uncommon at their age, she shook her head in sorrow and muttered disapprovingly that they must have gotten "the jab." More than once she had turned to Dale and told him that the only reason they were still alive was that they had refused to "drink the Kool-Aid," unaware that he was both vaccinated and boosted. If she were to find out, he suspected, she would consider it a betrayal on par with infidelity.

Being with Doris had devolved over the past year and a half into a delicate balancing act of peacekeeping and pure self-preservation. She and Dale couldn't talk or laugh like they used to. The loneliness he felt was excruciating; it sometimes kept him up at night missing her, even as she lay right there. But it was the little moments he used to share with her that were the hardest: When he saw their shih tzu make that adorably goofy face that Doris found so funny, with her tiny pink tongue just barely poking out. When the heirloom tomatoes and rutabagas in their community veggie garden began to ripen. When he heard a new song on the radio that he knew would make her smile. Those were the times when he felt the most alone.

It was exhausting too to be uncomfortable around his own wife in his own home. But no matter how desperately he wanted to mend their marriage, he couldn't bring himself to sit through her never-ending queue of insufferable videos detailing all the ways the "elites" were plotting to oppress and terrorize them. *That* was not how he wished to spend his remaining time.

He still had his hobbies. Some of them, at least. When he wasn't in the UA pool, he was counting down the hours until he could go back. It was all that remained of his once-active social life. In non-Covid times, he had gone to indoor cycling sessions on campus and senior cardio classes in which he and a group of fellow alumni danced to "The Twist" and other songs from the '50s and '60s, dusting off moves from days gone by. He had also volunteered now and then to pick up trash around the lake with other residents, mostly younger families. Though his body could ache for days afterward, the joy of being able to help out in his community lasted far longer.

Doris didn't have any of that. Dale wasn't normally one to dwell on what-ifs, but the crushing aimlessness he'd experienced during the lockdowns, when he was cut off entirely from the activities that made him feel whole, had left him wondering whether things might have been different if Doris had simply had a hobby of her own. Something that wasn't too physically taxing for her—even a book club. He recognized that broadcasting her QAnon beliefs satisfied many of the same psychological needs for her that his hobbies did for him: It seemed to give her a restored sense of purpose and value, feelings that naturally eroded with age. He could hear the excitement and the righteousness hiding behind the concern in her voice when she spoke of the Deep State. But if she'd already had a stimulating source of fulfillment in her life, outside their home, maybe the conspiracy theories that had initially piqued her curiosity wouldn't have spiraled into the all-consuming obsession they were now. They had become her everything. It was clearer by the day that that wasn't going to change.

Dale was trying his best to accept that. There wasn't a specific moment or episode of heartbreak when he realized that Doris wasn't coming back. His hope had just faded away over time. He'd read an article profiling people whose spouses had also been consumed by hardcore conspiracy theory beliefs. One was a woman whose husband had broken down in tears and accused her of "murdering" their kids upon hearing that she'd taken them to get vaccinated. Another was a man whose wife, like Doris, had first gotten sucked in by Del Bigtree videos years earlier, then graduated to QAnon. Along with others featured in the story, that man intended to get a divorce.

Leaving Doris had never crossed Dale's mind. It was far too late for him to start over in life, and he didn't want to, regardless. He still loved her. Though it agonized him, he viewed her conspiracy theory affliction not as who she was but as something that had happened to her, like an infection of the mind. One without a cure, it seemed. He wouldn't walk away from her if she were suffering from dementia, and he wasn't going to do so now. The vows he had made to her were unconditional.

He would be there for her—always and no matter what.

What that meant, in practice, was changing. Previously, Dale had thought that being there for Doris meant trying to save her with facts and evidence. Now, with the revelation of a terrifying wound that looked like it was rotting through her arm, it meant trying to literally save her.

No longer concealing her suffering, Doris sobbed openly from the pain. Dale was completely beside himself. He had no idea what had caused her rash or open sore to begin with, or what kind of treatment to seek, but taking her to a wound center seemed logical. To his surprise, she agreed without hesitation to go. He called to make the appointment right away, feeling mildly hopeful until hearing two words: "mask requirement."

Dale stepped outside into the cool morning air and shut the door, out of earshot from Doris.

"Ma'am," he said as kindly as he could to the nurse on the line, "is there *any* possible way that you could please make an exception? You see, my wife, she just won't wear a mask."

"No. I'm sorry, sir—"

"*Please*," he begged. "I'm afraid she's going to have to get her arm amputated if we can't get this resolved soon."

Before the nurse could respond, Dale told her that Doris was a good, caring person who'd lost her way. He told her candidly about his long struggle with Doris's conspiracy theories, listing the many online remedies that had already failed her. Getting to a point where she was willing to even consider conventional medicine, he explained, was a small miracle. This was probably his only chance to help her.

The nurse put Dale on hold. He wasn't a religious man, but he was on the verge of prayer.

"All right, sir," she said a couple minutes later. "We'll see her. You just make sure she comes straight back and doesn't go near any other patients."

Before hanging up, she added, "Good luck to you. With everything."

Dale thanked her profusely then went back inside and told Doris they were all set. He was afraid she might change her mind, but on the morning of the appointment, in tears, she rushed out the door ahead of him to the car, cradling her left arm in her right like a broken wing. Her pain was winning against her fear.

The wound center, however, wasn't the miracle Dale had hoped for. The attending practitioner didn't know what was wrong with Doris's arm, nor did she know how to heal it. But the nurses who delicately cleaned and dressed it for Doris, a pair of middle-age women with smiling eyes who called her *darlin'*, were so kind and warm to her, even without her mask, that she agreed to come back once a week for professional rebandaging. It was a major first step in a long and brutal road ahead of mask-optional visits with doctors and specialists all over western Alabama.

On their fifty-first anniversary, Dale and Doris ate ham sandwiches together in the kitchen. They still didn't have much to say to each other, beyond scheduling and discussing her appointments. But the silence between them was softening. Dale had started picking up all the household chores, which they had split from the beginning of their marriage: He had always done the laundry, she had emptied the dishwasher, and so forth. In her condition, though, he just wanted her to rest. With every task he took off her plate, she gently smiled and thanked him.

Dale cleaned up after they finished their sandwiches then drove to UA. It was a crisp and perfect fifty-three degrees out. With students busy studying for finals, the grounds were mostly empty, leaving him all alone to behold the magnificent Christmas tree aglow in twinkling gold near the base of the Quad, like a beacon of light. He and Doris used to admire it together. But she had turned away from the radiance of life to withdraw into the darkness, captivated by enemies and evils that didn't exist while beautiful days passed her by and the hourglass emptied. Dale wondered if there was still reason for hope after all. Maybe, if they could just find the right doctor to finally heal her, the entire horrid ordeal would be the wake-up call she needed to come back to reality and away from her delusions. . . . If ever he could use a silver lining, it was now.

The next few months brought only discouragement: befuddled clinicians, ineffective antifungals and antibiotics, more pain, and more crying. Dale had never seen Doris so depressed. She barely ate, barely slept. He went down a warren of rabbit holes of his own, unsuccessfully scouring the web for answers as her wound darkened and grew. He was beginning to think that losing her arm was inevitable. But in the late spring of 2022, they finally had a breakthrough.

A friend recommended Dr. Robbins, a pleasant, round-faced dermatologist about an hour out of town. He inspected Doris closely and told her that she appeared to have a rare tropical skin disease. He had seen it once before: Over the past decade or so, he explained, more and more cases had been cropping up among Americans who hadn't traveled out-side the country, suggesting that the condition could also be endemic in the United States. It would have been more easily identifiable in its early stages, had Doris sought proper care at the onset of symptoms. But at last—after more than a year—she had gotten an accurate diagnosis.

Dr. Robbins prescribed a medication to take twice daily for four weeks along with the correct antibiotics to treat a secondary bacterial infection, effectively tossing Doris and Dale a lifeline up out of the hell in which they'd been trapped. Before long, the wound began to heal. They both wept with relief.

After a roller-coaster of lows and lower lows, the end was in sight. Dale was optimistic that with Doris's health crisis mostly behind them, they could focus on healing their relationship. But the ride, it seemed, wasn't over yet.

During a checkup to assess Doris's recovery progress, Dr. Robbins looked at her arm and frowned. He noticed that a mole at the base of her shoulder appeared to have gotten larger. It could be cancerous, he said. Dale's heart dropped. His mind flashed back to the fateful day in 2016 when a doctor had told Doris, falsely, that she had pancreatic cancer. The trauma she had suffered as a result had kicked off a harrowing chain of events that had upended their lives and nearly blown apart their mar-riage. In a way, it had brought them to this very moment.

Dr. Robbins was still speaking. Surgically removing the mole would be the best course of action, just to be safe, he advised with a reassuring smile. It would be quick and painless.

Dale looked anxiously at his wife. She sat in the patient chair in si-lence, visibly shaken.

"Okay," she said after a few moments, taking a deep breath and exhal-ing slowly. "Let's schedule the surgery."

As Happy as Can Be

December 6, 2022, Dale and Doris's fifty-second anniversary, was a good day. Not the kind of *good* that Dale had once imagined for them at this stage of their life, but the kind that he had come to accept: as good as *good* was going to get.

They didn't make it to Tony's. Doris spent the morning and afternoon in the study on Facebook, like always. Dale went off to UA to swim and socialize, then returned home to read. But in the evening, they sat down on their navy velvet sofa to watch murder-mystery dramas together, an old, abandoned ritual that they had revived over the past year. It was a brief, daily window during which Dale felt connected to his wife again. They didn't talk about much of substance—just the show on TV—but they laughed and smiled and enjoyed each other. Dale savored every minute every night. He knew he had to be careful, though. If he got carried away and let things go too far, Doris would turn the conversation toward chemtrails or 5G or "the clot shot."

Her conspiracy theory–mongering hadn't abated. She trusted *her* doctors now—in particular, Dr. Robbins, who had indeed caught melanoma on her shoulder, as a biopsy had since revealed. But she continued to believe that the system at large was run by corrupt elites hellbent on massacring people with vaccines—and she still made no secret of that online.

It was easiest for Dale not to think about it. Being there for her, he had decided, meant accepting her as she was. That didn't mean he had to pretend to agree with her. They could coexist and, for an hour or two each night, set aside their differences to just be together with the time they had.

They turned on *Columbo,* a crime drama about a rumpled but genius detective. The series had first aired in 1968, the year Dale and Doris first met. They hadn't watched much TV at the time, though, choosing to spend their days out experiencing the world for themselves instead of through a screen. Things were simpler back then. There was no Facebook, no QAnon, and no doubt in their minds that they would live happily ever after.

After the episode ended, Doris complained of a discomfort in her shoulders. She asked Dale for a back rub, and he gladly obliged. He massaged her in tender silence, smiling down at the nape of her neck as he worked through her knots. When he was done, he sat back down beside her, wanting to draw out the moment just a little longer.

Then, in an instant, it was over.

"I want to show you something," Doris said keenly, sitting forward and gesturing for him to follow her to the study. "There's this video you *really* need to see."

Dale said nothing for a few seconds, caught in emotional whiplash. It felt like he'd been shaken from a pleasant dream. He had let it go too far.

"Oh," he replied, dropping his gaze. "It's just . . . I'm pretty tired, actually. I think I'd better go to sleep."

Doris's smile faded. She nodded as he made his way to the bedroom, book in hand.

"Well, good night, then."

LIKE MOONS AND LIKE SUNS

—Kendra and Jonah—

Once Buck was gone, Tayshia just couldn't.

She couldn't eat, couldn't sleep, couldn't function. She couldn't go to work or attend the racial justice rally that she herself had helped organize. She couldn't even bring herself to go outside. The first day that she mustered the strength to bring in the mail, there was a little package from Wish.com addressed to Buck. Inside were silver love-knot earrings with tiny purple gemstones, Tayshia's favorite color. She cried so hard she couldn't breathe. Were she to die there on the kitchen floor, she would be okay with it.

The reminders of Buck were everywhere. Tayshia took off her wedding ring and kept it with his on a necklace tucked under her shirt, out of sight but close to her heart. The house was full of their Lions paraphernalia, from Buck's chalice displayed in the center of their dish cabinet to the blue and white string lights hanging around their living room window, as well as all the little handmade cards he'd given to her over their six years together. The giant ones too: He'd been making cards out of posterboard lately, to show her "big love." Standing up, they nearly reached her shoulders. The last one, for Valentine's Day, had a heart on the front that was crafted with purple tissue paper pieces made to look like rose petals.

"I LOVE YOU MY QT π," he'd written.

Buck's glasses were still on the nightstand. His truck was still in the driveway. His cigar and cigarette butts were still in his ashtray. Every time Tayshia had pushed him to quit, he'd smirked and told her, "Smoking won't be what kills me, baby." But he was wrong, and now she was a widow before forty. That was her theory, anyway: that his smoking had worsened and worsened his heart disease until he suffered his fatal myocardial arrhythmia on their front porch steps while she watched helplessly on the Ring camera from her car.

Kendra had her own theory, and she had shared it with Jonah. And when he called Aunt Tayshia and accused her of killing the man she loved more than anything by getting him vaccinated, the pain was so blinding she started to disassociate. She wanted to run away. So she did.

Tayshia found a job on Indeed.com as an overnight shift worker at a halfway house in rural Ohio, then picked up and moved on a whim. Home for her and her two "fur bastards" was now a drab farming village of not two square miles sitting between Detroit and Cleveland. It had a church, a three-pump gas station, a tiny convenience store, a post office, and little else—not even a traffic light. On the drive in, she had done a double take at the image of a bloody, totaled car on an auto repair billboard promising people a free steak if they ran over a deer: "Hit A DEER, Get A STEER."

If Tayshia had to guess, her arrival had notched the not even five-hundred-person community's population down to 99 percent white. She was renting a room in an old double-wide trailer on a plot of farmland with hunting rifles mounted to the walls inside and an anti-Biden LET'S GO BRANDON sign out front. The owner, a retired widower in his midsixties with a scruffy mustache and beard, lived there too. Save for church on Sundays, he spent almost every waking hour slouched in his living room armchair watching Fox News on a thirty-two-inch flatscreen that sat atop a larger, broken TV. He and Tayshia had connected through Craigslist and corresponded exclusively via email; the day she showed up to move in, his eyes practically bulged out of his head.

That was the typical reaction Tayshia received when she was out. Most people would gawk at her, as if they'd never laid eyes on a Black person in their life, though some just ignored her completely. One morning, she got stuck on the side of the road in a snowstorm. Surrounded by farmland, she trekked to the nearest house, but when she knocked on the door, shivering, to ask for help, the couple inside just peered at her through the window and did nothing. She returned to her car and, after more than an hour spent stranded in the cold without cellphone service, was able to flag down a pickup truck driver to call the police. The dispatched officer wrote her a ticket for improper parking.

Once again, just like when she was a little girl thrust into an all-white private school in Milwaukee, Tayshia was unwelcome and out of place. Only this time, it was by choice.

Down for the Count

Somewhere out there, in some tattered, yellowed newspaper, there exists a grainy photo of six- or seven-year-old Tayshia bent over in a small crowd in front of the Wisconsin governor's mansion, mooning it. At the time, she didn't understand the concept of welfare reform, or why her mom had brought her and her little sister and cousins there to march and chant on her only day off work. It was just exciting.

The next time Tayshia was at a protest was as a timid, skinny tween in 1993. A parasite had contaminated the Milwaukee water supply, causing a third of the population to fall ill with cramps, fevers, and diarrhea. Brandy couldn't find bottled water at any of the supermarkets, so she and the kids were boiling tap water to drink and brush their teeth with. It was just she and Tayshia who descended on City Hall with other outraged residents, signs in hand, to demand action. They were demonstrating, not for themselves, but for Milwaukeeans with AIDS, who were dying by the dozens. The water, for their weakened immune systems, was like arsenic.

This time, Tayshia understood. Being there with her mom and everyone else who had come out to stand together for justice, using their voices and bodies as tools to peacefully advocate for accountability, was the most empowering thing she'd ever experienced. It wasn't just a right, it was a duty, her mom told her. The only way to build a better future was to fight for it.

That wisdom became part of who Tayshia was. Once she was relatively stable in life, with a college degree and a steady income, she put nearly all of her free time into activism. She got heavily involved with her community's Black Lives Matter chapter; she joined a local women's political engagement organization; she helped organize nonpartisan, citizen-led redistricting proposals; she rallied locals to protest at the airport against the deportations of undocumented immigrants. Before settling in the Detroit area, she had even served as a campaign volunteer for her city's mayor-to-be, advising directly on how to better support residents of color.

Racial justice was Tayshia's true cause. And after George Floyd was murdered, her mother's words rang in her head like a bell.

She was out protesting, making speeches, doing local media interviews, and organizing every single day, working around her full-time job as a hotel clerk. The nation was *finally* paying attention to the needs of Black America for more than a news cycle, and there were so many issues beyond police brutality that needed to be confronted, from criminal justice reform to education equity. And, as Tayshia was gradually realizing, one that she'd been blind to—a crisis within a crisis.

There had certainly been signs of disinformation operations targeting people of color and exploiting their historical trauma to sow division. While out canvassing for Joe Biden in her mostly Black, low-voter-turnout neighborhood, Tayshia had had a door slammed in her face more than once upon touting his plans to ensure equitable access to the Covid-19 vaccines. Multiple residents worried that Black people would be used as "guinea pigs"; one man said they didn't need to get immunized because the melanin in their skin protected them against the virus. But it wasn't until that chilling day when Kendra looked her in the eyes, told her Floyd's death was "a hoax," and proclaimed "*All lives matter!*" as little Jonah nodded along, that Tayshia understood just how dire things had become. Her community needed her more than ever—her family needed her more than ever. As the stakes climbed higher and her own life fell to pieces, Tayshia wanted to keep fighting for them.

She just couldn't.

Tayshia didn't talk to Jonah for months. His words were still ricocheting in her mind.

You killed him. Mom told me.

She wasn't angry with him. She felt like she'd failed him. Moving to middle-of-nowhere Ohio was, perhaps, not only an escape but a self-inflicted punishment. She still kept in touch with Jayden, calling him every couple weeks from her rented room in the trailer with her fur bastards cuddled up beside her in bed. He had just started high school; "only four more years to go," he'd say. Getting out and going to college was all he cared about. He was thinking about studying fine arts.

It was nice to hear Jayden's voice. He was the only close family Tayshia had left. After losing Buck, she felt as if she'd lost her sister too. It wasn't the first time a loved one had slowly slipped away from her. She had been there with their mother for eight months while her memory faded, watching her turn into a stranger before she died.

Tayshia was still too hurt to miss or mourn Kendra. But she missed her "twin best friend," with whom she had laughed and cried and cowered through the highs and many lows of their childhood. She wished she could understand why things had turned out so very differently for two little girls who'd grown up in the same environment with the same struggle and the same opportunities. She wished she could have done more to keep it from repeating with her nephews.

Jayden gave Tayshia updates on how his brother was doing. Most were devastating. He wasn't just consuming conspiracy theories—he was spreading them. At the beginning of his third-grade year, Jonah had gotten into a dramatic argument with his bus driver over his refusal to wear a face mask, repeatedly shouting that doing so made people sick, a false claim he'd surely heard while watching YouTube videos with Kendra. As a result, he'd been banned from riding for the rest of the school year, meaning she had to drive him in every morning. She was often late, Jayden said, so Jonah was missing out on part of his education.

Even more distressing were Jayden's reports that some of Jonah's friends no longer wanted to play with him. The more paranoid his view of the world became, the harder it was for him to relate to his classmates, who still cared about things like Roblox and basketball. Jayden wasn't sure if it was their decision to avoid him or if their parents were insisting they do so out of alarm over the conspiracy theories being repeated at home. He just knew his little brother was lonely.

Tayshia was so heartbroken upon hearing this that she mailed Jonah a black Moleskine notebook with instructions to jot down the things he heard on YouTube instead of sharing them at school. One day, she wrote to him, the two of them would go through his notes together and turn them into a series of short stories. She doubted he would do it; she was, in his eyes, still the person who'd taken his Uncle Buck away. Even Jayden couldn't change his mind on that. But Tayshia didn't know what else to do.

No one really did. There wasn't any research into deprogramming conspiracy theorist children, or any data quantifying the scope of the issue. But given that Tayshia had recently read a *New York Times* article headlined "QAnon Now as Popular in U.S. as Some Major Religions," it was hard for her to imagine that there weren't plenty of other kids like Jonah who were frequently exposed at home to terrifying—even traumatizing—tales of a murderous cabal plotting global domination, and other frightening falsehoods.

The closest indication of a trend was a BuzzFeed News survey put out to American teachers in late 2020 asking which conspiracy theories, if any, they were hearing in the classroom. Responses flew in from exasperated educators all over the country, who said they'd heard it all, from Covid being a hoax to "pedophile Satanist liberals feeding on kidnapped babies' adrenal glands." QAnon was a big one. Their students were picking up these false narratives on social media apps like TikTok, they noted, or, in many cases, directly from their parents—then resharing them online. Yet official guidance from school leaders on how to address the issue had reportedly been nonexistent or unproductive. One middle school teacher said her administration had told her and her colleagues to avoid engaging in discussion about such things altogether.

Such advice ran contrary to the findings of a growing pool of research: The single best way to counter fake news was to inoculate against it, with teachers—and, ideally, parents—leading the charge. There was simply no avoiding kids' exposure to it. They were traversing the most difficult-to-navigate information landscape in history. As it got muddier and muddier, they were getting online younger and younger. While media literacy training wasn't a silver bullet, it had been found to significantly improve their critical thinking skills, ability to judge the credibility of digital content, awareness of media bias, and desire to consume quality news. The problem was that it wasn't being widely taught in schools.

But for Jonah, Tayshia feared, it was already too late—not despite his age, but because of it. The distorted reality in which he was now so firmly planted, and in particular, the resulting trauma and toxic stress she believed he had suffered during his formative years, could influence the rest of his life: his psychological development, his relationships, his sense of self and of the world. Caught in a web of conspiracy theories pushed for power and profit, he was, at eight years old, collateral damage in a crisis he was too young to understand.

A New Fight

At the halfway house, four nights a week, Tayshia worked a split shift from 8 p.m. to 8 a.m.

Adjusting to nocturnal living wasn't hard; she hadn't been sleeping much anyway. It was a small place with two floors, twelve bunk beds, very little natural light, and a perpetually messy kitchen stocked with camping-type foods, like peanut butter and Kool-Aid mix. Tayshia's job was just to keep an eye on people, essentially, to ensure that nothing illegal was taking place, and to provide support as needed. It was mostly downtime.

Some residents were addicts, some were formerly incarcerated, and some were survivors of abuse. Several fell into at least two of those categories. The youngest was Bailey, a recovering teenage opioid user who probably weighed no more than one hundred pounds at around five foot five. She'd been there for months and stayed there every single night, but close to two weeks went by before Tayshia even saw her face.

Bailey never said much to anyone. She kept her hood up and her head down, and mostly remained in bed with her body turned toward the wall. When Tayshia approached her on her very first shift while making her rounds to introduce herself, Bailey didn't even flinch; she just told her to go away.

Over the next several nights, Tayshia kept trying, unsuccessfully, to talk to her. She wasn't sure what it was, but something about Bailey called to her. She was so young and seemed so defeated. Tayshia hated wondering what was wrong or if there was something she could be doing to help. So one evening, after being ordered away, she lingered.

"Girl, why are you so angry?" she asked, crouching down next to Bailey's bunk.

Bailey glared over her shoulder. Her face was gaunt and her eyes were red. It looked like she'd already been crying, or was on the verge.

"What's wrong?" Tayshia pressed. "I want to know."

Bailey covered her face with her hands and sobbed. She didn't want to be there, she said, but she had nowhere else to go.

"It's just fucked up where I am."

Tayshia told her she knew the feeling.

Bailey's story was a familiar one. She divulged it little by little during late-night conversations, first by her bed, then, eventually, in the kitchen over Kool-Aid. Tayshia sometimes cried with her, despite her efforts not to. Like her, Bailey was the eldest child in a single-mother home plagued by poverty and trauma. But she reminded Tayshia more of Kendra than of herself. Her outlook on life was so fatalistic. Some days, Bailey said, it felt like there was nothing worth living for anymore.

Tayshia shared with Bailey some of her own story, recalling the many hardships of growing up on the impoverished north side of Milwaukee, and the immense joy of finding her passion in activism later in life. Talking to her, and listening to her vent, cry, and—on rare nights—even laugh, was privately therapeutic for Tayshia. Bailey liked her blue hair, her faint *Wis-cahn-sin* accent, and her face mask, which featured Bender the robot's toothy grin, complete with a lit cigar. It was from *Futurama*, one of Tayshia and Buck's favorite shows.

Tayshia never mentioned Buck, but talking through Bailey's pain was slowly loosening the binds of her own. At the end of particularly rough days, sitting down with her and sipping Kool-Aid until their tongues turned purple kept Tayshia from spiraling.

Bailey seemed to be doing better too as the weeks passed. She perked up every time Tayshia arrived at work, and her mood was noticeably, consistently brighter. Their conversations began to focus more on the good than the bad. One night, Bailey told her with a cautious smile that she had always wanted to have a baby. A little girl, she hoped. She would name her Ava and give her pigtails with ribbons. It was bittersweet to hear. Tayshia and Buck had wanted one too, more than anything. But it was the first real hint of optimism Bailey had expressed. Tayshia smiled back at her. It felt like she was making a difference again. She wasn't dismantling the police state or solving the disinformation crisis in communities of color. She was helping to create a better future for *one* person—and that mattered to her. She could pick up her old fight when she was ready.

A few months into her time at the halfway house, Tayshia printed out an image of an uplifting quote she had come across on Instagram. Posts of that nature, while just words on a screen, were what had gotten her out of bed or off the couch on her darkest days after Buck's death—a tiny dose of positivity to keep her going. Before ending her shift in the morning, she slipped the note into Bailey's mailbox slot, beginning a new daily routine, then made her way back to the trailer. It was part of a Maya Angelou poem.

> Just like moons and like suns,
> With the certainty of tides,
> Just like hopes springing high,
> Still, I'll rise.

16

ONE STEP BACK

—Alice—

On December 31, 2021, Alice and Christopher went to a party south of San Francisco to usher in the new year. The theme was "steampunk." She put her own hippie twist on her attire, wearing lacy bell-bottoms with a beaded wrap around her waist and a gold halter top. He wore a plain dress shirt and trousers, playfully blaming his new bride for the lack of variety in his wardrobe.

It had been just two weeks since they eloped in Hawaii—one of many things to celebrate in closing out the year. Alice was staying true to her commitment to enrich her life by focusing on herself and the things within her control. She had leaned back deeply into her compassionate communication work, earning new certifications in the field, and she and Christopher were spending as much time offline as possible, taking full advantage of the Bay Area's many gorgeous beaches and hiking trails. YouTube had become a place only for meditation videos, yoga sequences, and stretching routines.

Alice had even gotten vaccinated. It took two attempts: The first time, she got spooked and canceled her appointment at the final hour as old fears and suspicions crept back in. Her strategy of simply putting conspiracy theory–type thoughts out of her head by paying attention to the here and now was put to the test when it came to sticking a needle in her arm. The second time, though, she boosted her immune system with herbal antioxidants and red marine algae supplements, then cried silently through the shot while playing soothing hymns with Christopher there to comfort her. And she was fine.

Most of Alice's friends had gotten their vaccines ages ago and were finally feeling comfortable enough to attend social gatherings, like this party. She missed them with every fiber of her being.

Reality Check

Shortly after arriving, Alice noticed her friend Hazel, a woman in her midfifties with wavy brown hair, standing over by the stone fireplace. They had known each other since working together at a massage therapy clinic more than twenty years ago, though it had been some time since they'd last spoken. Alice greeted her with a big smile and pulled her in for a hug.

"Oh. Hi, Alice," Hazel said delicately. "How are you? I've been thinking of you these last two years."

There was a jarring sorrow in her voice, as if she believed Alice had been battling some sort of disease.

"Really?" Alice asked. "Why's that?"

"Well . . . I just remember you as being the most compassionate, heart-centered person," Hazel replied. Her tone soured.

"And then I heard you became a *QAnon* believer and a *Trump* supporter."

Alice's joy left her body like air escaping a balloon. Her eyes flashed around the room. *How many of her friends still felt this way? Had they been talking about her?*

Hazel was frowning at Alice silently—scrutinizingly—waiting, it seemed, for reassurance that she had snapped back into the uber-liberal, Trump-detesting person she was before. But she hadn't. While she no longer endorsed the Far Right conspiracy theories of QAnon, she now found herself to be a bit of a political nomad, unsure of where she belonged. She didn't like Trump or Biden. She had emerged from the rabbit hole with new empathy for the concerns held by people on the right, like anticonservative censorship, which she knew Hazel and her other old friends wouldn't understand. That was why she had stepped away from politics altogether.

"I—I'm not in QAnon anymore," Alice stammered. "And I still have the same values, Hazel. I'm still compassionate and heart-centered. Do people not see that about me?"

Hazel looked unsatisfied with her response.

"Let's just enjoy the party," she said. Then she walked off.

The party, for Alice, was over. Fighting back tears, she found Christopher and told him they had to leave. They spent the countdown to midnight asleep in bed.

It wasn't the first time Alice had felt the ostracizing effects of QAnon since getting out. After realizing how many people had blocked her on Facebook, she'd gone in search of a community that would understand her experience, and came upon r/QAnonCasualties, the enormous Reddit support group for loved ones of QAnon believers. It seemed perfect: She considered herself to be a casualty of the movement too, and she could engage there anonymously to test the waters. She thought it could even be valuable to others if she shared her story, along with tips on what *not* to do when trying to deprogram someone. So she drafted a short essay emphasizing how counterproductive she believed it had been when her friends accused her of being ignorant and hateful.

"People who have known me for more than a decade—people who have seen that I have friends of all nationalities, LGBTQ+—were accusing me of being a racist, sexist, and supporter of fascism . . . WTF?" Alice wrote, recalling how she had felt at the time. "How did Bill Gates and vaccines have anything to do with racism, sexism and fascism???"

QAnon supporters needed understanding, not criticism, she stressed; only then could they find the space for growth that they needed in order to escape the movement.

Feeling nervous—and hopeful—she published her post.

Attention came quickly. Former believers were rare. To Alice's delight, early commenters lauded her for her bravery and thanked her for her advice. But before long, the conversation turned to anger. In comments that were heavily upvoted, or liked, people accused Alice of invading a safe space and playing "the victim."

"You were part of a terrible problem," one wrote. "You're an asshole, and an idiot for seeking comfort from people who are being traumatized by people like YOU every day."

An emerging consensus in the thread—expressed in manners both gentle and harsh—was that Alice hadn't grown quite as much as she seemed to think she had.

"It doesn't look like you're fully taking accountability for what has happened," someone said, echoing others. "Even if you weren't personally racist, sexist, etc. you enabled the people that [were] by subscribing to these views."

Alice was devastated. People questioned how she had failed to see the intrinsically hateful elements of QAnon for so long. Some suggested it was due to willful blindness that she had yet to acknowledge, and tried to educate her about the harmful ideologies that she had helped perpetuate. It was a painful reality check. But in her fragile state, it felt more like an attack. Her body trembled as she scrolled in tears through one critical comment after another. She felt as if she already *had* taken accountability for what happened by accepting blame and taking stock of the hurt that she had caused others, and she still didn't believe that internalized white supremacy or antisemitism had played any part in her attraction to QAnon. Replying as nicely as she could to several comments, Alice explained that she herself was part Jewish. That only stoked further backlash.

She couldn't take it. These people were just using her as a punching bag, she told herself; she clearly wasn't welcome in their support network. So she left.

Back to the Edge

A little over a year after the New Year's Eve party, Alice went to the "Conscious Life Expo" down in Los Angeles.

The annual event, America's biggest New Age exposition, was like a three-day carnival for dreamers and gurus of all stripes. Chimes tinkled. Incense burned. Vendors donning long, flowing robes and flower crowns packed into a bustling marketplace to sell chakra crystals, psychic readings, gemstone amulets, magic remedies, and "shamanic moon ceremony experiences." Crowds gathered round to listen to the teachings of "truthtellers," energy healers, lightworkers, UFO experts, and "starseeds," humans who identified as aliens.

Christopher had pleaded with Alice not to go. He feared that it could be a slippery slope back into conspiracy theories. Several of the talks scheduled for this year's expo troubled him. Previewed in the online program for the keynote panel were questions such as *Are we in the middle of the Great Reset or the Great Awakening? What is the Illuminati's master plan? Are the technocratic elites engineering an AI takeover?*

For four terrible, tearful days, Alice and Christopher had argued about her plan to attend. It was intensely triggering for both of them, evoking traumatic memories of the blow-out fights that had nearly destroyed their relationship in 2020. Alice tried to explain that it was the *people*, not the subject matter per se, that called to her. She still didn't feel fully comfortable in her pre-QAnon community in the Bay Area, to the extent that she and Christopher had recently moved into a rental home a couple hours away to shoot for a fresh start. She desperately craved human connection—to be in a place where she could feel like she belonged again. This rift with her "beloved" wasn't helping. The Conscious Life Expo, she told him, would be a gathering of kindred spirits: curious, peace-loving, mystical beings, like her, who shared her values. People who would accept her.

She didn't just want to go, she said. She *needed* to.

Among the many people she met at the twelve-thousand-attendee event was Mikki Willis, the creator of the viral *Plandemic* film, whom she'd admired online for a decade. He'd been a light in the dark for her and so many other die-hard Bernie Sanders supporters after their crushing loss in 2016. They chatted briefly, laughed deeply, and hugged tightly. Alice also connected with old, faraway friends she'd met at other New Age events and easily made new ones between perusing the shopping booths and attending panels. It was medicinal: Her heart was happy and her soul was singing.

Toward the end of the expo, Alice went to a rough-cut screening of *Plandemic 3: The Great Awakening*, Willis's forthcoming documentary about the "Covid industrial complex." The energy in the room was intoxicating. Despite the time—8 p.m. on a Sunday—it was packed wall-to-wall, and it was buzzing. To be there was to be in the know, like VIPs in an exclusive club. As they filed into their seats, strangers swapped stories of being suspended on Facebook or blocked by relatives for sharing the original *Plandemic*, featuring Judy Mikovits, who was there in the audience and turned heads like a celebrity.

Willis had addressed this issue in a speech earlier in the expo. He'd spoken of the social alienation that too often came with standing up for "the truth"—something he'd been chasing since losing his mother to cancer and his brother to AIDS, both deaths he'd blamed in part on "harmful medical treatments." He also claimed with a hint of pride that he and his family had been driven from their hometown in retaliation for his *Plandemic* works.

"This thing gets hairy when we step out," he said, to nodding applause. "But we don't lose friends. We lose people that we thought were our friends."

Once the film began, the hum of excitement gave way to gasps of unified dismay. Over more than an hour, it created the impression that completely healthy people were suddenly dropping and dying all over the place after getting their Covid shots. Then it painted a haunting picture of the ongoing provaccination campaigns pushed by TV stars, politicians, and the media as a coordinated psyop foreshadowing an attempted authoritarian takeover in America.

As she watched, looking beyond Voltaire's garden once more, Alice could feel something deep inside her flicker back to life. The documentary was terrifying. But it was also a call to collective action to rise up and resist as one. After the disappointments of the Bernie Revolution, and of QAnon, Alice ached to be a part of something again. To feel like she belonged. She was at once afraid, empowered, and inspired. These people—her people—they *got it*. And they weren't going to take it.

Upon returning home, Alice was lonelier than she'd been before. She had missed her beloved and she was happy to see him. But there was a familiar distance already trickling back in between them. She couldn't talk to him about the hope or excitement still racing through her mind and soul. Or to her dad. Or to anyone, really, except the types of people she had sworn to cut ties with for good—the ones who weren't afraid to question the official narrative. There was nothing as isolating as keeping a secret.

After escaping the rabbit hole, Alice had returned to the edge. She was peering over. And her need for community, once again unmet, threatened to pull her right back in.

THE UPSWING

—Matt—

From the time Matt was young, he was told that death was nothing to fear. Good Christians went to heaven; all he had to do was believe and serve. So he did. When the moment came to leave this life for the next, be it on Judgment Day or sooner, he was certain that he would be ready. It was living—not dying—that seemed like the hard part.

Matt had learned about his duties as a follower of Christ from a handful of religious teachers. By far the most influential were his bosses at the radio station, Joseph and Dawn. Over his nearly two decades there, he had listened to countless hours of staff meetings-turned-fundamentalist sermons in which they had implored him and his co-workers to rise up against the secular evils of the Left, as they'd been put on earth to do. But it was QAnon soothsayers like Dave Hayes, the "Praying Medic," who taught him how to take real action. For more than two years, he trained via YouTube as a digital soldier to help fulfill the divine mission laid out in "The Plan to Save the World." If successful, Hayes had prophesied, the result would be "heaven on earth." There was no greater calling Matt could imagine for his life.

So, in the spring of 2021, when his faith came crashing down around him in pieces, so too did his reason for being. Stripped of purpose, he had nothing, was nothing. There would be no Great Awakening and no afterlife. He didn't fear death, regardless. He invited it.

A Hard Reset

The psychiatric ward was pretty much exactly what Matt had seen portrayed onscreen.

There were dull, off-white walls; long hallways with fluorescent ceiling lights reflected along squeaky floors; a recreation room with books and board games and people milling about, sometimes muttering to themselves; and lumpy chicken sandwiches on plastic cafeteria trays. Matt had been admitted following his suicide attempt. His days were full of group therapy sessions and private appointments with psychiatrists and mental health counselors who listened intently and asked him lots of intimate, often repetitive questions. He wasn't normally a talkative man around strangers, particularly when it came to the personal stuff. But at this point, he figured, what did it really matter? That was the thing about rock bottom: It was a profoundly liberating place to be.

In honest, unvarnished detail, he went over every domino that had shattered his sense of self and led him to the pills, from his former disability to his QAnon indoctrination to Andrea's ensuing serial infidelity to the collapse of his entire religious and political belief systems. It was a sad story to hear out loud, even from his own lips. But all of it was now behind him, his primary psychiatrist said. He was barely forty. He could dwell on the past and punish himself for as long as he wished, languishing in his regret and disillusionment, or he could seize this opportunity to heal, reinvent himself, and move forward in life as whoever he wanted to be.

Matt thought about that deeply over his weeklong stay. For better or for worse, he was still alive. Why *not* try to forge a new path and see where it took him? What did he have to lose?

Two things, to start: The first was his marriage. He found a lawyer to file the paperwork as soon as he was discharged, with no resistance from Andrea. She was still involved with her most recent affair. Next was his job. When he had described his work culture—and Joseph and Dawn—during a group sharing session at the hospital, people had literally gasped at some of the details. It sounded more like a religious cult than a workplace, observed one man, who was himself a Christian. Matt's plan was to find a new job first, but the decision was quickly taken out of his hands. Not long after his return to work, nineteen years into his tenure at the station, Joseph informed him that his services were no longer needed. (In an ostensibly unrelated parting lecture, he reminded Matt that God didn't look kindly upon divorce or suicide.)

Matt turned back to his side gig doing on-call tech support work. He had picked it up back in 2019, following his series of hasty, QAnon-inspired financial decisions that had depleted his and Andrea's savings without her knowing—a betrayal that he had since confessed to, and that she considered to be worse than her own. The small silver lining of their separation—or at least the timing of it—was that the housing market was red-hot. Selling their home would more than cover what he had lost, along with the rest of their debts. They found a realtor in April. In the meantime, they were sleeping in separate bedrooms, with the intention to each get their own place and split custody of the children.

Everything was happening so quickly it made Matt's head spin. The pain didn't hit until the listing went up. As he clicked through Zillow photos of their unnaturally tidy house, with sparkling floors and perfectly made beds, his heart broke. This place was the dream that he and Andrea had imagined for years as young lovers with their whole lives ahead of them. The wood-paneled living room, where they sat every Christmas with their matching "Hubby" and "Wifey" mugs as Abby and Hayden tore into their presents, sugar-high on little stocking-stuffer chocolates, now appeared sterile and lifeless. So did the kitchen, where the kids plunked down on the floor each October surrounded by slimy orange guts and seeds, laser-focused on carving their Halloween pumpkins. Matt blinked back tears as it dawned on him that his fondest memories from the past couple years were limited to holidays: the rare occasions when he had stepped away from his conspiracy theory content in the basement to spend time with his family. Now the dream was over.

All Matt could do was focus on starting anew. It was time for a hard reset. Between scouring online for jobs and apartments, he made a deliberate effort to do what had once been unthinkable: He tried honestly to investigate and understand the liberal perspective. It wasn't his idea but that of his therapist, Ralph, a kindly older man with a white goatee. Matt's continuing treatment plan after leaving the hospital included weekly therapy and new medications to improve his mental health; the antidepressants he'd been taking, he learned, had been overstimulating him, contributing to his compulsive behaviors. When Matt explained that he wanted to rediscover who he was, Ralph pointed out that he'd been deeply embedded in a groupthink echo chamber for a long time. It could be worth exploring alternative viewpoints to broaden his perspective, he said. Then he suggested with a smile that Matt do his "own research," unwittingly echoing a common QAnon refrain. Matt could only laugh. He went back down to his neatly staged basement and into his office, the place where it all began, and took a closer look at some hot-button issues with fresh eyes—and without the likes of Joseph, Dawn, Trump, Praying Medic, or Q telling him what to think.

The climate crisis seemed as good a place to start as any. Matt had always heard that it wasn't real; Trump and other Republicans even called it a "hoax" invented by the Chinese. And just a couple months earlier, a deadly deep freeze in Texas had blanketed the state in snow, which appeared to disprove the concept of "global warming" entirely. Matt did a Google search and clicked on a CNN article headlined "Why Temperatures Still Plummet to Dangerous Levels Even as the Planet Warms." He was still averse to mainstream news, but the whole point of this process was to hear the other side of things.

In the article, quoted beneath a corresponding diagram, a climate scientist explained that freezing Arctic air was confined by strong atmospheric wind currents known as the "jet stream," which had been weakened due to warming temperatures, allowing the dense polar vortex to spill south. It was surprisingly simple to Matt, but it made sense. And that was the most surprising thing of all: In QAnon, he never would have accepted that explanation, despite its logic. It was becoming embarrassingly, disturbingly clear to him that his beliefs had been rooted simply in a desire to believe. Being a digital soldier had made him feel good. Logic had nothing to do with it.

Matt read about QAnon too. It was a big topic in the news, especially in the wake of what had happened at the Capitol. The coverage was shifting in tone from that reflected in the mocking headlines Matt had previously dismissed as Deep State media hit jobs. Now adherents weren't just cast as psycho; they were *dangerous*. But the coldest splash of water in Matt's face came from watching Q: *Into the Storm*.

The six-part HBO documentary charted QAnon's explosive growth from the entrails of the internet to the front lines of the insurrection. On a mission to unmask Q once and for all, filmmaker Cullen Hoback had gained unprecedented access to the public-facing figures with known ties to the movement. Among them was thirty-four-year-old Ron Watkins, an odd, slow-speaking man in Japan with dark-rimmed glasses, shaggy black hair, a sparse goatee, and an affinity for cowboy hats. One scene showed him watching porn on his dashboard while driving. Known online as "CodeMonkeyZ," Watkins was a longtime administrator of 8kun (formerly 8chan), where Q communicated with anons, as well as a major spreader of pro-Trump election disinformation in 2020. In the series' final episode, during a video-call interview with Hoback, he appeared to slip up. He casually divulged that he had spent the past three years anonymously "teaching normies how to do intelligence work." Then he quickly turned and looked directly into the camera.

"*Never* as Q," he exclaimed.

He let out a flustered laugh, then cleared his throat.

"Nev-never as Q. I promise. . . . 'Cause I am not Q . . . and I never was."

Matt was speechless.

That fucking guy?!

For two and a half years, he had turned away from his wife and children, deluded into believing that he was on a mission to save the world by some perverted troll overseas. *This* was rock bottom.

Q: Into the Storm laid bare in visceral detail the extraordinary harm that QAnon had wrought on American democracy. But missing from the film's six hours—and from the roaring national discourse surrounding the movement—was the quiet damage to families like Matt's.

It was staggering. Matt had seen polls revealing that tens of millions of people in the United States now agreed that the country was secretly run by Satan-worshipping pedophiles. And he wasn't surprised: QAnon conspiracy theories had dissolved into America's cultural bloodstream like salt in water. Trump, Fox, and a collective of other self-serving opportunists had diluted and normalized its lies to meet their own ends—galvanizing voters or viewers or customers through populist paranoia, at an immeasurable cost. Trump alone had amplified QAnon-promoting social media accounts hundreds of times during his presidency while acting as if he knew hardly a thing about the movement. He had even retweeted a post tagged #PedoBiden. Now such smears were being tossed around as if the country was in a new Red Scare era.

At Q's direction, anons had begun to shed the label of "QAnon," evidently aware that they could sway more minds without it. But no matter the packaging, Matt knew that QAnon's insidious influence on American life would endure. More and more, he had been encountering variations of its delusions all over the place, regurgitated by people who would never wittingly align with the movement.

Even at his own dinner table.

On a somber summer evening, Matt, Andrea, and the kids were quietly picking at their spaghetti on paper plates. The dishes, like most of the rest of their possessions, were already packed away in cardboard boxes. This was one of their final meals as a foursome. When the house closed in a few days, Matt would be moving into a small three-bedroom apartment over a roadside beauty salon.

Abby broke the silence.

"I want to get vaccinated," she said. "Twelve-year-olds are allowed to now, and my friends already—"

"Absolutely not," Andrea cut her off. "It's unsafe and you don't need it."

Matt looked up from his fork-twisted noodles. He had already gotten his shots.

"Unsafe how?"

"There are all kinds of super messed-up side effects. Have you seen the videos of vaccinated people sticking magnets to their bodies? The vaccines literally made them magnetic! It's horrible."

Matt was shocked.

"Come on. Seriously, Andrea? They probably just need to shower."

Abby and Hayden laughed, but Andrea didn't find it funny.

"It's not a joke," she snapped. "And Abby, it's not happening. I'm sorry."

Andrea had never been wary of vaccines before; both kids had gotten all their childhood immunizations. These days, though, the entire country seemed to be more suspicious and less discerning—the "QAnon Lite" effect, Matt thought to himself. He let it go. He didn't want his last memories at home to be arguments. But the following week, while unpacking at his new place, he turned on the news and saw a report about pediatric hospitals overflowing with sick children in areas where the Covid Delta variant was spreading. Hayden was still too young, but if Andrea would let Abby get vaccinated before school started, Matt would feel at least slightly at ease.

He sent her a Facebook message asking her to consider meeting with their family doctor or someone from the health department to discuss her concerns about potential side effects. She promptly referred him to a video that she had shared the day before, which supposedly proved that the Covid vaccine was more dangerous than the disease itself. Matt clicked, but it had already been removed for violating YouTube's policy against Covid misinformation.

"Yeah I'm gonna go out on a limb and say that was a bunch of crap," he wrote.

"Of course it was removed," Andrea replied. "No one wants any opposition."

Matt shook his head and sighed to himself.

"I will take info from professionals over a YouTube video."

It was an astonishing about-face for a man who'd been radicalized on YouTube. He and Andrea went back and forth intermittently over the next several hours, until she eventually acquiesced—with a threat: If anything were to happen to Abby post-vaccination, she would take legal action against him. She peppered him with a stream of TikToks and a few videos from Rumble featuring a mishmash of conspiracy theories, including the vaccine "shedding" rumor and the false claim that the shots actually gave people Covid.

Matt couldn't make it through all of them. He told Andrea that the vast majority of hospitalized Covid patients were unvaccinated, a widely reported fact. Her three-word response was jarring.

"Are they though?"

It felt like he was arguing with a former version of himself.

Movie Nights

Matt had the kids for half of each week and every other weekend, time that he intended to make the most of. He hadn't been in "Dad mode" for far too long. Fridays became movie-and-pizza nights. Saturdays were typically spent lounging around playing video games together, and on Sundays they went to the mall. If he could swing it, during months when his gig work picked up, Matt also splurged on fun family activities. On one weekend, he took Abby and Hayden to a hotel with an indoor pool and an arcade. On another, he bought the parts for a gaming PC, and then they spent the night putting it together on the floor of his apartment.

Matt was getting to know his own children all over again—and they were *cool as hell:* kind, funny, industrious, intelligent. And, mercifully, forgiving. His relationships with both of them had never been better. He was having such a good time hanging out with them that his weekends on his own felt empty.

In the new year, he decided to try dating again. Maybe 2022 could bring some romance back into his life. He signed up for Bumble, a Tinder-like app requiring female users to initiate contact with their matches. That was what appealed to him. He hadn't asked someone out in seventeen years; flirting, by this point, was like a foreign language.

As he swiped through profiles, it occurred to him that he didn't really know what he was looking for. Someone on the introverted side, like him, he guessed. Close by. Kids would be fine. Not a political fanatic. *Definitely* not a Trump supporter—he didn't need to go back down that path.

Small talk was harder than Matt remembered. He fumbled his way through a handful of conversations and managed to get a couple coffee dates, but never knew what to say or what kind of expression to wear on his face. Trying to act natural felt entirely unnatural. And whenever his dates asked him to tell them about himself, he had no clue how to respond beyond his job title and parental status. He still hadn't figured out who he was—just who he wasn't.

In late January, he came across a profile belonging to a woman named Rylee. She was forty, about a year younger than him, and lived an hour away—not ideal. But she was cute. She had jet-black hair with hot pink streaks, a curvy figure, and a coy smile. Matt swiped right and was excited to receive a match and simple "Hello" a short time later. They chatted a bit and agreed to keep things on platonic terms, given the distance. Both felt like they could use a friend. As they got to know each other, they were surprised to discover how much they had in common: Rylee was also a single parent who had been cheated on the year before by her longtime partner. She was raised Christian and had since drifted from her faith too. And, to Matt's delight, she didn't give a damn about politics. Beyond the major, unmissable news stories, she seldom knew what was going on, and she preferred to keep it that way.

Matt immediately felt comfortable opening up to her. She was a good listener. She was also effortlessly hilarious—even unintentionally so. When he asked what she did for fun, she told him without hesitation that she liked going to Disney World and taking naps. Pretty soon, Matt realized that she was the person he was most excited to hear from. Seeing her name pop up on his phone gave him a rush every time. They decided to meet in person, just to see how things would go, and ended up having a blast simply wandering around talking in an empty park.

Within a month, Matt was calling Rylee his girlfriend. She was the complete opposite of his ex: Andrea was a bubbly people pleaser; Rylee was grumpy—in a lovable, Garfield-type way—and didn't sugarcoat anything for anyone. Matt liked that she wore flip-flops year-round, even in an inch of snow, entirely unbothered by what people thought. He liked that she gave the best hugs he had ever received, squeezing him tightly and holding him there. He especially liked that she was loyal to a fault, from relationships to brands and food preferences. It wouldn't matter if everyone she knew was raving about a viral new Starbucks drink, her order would never change: grande vanilla sweet cream cold brew with cold foam and one extra pump of vanilla syrup. And for reasons Matt couldn't articulate, he found it comically, adorably endearing that Rylee had a backscratcher. She was the only person he'd ever known to own one. It was made of wood and she kept it beside her bed. Whenever he woke up to see her hunched over in her pajamas, practically purring while reaching over to itch between her shoulder blades, it made him melt.

When he was with her, it was easy to forget about the culture wars raging in the background of his life. Beyond the inescapable vaccine fearmongering, which often had little to do with actual science, national right-wing campaigns against critical race theory and the purported "trans agenda" were already dividing parents at his kids' school. Rylee's place was like a haven from the ugliness of the outside world. But one night in June, between movies and episodes of *90 Day Fiancé*, she wanted to talk politics. Mostly to vent. She had just heard about the feud between Florida governor Ron DeSantis and Disney, which had begun with the CEO disavowing Florida's so-called Don't Say Gay bill, and had escalated with DeSantis accusing the corporation of "sexualizing kids." Now, for months, "Save Our Children" activists had been holding "antigrooming" rallies at Disney headquarters and promoting all kinds of unhinged conspiracy theories, including that at night, Disneyland—"the Tragic Kingdom"—turned into a gathering place for pedophiles to rape and traffic lost children.

"It's insane!" Rylee marveled, her eyes wide. "I mean, seriously, can you believe people buy into this garbage?"

Matt could.

Most of the rallies she had described were undoubtedly organized by QAnon believers. Incidentally, Q had just reemerged after an eerie eighteen-month hiatus, sending intel-starved anons into a frenzy. Matt had seen the new Q Drops reposted all over Twitter. He wondered if it was Watkins, who had moved to Arizona and leveraged the political capital he'd squeezed from QAnon—including hundreds of thousands of followers across his personal social media accounts—into a congressional run. QAnon had never come up in Matt's conversations with Rylee. He wasn't ready to tell her about his involvement, but this discussion about Disney seemed like a good opportunity to lay the groundwork for a future conversation when he could work up the nerve.

"Have you ever heard of QAnon?" he asked her, apprehensively.

Rylee shook her head.

"It's this big conspiracy theory group," Matt explained, trying to choose his words carefully as he went. "They think Trump is God, basically, and he's saving us all from these liberal elites and celebrities who rule the world and are secretly satanists and pedophiles. And, uh, drink kids' blood."

He winced. Having to actually verbalize the sheer absurdity of the belief system he once took as gospel was privately humiliating. He looked at Rylee, who giggled.

"Well, that's pretty dumb," she said.

She pulled out her phone.

"I'm hungry. Should we order Chinese?"

Divine Intervention

January 13 was a Friday.

Matt didn't think anything of it. He no longer believed in the superstitious or supernatural, like bad omens and miracles. Early on in his religious disillusionment, he had looked back over his life without the filter of his faith and had reinterpreted events that he had once attributed to a higher power—like Andrea's swift, unexpected recovery from the head trauma she'd suffered in a brutal car accident just before they were married. That wasn't the work of God, Matt had determined; it was a testament to the top-notch care she had received at the state's best hospital. Likewise, his discovery of her infidelity on a Friday the 13th in 2019 was nothing more than a meaningless coincidence.

On this soon-to-be-fateful day, in 2023, Matt was at Rylee's place watching *The Flight Attendant* on Netflix while she dashed around the bedroom folding warm clothes into a bag. They were planning to leave bright and early the next morning for a trip out of state with her kids to visit her mom's side of the family. Matt had been looking forward to it, but he was starting to feel out of sorts. He realized that he had accidentally mixed up his daily medications, tipping him into a gloomy funk that would likely take a couple days to run its course. The thought of being around a bunch of people while he wasn't quite himself—especially his girlfriend's loved ones—was miserable. He ended up apologizing to Rylee and heading out into the snow to go home by himself just before 10:30 p.m.

The drive was a straight shot east on the interstate; he could be snug in bed by midnight. He cranked the heat, turned on his Weezer playlist, and thought about nothing at all as he zipped along in the left lane. It was a quiet night. Being alone was already making him feel a little bit better. But about a quarter of the way there, drowsiness crept in. Matt lightly slapped his face a couple times as he looked for a place where he could pull over to take a break. Just for a few moments, to rest his eyes . . .

He woke up to the ear-splitting screech of his van smashing through the metal guardrail at eighty miles an hour. His face bounced off the wheel and his seatbelt crunched into his chest as his body lurched forward on impact. Suddenly, he felt weightless, like he was flying through the air. A searing coldness enveloped him. Then everything went black.

By all accounts, Matt should have died under the bridge that night.

In fleeting flashes of consciousness, before emergency responders showed up on scene, he felt a pair of hands lift his head out of the dark, icy water. Then came muffled shouting and pulsing red-blue lights illuminating the snowflakes softly falling from the sky.

"I c-can't f-feel anything," Matt cried out. He had no sensation from the neck down.

He saw the blurry interior of an ambulance, then the inside of a CT machine. Then Rylee's harrowed face staring down at him surrounded by bright lights. When he hadn't answered his phone to confirm that he'd made it home safely, she had searched online and found an article from a local NBC affiliate reporting a single-vehicle car wreck along Matt's route. The male driver, it reported, was believed to be "seriously hurt."

And yet, somehow, he wasn't.

The injuries Matt sustained turned out to be relatively minor, all things considered: He had hypothermia, a broken clavicle, several broken ribs, a deep cut over his left eye, and a fractured pelvis, requiring him to temporarily use a walker. He was expected to make a full recovery. But when he saw photos of his van, which fire crews had extricated from the creek into which it had nosedived, the assessment in the news story made sense. The front half was obliterated; it looked like it had slammed full-speed into a rock wall. Matt didn't understand how he had survived. No one did.

A few days into his hospital stay, still groggy from pain meds, he got a call from his ex. She had posted on Facebook describing the accident and asking their family friends to donate money toward the medical bills. In response, she said, an acquaintance had reached out to say that her husband had saved Matt from drowning. In the time since, he had been trying to figure out who Matt was and how to get in touch with him to make sure that he was all right.

The man's name was Hayden, like Matt and Andrea's youngest. Hayden wouldn't have normally been on the interstate on a Friday night, but it just so happened that a friend had given him last-minute tickets to a concert in the area. He was on his way home when, in his rearview mirror, he saw Matt veer off the road and vanish over the edge of the overpass. Hayden pulled over and raced down the embankment through the brush in the darkness, where Matt's van had crashed and cradled onto the driver's side in the creek. His head was submerged. Hayden yanked him up above the surface but couldn't pull him loose, so he stayed there with him in the water in the thirty-degree cold, holding him in place until help arrived.

Matt extracted these details from Hayden himself, a humble, quiet guy who lived twenty minutes from him and looked strikingly similar to him, with a pointed brown beard, light eyes, and a medium build. He was a cybersecurity specialist and a volunteer pastor—and, Matt was convinced, an honest-to-God guardian angel.

Since coming out of QAnon, Matt had learned to form his beliefs around not dogma but evidence. Perhaps most importantly, that meant taking off his blinders and being receptive when presented with evidence that countered his existing views.

This felt like one of those occasions.

God was real after all: The proof was Matt's own beating heart. His survival of the surely unsurvivable was a *true* miracle that he couldn't explain away with logic or reason. Even after he had turned his back on his faith, God had reached down to tap him on the shoulder and say, *I'm still here. I still love you.*

It was an abundantly comforting epiphany. But it was equally confusing. Matt was back to the drawing board of his identity, trying to figure out who he was and what his purpose in life would be now. He felt unworthy of—and overwhelmed by—God's grace, and he had no religious mentors left to turn to for direction. So he decided to talk to Hayden. The two had quickly formed a unique friendship, mostly via text, discussing things big and small, from life and death to bland, rubbery hospital food. If anyone could help, Matt thought, it would be his God-sent savior. He called him shortly after being discharged into Rylee's care and explained how very lost he'd been feeling.

"To be honest, I don't know why I'm still alive," Matt confessed. "God refused to let me die. There's gotta be a reason, right? He must have a higher calling for me . . . something important He needs me to do here on earth, don't you think? I just don't know what it is."

Hayden thought for a moment before responding.

"Well," he said, "I think that's up to you, man."

Matt didn't understand.

"Look at your life," Hayden explained. "Look at all that God has blessed you with. You're a lucky dude! You can honor Him by just appreciating it as best you can, and using it to do good for others."

That night, as Rylee slept, Matt stared at the ceiling and reflected on the confounding simplicity of Hayden's advice. It was unlike anything he'd been taught by Joseph and Dawn, or by QAnon luminaries like Praying Medic. They had preached of upholding one's Christian duty through fear-driven militance—of primordial us-versus-them, good-versus-evil, and "right"-versus-Left. What Hayden had described sounded like a different religion entirely. Matt called him again a few days later. Over a series of uncomfortably enlightening conversations, he arrived at the revelation that the genre of Christianity he'd been absorbing since joining the radio station back in college wasn't actually all that Christian. It was Christian nationalism: a theocratic ideology rejected by many mainstream Christians as a perversion of their faith and a cover for white supremacy.

Yet again, Matt was left feeling ashamed and questioning everything he thought he'd known to be true—even sacred—for so long. But at a time when he was struggling to integrate his abandoned faith back into his recently spared life, he more than welcomed this new understanding. Per Hayden's telling, being a good Christian wasn't about conquering an enemy or living in existential fear of what could be taken from you. Quite the opposite, he said: In short, it came down to loving one another and being generous with what you had.

It was, for Matt, a veritable come-to-Jesus moment. After a years-long identity crisis that had completely upended his political, ideological, and religious views of the world and his place in it, this felt right.

In April, Hayden got Matt a job with his employer. He was responsible for handling surveillance cameras on location at stores scattered all around the Midwest, the Northeast, and the South. He drove more than five thousand miles in his first month—and he loved it. His time on the road in a company car gave him a chance to sit back and binge through podcasts, a habit he'd gotten into during his QAnon days. Back then, decoders would rage into his ear about demonic globalist elites and "banksters" between ads urging listeners to stock up on precious metals and doomsday survival kits—which Matt had leapt to do (and lived to regret). But these days, for his long drives winding through the Appalachian Mountains or inching through city traffic, his podcast of choice was called *Scamfluencers*. Hosted by a pair of female journalists, it delved into the methods and motives of cunning online grifters.

The best part of the job was the pay. Matt was earning more than he ever had, by far, and not a moment too soon: He and Rylee were saving up for a home of their own. After living together for six weeks while he was laid up from his injury, they decided that they wanted to make it permanent. It would have to be somewhere midway between their current places, so the kids' trips to school wouldn't be too long. Having at least five bedrooms was also a must; everyone needed their own space. Multiple bathrooms too. As of now, Matt and Rylee both had just one; mornings were chaos. The dream would be a big, modern house with a fenced-in backyard for their dogs to run around in and a master bedroom big enough for a king-sized bed. Maybe, if they were lucky, they could find one on a quiet, tree-lined street.

Though they were already excitedly scrolling through Zillow almost nightly in bed, the plan was to wait until the fall of 2024. That way, Matt would qualify for Missouri's First Place Loan, a homebuyer's assistance program available only to those who hadn't owned a house for at least three years. It was something to look forward to.

The last time Matt had been this excited for the future was when he was in QAnon, breathlessly awaiting the Great Awakening that he and so many others had worked ever so dutifully to accomplish. He had believed in earnest that it would bring salvation to humanity—and, also, meaning to his existence.

Since reexamining his faith, however, Matt had come to understand things differently. He didn't need to be a digital soldier or even a servant of God to find purpose in life. It wasn't his job to save the world one way or another. He just needed to be a good parent, a good partner, and a good person. That was enough.

Epilogue: Dear Adam

—Emily—

After twelve long years spent living alone, and one completely estranged from her children, Emily sold her estate. It went to a Christian couple from the Rockies looking for a place large enough to raise their own five kids.

A lot had changed in Emily's life leading up to that point. In the time since she had disowned her son in her emailed letter calling him a "huge disappointment" who would end up like his father, severing their contact indefinitely, she had abruptly retired, shuttered her law practice, and nearly died in the hospital with only her hairdresser by her side. Now she was relinquishing her rural lifestyle of land—and seclusion—to move into a one-bedroom apartment in the suburbs.

Emily had been living out in the country since the '80s, upon settling down with Dan. In her new environment, a densely populated city full of young families, she thought about the past and about her children. She thought about how everything had fallen apart.

A few weeks after relocating, on a cool Saturday afternoon, she put those thoughts down in writing in another letter to Adam. It was titled "Truce and love."

"This life of ours has had more than a fair share of hurt, pain and anger," she reflected. "Nothing gets resolved; it just festers, producing more pain, anger and hurt."

She wrote of Dan's death and the trauma it had caused them both, stripping Adam of his joy at such a tender age and leaving her all alone to raise him and his sisters. He had once said she was his hero for doing so, she recalled; the truth was, she had carried with her deep resentment and fear, always bracing for the next tragedy to bring her down. Given all they'd been through, it was understandable that they both had their "defenses" up, but now was the time to end the cycle, she urged—to put their differences aside and start over before it was too late.

She was no hero, she said. She had only ever been—and would only ever be—his mother, flawed and filled with unconditional love for him.

She longed for the way things used to be, and she was sorry, she offered briefly at the end of the letter. For what, specifically, she didn't say. In nine hundred words, there was no mention of QAnon, conspiracy theories, or the hurtful things she'd said and done—only references to a "past war" between them, and requests for a "truce."

"I love you my beautiful boy, and pray this day and my email greets you with all the love it intends and opens a dialogue for you and I being 'us' again. Until such time, I will wait, patiently."

Adam used to view his life in two parts: life before losing his dad, and life after. But with time, he had come to accept the third part.

He never responded.

Afterword

When I set out to write this book, I saw a daunting crisis and a clear culprit.

The nation, it seemed, was losing its grip on reality. At least one in five Americans believed that coronavirus vaccines were being used to implant secret microchips and that a "storm" would soon "sweep away the elites in power and restore the rightful leaders," among a litany of other false yet stunningly popular conspiracy theories. On a grand scale was a democracy at risk; up close, behind closed doors, were countless fractured families, like those of Emily, Matt, Doris, Alice, and Kendra. And mostly to blame, I was convinced, was our greed-corrupted information ecosystem.

As a tech reporter, I'd written extensively about the insidious ways in which profit-maximizing social media algorithms were driving tribal polarization and amplifying fake news while foreign powers leveraged the platforms to do the same from afar. Adding fuel to the fire, media personalities and influencers with audiences of millions were preaching lies and hate for clicks and views with increasing success, while a growing faction of the nation's leaders was doing the same for political ends. And, in the background of it all, QAnon had risen from the fringes and cranked up the madness to a fever pitch.

Inside this ecosystem, a battleground for the world's attention, the scales were progressively tilting away from truth: Rapacious peddlers of unevidenced conspiracy theories could easily go viral on Facebook, YouTube, TikTok, and Twitter, even outperforming major news outlets in their vast, rapid reach, as we'd seen with *Plandemic*. The problem was clear, and so too appeared the fix.

In theory, the scales had to be tilted back. In practice, that meant doing things like reining in Big Tech, teaching media literacy to help people parse real from fake, and countering false information with fact-checking labels.

It would seem entirely logical to fight fiction with fact. But therein lies a fraught assumption. Beneath these kinds of delusional beliefs, in many instances, is not a desire to be accurately informed, but a need to be internally comforted. Matt was seeking a restored sense of purpose following his debilitating injury, just as Alice craved security and answers during a period of petrifying uncertainty. Neither of them was crazy or unintelligent, and neither of them, at the deepest level, was interested in objective truth. Simply, they were vulnerable, and espousing conspiracy theories met their needs.

This was the case for many of the hundreds of families I spoke with in the process of my reporting. In QAnon, the lonely found belonging, the aimless found direction, and the hurt and the angry found validation. The truth is that *the truth* is almost beside the point. Facts alone won't fix this; to get bogged down in debunking falsehoods is to tackle the symptom, not the cause. What we're facing is as much a wellness crisis as it is a disinformation crisis. Our interventions need to reflect that.

"I could teach you all the media literacy tips in the world," says Dr. Joanne Miller, an expert in political psychology and a professor at the University of Delaware, "but if you're feeling uncertain; if you're feeling a lack of control; if you're feeling socially isolated; if you're feeling helpless and searching for answers, because answers will make you feel better, then media literacy won't help you. You'll throw it all out the window."

Miller's years of research into the motivations behind conspiracy theory belief had been of growing interest to me as I worked through the book. She'd found that people with a weaker ability to "bounce back" from adversity were more susceptible, supporting her understanding that conspiracy theories were, for many, a *coping mechanism*—a more easily accessible and ostensibly less harmful one than others, like drugs or gambling.

"If you really, really want to believe, then you'll find a way, regardless of facts and evidence," Miller says. "So the question is: Why do so many of us want to believe right now?"

A key issue underlying our collective vulnerability is mental-emotional health. America, by that measure, is seriously unwell. Depression rates among adults soared from 11 to 40 percent over the pandemic, with higher numbers inside disproportionately hard-hit communities of color—and with lasting effects: Researchers detected changes not only to our health but to our *personalities,* including significant declines in traits related to socializing and interpersonal trust. Young people in particular became moodier and more prone to stress. And when the outbreak finally subsided, the world we returned to was in many ways worse than the one we'd left behind.

Rents and eviction filings in many parts of the United States spiked to above their prepandemic levels after Covid protections and assistance came to an abrupt end, causing surges in bankruptcies and homelessness that will be felt for generations. Millions and millions were laid off amid fears of a recession. School shootings leapt to an all-time high, then more than doubled. Hate crimes in big cities reached unprecedented levels. America broke its record of billion-dollar climate disasters in a single year. Looking to the future, more seniors are living alone than ever before—nearly half without retirement savings. Leaders of the artificial intelligence industry, meanwhile, warn that the technology poses a "risk of extinction" on par with nuclear war.

Is it really any wonder that so many people are coping with conspiracy theories?

Unlike QAnon's silver-bullet "Great Awakening" to bring an end to the world's woes, there is, of course, no simple solution here. But a good place to start would be broadening access to mental health services using a community-based approach, and, critically, fostering emotional resilience in kids. Miller advocates for culturally informed social-emotional learning, an educational program that's already being taught in many schools nationwide, which helps students develop vital life skills including healthy coping strategies and self-awareness. The idea is that this would prepare young people to navigate hardships like Doris's cancer misdiagnosis, or even Kendra's acutely disadvantaged upbringing, without leaning on conspiracy theories as a crutch. On the flipside, for the many people in a position like Adam's, it could give them the tools to deal with losing a loved one down the rabbit hole without spiraling.

Dr. Shauna Bowes, a clinical psychologist studying the "conspiratorial mind," stresses that we must also "target social motives pertaining to mistrust and outgroup threat perception." She points to "social contact theory," which holds that under appropriate circumstances, interactions between different social groups, such as interfaith dialogue initiatives, can decrease prejudicial attitudes—and, she believes, could also be effective in reducing tribalist conspiracy theory ideation.

Despite the scale of delusion with which we're grappling—by late 2023, one in four Americans were in agreement that "Satan-worshipping pedophiles" controlled the government and media—few resources exist for afflicted families and individuals. Many people, in their desperation, become self-taught deprogrammers, hunting for tips and tricks online to help relatives and friends, as Adam did. But even those fortunate enough to have access to therapists and other industry professionals often still have a difficult time finding someone with the specific skill set that this highly complex and delicate phenomenon demands.

"Mental health clinicians have been running into issues, throwing their hands up in the air, saying, 'We don't know how to deal with this stuff, because once we try, we become part of the conspiracy [in the eyes of the client],'" explains Charlie Safford, a licensed clinical social worker in Olympia, Washington.

Safford was tapped by chapters of the National Association of Social Workers to develop a training program for practitioners to use when working with QAnon believers or their family members. The strategies he recommends align closely with the approach that Christopher and Ted used with Alice: a combination of the Socratic method and motivational interviewing. This kind of applied technique is, at its heart, about storytelling, Safford says. Conspiracy theories may cast someone as a digital soldier or a patriot or a righteous activist—a fantastical narrative that the reality of their ordinary life likely just can't compete with. The process, therefore, involves gently chipping away at the fantasy while helping the person reach a point at which they can begin to rewrite their story in real life.

But the need for support doesn't end when someone breaks free from this way of thinking—it increases. Getting out is half the battle; as Alice came to find, *staying out* can be just as challenging, especially when the issues that led to conspiracy theory belief in the first place might never be fully resolved.

"When you leave, you're more vulnerable than when you got in," Diane Benscoter, a former member of the Moonies (Unification Church) cult, says of QAnon and movements like it. "You may still be in a state of crisis. Because it's not just that you believed this—it became who you were. It's what you were proud of."

The single most valuable resource to keep people from returning to cult-like environments, and what's urgently needed for people in Alice's position, Benscoter says, is an organized support group of others in re-covery, not unlike Alcoholics Anonymous.

"That's where they can really start rebuilding their identity and start to grow stronger. People who've been through it and have gotten the support that they need are incredibly powerful in the fact that they won't be had again like this."

Some of these steps toward possible solutions, like bettering America's mental healthcare system, are ambitious, yes. But recasting this crisis through the lens of well-being should be cause for hope, not discourage-ment. Because the alternative—playing Whac-A-Mole cracking down on an endless lineup of lies and liars—is surely unwinnable in a world of runaway tech. Already, seeing is no longer believing; deepfakes will al-ways outpace deepfake detection tools, just as increasingly sophisticated agents of disinformation, from click-chasing hucksters to election-meddling foreign governments, will always find new and innovative ways to sow chaos.

Trying to improve our information ecosystem and to arm people with the knowledge to navigate it, while both crucial endeavors, will never be enough. Confronting the foundational, systemic wellness issues, how-ever, is something we can do, and must. As the characters of this book and the myriad other Americans who've lost loved ones into the realm of con-spiracy theories can attest, the stakes are staggering.

Notes

PROLOGUE

xix **rocketed to 25 percent:** Public Religion Research Institute, "Threats to American Democracy Ahead of an Unprecedented Presidential Election," PRRI, press release, October 25, 2023, https://www.prri.org/research/threats-to-american -democracy-ahead-of-an-unprecedented-presidential-election/.

xix **elected—and reelected—as House representative:** M. Astor, "Marjorie Taylor Greene Is Re-elected and Poised for More Power in G.O.P.," *New York Times,* November 8, 2022, https://www.nytimes.com/2022/11/08/us/politics/marjorie -taylor-greene-georgia-wins.html.

xix **even murderous:** Center for Strategic and International Studies, "Examining Extremism: QAnon," *Examining Extremism* (blog), June 10, 2021, https://www.csis .org/blogs/examining-extremism/examining-extremism-qanon.

CHAPTER 1

5 **a YouTube video:** "Q—The Plan to Save the World," 2018, https://www.bitchute .com/video/r50sMdc3ZGxf/.

7 **Amazon, owned by hectobillionaire Jeff Bezos:** Alex Kasprak, "Did Amazon Pay No Federal Income Taxes in 2017?," Snopes, September 26, 2018, https://www .snopes.com/fact-check/amazon-federal-taxes-2017/.

9 **Amazon-bestselling book:** B. Collins, "On Amazon, a Qanon Conspiracy Book Climbs the Charts—with an Algorithmic Push," NBC News, March 4, 2019, https://www.nbcnews.com/tech/tech-news/amazon-qanon-conspiracy-book -climbs-charts-algorithmic-push-n979181.

10 **"tip top shape":** "Remarks by President Trump at the 2018 White House Easter Egg Roll," White House, April 2, 2018, https://trumpwhitehouse.archives.gov /briefings-statements/remarks-president-trump-2018-white-house-easter-egg -roll/.

10 **a phrase they misattributed:** A. Chabria, "Lizard People, Deadly Orgies and JFK: How QAnon Hijacked Hollywood to Spread Conspiracies," *Los Angeles Times,* December 7, 2021, https://www.latimes.com/california/story/2021-12-07/how -qanon-has-hijacked-hollywood-movies-for-conspiracy-theories.

12 **"a stumbling drunk" Kavanaugh:** E. Brown, "California Professor, Writer of Confidential Brett Kavanaugh Letter, Speaks Out About Her Allegation of Sexual Assault," *Washington Post,* September 27, 2018.

12 **actually showed Clinton with her official campaign photographer:** D. Evon, "Is This a Photograph of Christine Blasey Ford's Lawyer with Hillary Clinton?," Snopes, September 26, 2018, https://www.snopes.com/fact-check/ford-lawyer -hillary-clinton/.

CHAPTER 2

18 **"They hate you":** K. Yourish et al., "Inside the Apocalyptic Worldview of 'Tucker Carlson Tonight,'" *New York Times*, April 30, 2022, sec. U.S., https://www.nytimes.com/interactive/2022/04/30/us/tucker-carlson-tonight.html.

18 **trust fund baby:** A. Chávez, "Tucker Carlson on Rupert Murdoch in 2010 Radio Segment: 'I'm 100 Percent His Bitch,'" The Intercept, March 12, 2019, https://theintercept.com/2019/03/12/tucker-carlson-tapes-rupert-murdoch/.

18 **Fox's overwhelmingly white audience:** Public Opinion Strategies, "Who's Watching? A Look at the Demographics of Cable News Channel Watchers," February 1, 2019, https://pos.org/whos-watching-a-look-at-the-demographics-of-cable-news-channel-watchers/.

19 **paying hundreds of Fox News watchers:** D. Broockman and J. Kalla, "Consuming Cross-Cutting Media Causes Learning and Moderates Attitudes: A Field Experiment with Fox News Viewers," OSF Preprints, April 1, 2022, https://doi.org/10.31219/osf.io/jrw26.

22 **"folie à deux":** A. Mohdin, "This Bizarre Road Trip Gone Wrong May Be a Case of a Rare Shared Psychosis in Action," Quartz, September 11, 2016, https://qz.com/777918/a-shared-psychosis-called-folie-a-deux-may-explain-why-the-tromp-family-went-missing-on-a-bizarre-road-trip.

22 **a nationally shocking 2014 assault:** G. Cipriani et al., "A Contagious Disorder: Folie à Deux and Dementia," *American Journal of Alzheimer's Disease and Other Dementias* 33, no. 7 (2018): 415–22, https://doi.org/10.1177/1533317518772060.

22 **Media coverage was partly responsible:** S. Gorman and J. M. Gorman, "Do QAnon Followers Have High Rates of Mental Illness?," Psychology Today, *Denying to the Grave* (blog), May 4, 2021, https://www.psychologytoday.com/us/blog/denying-the-grave/202105/do-qanon-followers-have-high-rates-mental-illness.

22 **conspiracy theory belief and depression:** J. Green et al., "Depressive Symptoms and Conspiracy Beliefs," *Applied Cognitive Psychology* 37, no. 2 (2023): 332–59, https://doi.org/10.1002/acp.4011; D. De Coninck et al., "Beliefs in Conspiracy Theories and Misinformation About COVID-19: Comparative Perspectives on the Role of Anxiety, Depression and Exposure to and Trust in Information Sources," *Frontiers in Psychology* 12 (2021), https://www.frontiersin.org/articles/10.3389/fpsyg.2021.646394.

22–23 **Psychological stress as well as state:** V. Swami et al., "Putting the Stress on Conspiracy Theories: Examining Associations Between Psychological Stress, Anxiety, and Belief in Conspiracy Theories," *Personality and Individual Differences* 99 (2016): 72–76, https://doi.org/10.1016/j.paid.2016.04.084.

23 **circumstantial vulnerability in some cases:** M. Grzesiak-Feldman, "The Effect of High-Anxiety Situations on Conspiracy Thinking," *Current Psychology* 32, no. 1 (2013): 100–118, https://doi.org/10.1007/s12144-013-9165-6.

23 **Emotional trauma had the power:** H. U. Voss and E. Temple, "Exposure to Trauma Can Affect Brain Function in Healthy People Several Years After Event," https://www.apa.org/news/press/releases/2007/05/brain-function.

23 **Social isolation and loneliness:** S. Cacioppo et al., "Loneliness and Implicit Attention to Social Threat: A High-Performance Electrical Neuroimaging Study," *Cognitive Neuroscience* 7, nos. 1–4 (2016): 138–59, https://doi.org/10.1080/17588928.2015.1070136.

23 **a robust predictor of conspiracy theory thinking:** A. Cichocka, M. Marchlewska, and M. Biddlestone, "Why Do Narcissists Find Conspiracy Theories So Appeal-

ing?," *Current Opinion in Psychology* 47 (2022): 101386, https://doi.org/10.1016/j
.copsyc.2022.101386.

CHAPTER 3

25 **Marshall McLuhan, a philosopher:** M. McLuhan, *The Gutenberg Galaxy: The Making of Typographic Man* (Toronto: University of Toronto Press, 1962).

28 **three dominant television networks:** T. Brownfield, "The Origins of America's First TV Networks," *Saturday Evening Post,* March 4, 2019, https://www.saturday eveningpost.com/2019/03/the-origins-of-americas-first-tv-networks/.

29 **The number of seniors on the site:** E. A. Vogels, "Millennials Stand Out for Their Technology Use, but Older Generations Also Embrace Digital Life," Pew Research Center, September 9, 2019, https://www.pewresearch.org/short-reads/2019/09/09/us-generations-technology-use/.

29 **more likely than so-called digital natives:** A. Guess, J. Nagler, and J. Tucker, "Less Than You Think: Prevalence and Predictors of Fake News Dissemination on Facebook," *Science Advances* 5, no. 1 (2019): eaau4586, https://doi.org/10.1126/sciadv .aau4586.

29 **a third of "digital immigrants" over sixty-five:** L. H. Owen, "Old People Are Most Likely to Share Fake News on Facebook. They're Also Facebook's Fastest-Growing U.S. Audience," Nieman Lab, January 11, 2019, https://www.niemanlab .org/2019/01/old-people-are-most-likely-to-share-fake-news-on-facebook -theyre-also-facebooks-fastest-growing-u-s-audience/.

31 **"the largest false flag since 9/11":** "Debbie Lusignan Sane Progressive," BitChute, October 21, 2022, https://www.bitchute.com/video/oedkByucRQBn/.

31 **a product of parasocial attachment:** C. A. Hoffner and B. J. Bond, "Parasocial Relationships, Social Media, and Well-Being," *Current Opinion in Psychology* 45 (2022): 101306, https://doi.org/10.1016/j.copsyc.2022.101306.

31 **Influencer marketing was already a booming:** "Influencer Marketing Market Size," Oberlo, updated June 2023, https://www.oberlo.com/statistics/influencer -marketing-market-size.

31 **Older adults were more susceptible:** M. J. Poulin and C. M. Haase, "Growing to Trust: Evidence That Trust Increases and Sustains Well-Being Across the Life Span," *Social Psychological and Personality Science* 6, no. 6 (2015): 614–21, https:// doi.org/10.1177/1948550615574301.

32 **algorithmically promoted content:** J. Nicas, "How YouTube Drives People to the Internet's Darkest Corners," *Wall Street Journal,* February 7, 2018, sec. Tech, https://www.wsj.com/articles/how-youtube-drives-viewers-to-the-internets -darkest-corners-1518020478.

32 **Alex Jones's Infowars:** J. Kaiser and A. Rauchfleisch, "Unite the Right? How You-Tube's Recommendation Algorithm Connects the U.S. Far-Right," Medium, April 11, 2018, https://medium.com/@MediaManipulation/unite-the-right-how -youtubes-recommendation-algorithm-connects-the-u-s-far-right-9f1387ccfabd.

32 **labeling school shooting survivors as "crisis actors":** M. Strachan, "A Conspiracy Theory About a Stoneman Douglas Student Reaches No. 1 on YouTube," Huff-Post, February 21, 2018, https://www.huffpost.com/entry/youtube-stoneman-do uglas_n_5a8d9389e4b00a30a2517348.

32 **"Partner Program" as an incentive:** B. Lewis, "Alternative Influence," Data & Society Research Institute, report, September 18, 2018, https://datasociety.net/ library/alternative-influence/.

32 **Laura Eisenhower, the great granddaughter:** J. Cabral, "This Alien Expert Says Eating Vegan Food Is Best to Attract 'Sky Beings,'" *Vice,* March 28, 2016, https://www.vice.com/en/article/nzkkd7/this-alien-expert-says-eating-vegan-food-is-best-to-attract-sky-beings.

33 **vaccine falsehoods were not only allowed but amplified:** C. O'Donovan and L. McDonald, "YouTube Continues to Promote Anti-vax Videos as Facebook Prepares to Fight Medical Misinformation," Buzzfeed News, February 20, 2019, https://www.buzzfeednews.com/article/carolineodonovan/youtube-anti-vaccination-video-recommendations; J. C. Wong, "How Facebook and YouTube Help Spread Anti-vaxxer Propaganda," *The Guardian,* February 1, 2019, sec. Media, https://www.theguardian.com/media/2019/feb/01/facebook-youtube-anti-vaccination-misinformation-social-media.

33 **making a rising salary of nearly $150,000:** A. Suozzo et al., "Informed Consent Action Network," Pro Publica, Nonprofit Explorer, accessed May 9, 2013, https://projects.propublica.org/nonprofits/organizations/814540235.

33 **wearing the Nazi-era yellow Star of David:** Anti-Defamation League, "Anti-vaccine Protesters Misappropriate Holocaust-Era Symbol to Promote Their Cause," *ADL Blog,* April 5, 2019, https://www.adl.org/resources/blog/anti-vaccine-protesters-misappropriate-holocaust-era-symbol-promote-their-cause.

CHAPTER 4

35 **documented breaches of public trust:** G. Greenwald and E. MacAskill, "Boundless Informant: The NSA's Secret Tool to Track Global Surveillance Data," *The Guardian,* June 11, 2013, sec. US News, https://www.theguardian.com/world/2013/jun/08/nsa-boundless-informant-global-datamining.

35 **surveillance programs to MKUltra:** S. Fore, "The Psychological Torture of MK ULTRA," *IU South Bend Undergraduate Research Journal* 18 (2018): 27–34.

36 **Democratic Party officials' extraordinary bias:** T. B. Lee, "DNC Email Leaks, Explained," Vox, July 25, 2016, https://www.vox.com/2016/7/23/12261020/dnc-email-leaks-explained.

37 **surging numbers of hate crimes:** E. Smith, "Hate Crime Recorded by Law Enforcement, 2010–2019," Bureau of Justice Statistics, Statistical Brief NCJ 301554, September 2021, https://bjs.ojp.gov/sites/g/files/xyckuh236/files/media/document/hcrle1019.pdf.

38 **a "highly sensitive person":** S. Bas et al., "Experiences of Adults High in the Personality Trait Sensory Processing Sensitivity: A Qualitative Study," *Journal of Clinical Medicine* 10, no. 21 (2021): 4912, https://doi.org/10.3390/jcm10214912.

38 **an individual prone to intense emotional reactions:** "Highly Sensitive Person," Psychology Today, accessed October 24, 2023, https://www.psychologytoday.com/us/basics/highly-sensitive-person.

41 *The Fall of the Cabal:* "The Fall of the Cabal: The End of the World as We Know It [2020]," March 22, 2020, https://www.bitchute.com/video/MYHTpUW9KAXQ/.

42 **the hardly extraordinary truth:** T. Spry Jr, "Why Do Some Trees Survive Fires While Buildings Don't?," Wusa9.com, Verify, September 21, 2020, https://www.wusa9.com/article/news/verify/trees-survive-fires-buildings-dont-explained/507-a3fac229-1fe1-4677-9976-392c72b15617.

42 **crop circles were crafted by supernatural forces:** "About Janet," Circular Site, accessed October 24, 2023, https://www.circularsite.com/en-verder/about-janet/.

44 **scathing condemnations of the "corporate media":** F. Sonmez, "Sanders Accuses

the Post of Biased Coverage Due to His Criticism of Amazon, Cites No Evidence," *Washington Post,* August 13, 2019, https://www.washingtonpost.com/politics/ sanders-accuses-the-post-of-biased-coverage-due-to-his-criticism-of-amazon -cites-no-evidence/2019/08/12/9846878e-bd67-11e9-a5c6-1e74f7ec4a93_story .html.

45   **not an unprecedented era of paranoia:** J. Uscinski et al., "Have Beliefs in Conspiracy Theories Increased over Time?," *PLOS ONE* 17, no. 7 (2022): e0270429, https://doi.org/10.1371/journal.pone.0270429.

45   **more than five hundred hours:** D. A. Williamson, "US Social Media Usage," Insider Intelligence, June 2, 2020, https://www.insiderintelligence.com/content/ us-social-media-usage.

46   **declared, an "infodemic":** World Health Organization, "Novel Coronavirus (2019-nCoV)," Situation Report 13, February 2, 2020, https://www.who.int/docs/ default-source/coronaviruse/situation-reports/20200202-sitrep-13-ncov-v3 .pdf.

46   **More than a quarter of Americans:** L. Sanders, "The Difference Between What Republicans and Democrats Believe to Be True About COVID-19," YouGov, May 26, 2020, https://today.yougov.com/politics/articles/29917-republicans-demo crats-misinformation?redirect_from=%2Ftopics%2Fpolitics%2Farticles-reports %2F2020%2F05%2F26%2Frepublicans-democrats-misinformation.

46   **"purposely created and released":** J. E. Uscinski et al., "Why Do People Believe COVID-19 Conspiracy Theories?," *Harvard Kennedy School Misinformation Review* 1, no. 3 (2020), https://doi.org/10.37016/mr-2020-015.

47   **Cornell University study:** S. Evanega et al., "Coronavirus Misinformation: Quantifying Sources and Themes in the COVID-19 'Infodemic,'" Cornell Alliance for Science, September 2020, https://allianceforscience.org/wp-content/uploads/ 2020/09/Evanega-et-al-Coronavirus-misinformationFINAL.pdf.

47   **"time to #FireFauci":** T. Nguyen, "How a Pair of Anti-vaccine Activists Sparked a #FireFauci Furor," *Politico,* April 13, 2020, https://www.politico.com/news/2020/ 04/13/anti-vaccine-activists-fire-fauci-furor-185001.

47   **Fox News anchors quickly ginned up populist suspicion:** J. Feldman, "Tucker Carlson, Sean Hannity, Laura Ingraham Slam Fauci," Mediaite, May 13, 2020, https://www.mediaite.com/tv/tucker-carlson-sean-hannity-laura-ingraham -slam-fauci-after-senate-testimony-on-pandemic-lockdowns/.

47   **shifting public health advice:** Quinnipiac University Poll, "Fauci, Governors Get Highest Marks for Response to Coronavirus, Quinnipiac University National Poll Finds; Majority Say Trump's Response Not Aggressive Enough," April 8, 2020, https://poll.qu.edu/Poll-Release?releaseid=3753.

47   **polls found trust in him souring:** L. Lopes et al., "KFF Health Tracking Poll— September 2020: Top Issues in 2020 Election, the Role of Misinformation, and Views on a Potential Coronavirus Vaccine," KFF, September 10, 2020, https:// www.kff.org/coronavirus-covid-19/report/kff-health-tracking-poll -september-2020/.

48   **gave rise to the term *QAmom*:** M. Deckman, "Tea Party Women: Mama Grizzlies, Grassroots Leaders, and the Changing Face of the American Right," NYU Press, May 2016, https://nyupress.org/9781479866427/tea-party-women.

49   **burden of caregiving on women:** K. Power, "The COVID-19 Pandemic Has Increased the Care Burden of Women and Families," *Sustainability: Science, Practice and Policy* 16, no. 1 (2020): 67–73, https://doi.org/10.1080/15487733.2020 .1776561.

CHAPTER 5

54 **one of the most hypersegregated cities:** D. S. Massey and N. A. Denton, "Hyper-segregation in U.S. Metropolitan Areas: Black and Hispanic Segregation Along Five Dimensions," *Demography* 26, no. 3 (1989): 373–91, https://doi.org/10.2307/2061599.

54 **median income of a Black Milwaukee resident:** M. Levine, "The State of Black Milwaukee in National Perspective: Racial Inequality in the Nation's 50 Largest Metropolitan Areas, in 65 Charts and Tables," Center for Economic Development Publications No. 56, July 1, 2020, https://dc.uwm.edu/ced_pubs/56.

56 **Stella Immanuel, a Cameroonian American pastor:** M. Biesiker and J. Dearen, "GOP Fronts 'Pro-Trump' Doctors to Prescribe Rapid Reopening," AP News, May 20, 2020, https://apnews.com/article/health-us-news-ap-top-news-politics-virus-outbreak-4ee1a3a8d631b454f645b2a8d9597de7.

57 **hydroxychloroquine, an antimalarial drug:** N. Robins-Early, "The Hucksters Pushing a Coronavirus 'Cure' with the Help of Fox News and Elon Musk," Huff-Post, March 20, 2020, https://www.huffpost.com/entry/chloroquine-coronavirus-rigano-todaro-tucker-carlson_n_5e74da41c5b6eab77946c3b3?tnv.

57 **supremely bizarre claims:** W. Sommer, "Trump's New COVID Doctor Says Sex with Demons Makes You Sick," Daily Beast, July 28, 2020, sec. Politics, https://www.thedailybeast.com/stella-immanuel-trumps-new-covid-doctor-believes-in-alien-dna-demon-sperm-and-hydroxychloroquine.

57 **media personalities condemned:** "The Female-Black-Immigrant Doctor They Didn't Want You to Hear," *The Rush Limbaugh Show*, transcript, July 28, 2020, https://www.rushlimbaugh.com/daily/2020/07/28/the-female-african-american-doctor-they-dont-want-you-to-hear/.

58 **Black Americans, as well as Hispanics:** Brian Schaffner, "Survey on QAnon and Conspiracy Beliefs," Institute for Strategic Dialogue, October 2020, https://www.isdglobal.org/wp-content/uploads/2020/10/qanon-and-conspiracy-beliefs-full_toplines.pdf.

58 **Asian Americans in QAnon:** "Why Some Chinese Dissidents Love QAnon," YouTube, Vice News, January 9, 2022, https://www.youtube.com/watch?v=US0Rfav2qBA.

58 **conspiracy theories transcended race:** D. Sullivan, M. J. Landau, and Z. K. Roth-schild, "An Existential Function of Enemyship: Evidence That People Attribute Influence to Personal and Political Enemies to Compensate for Threats to Control," *Journal of Personality and Social Psychology* 98, no. 3 (2010): 434–49, https://doi.org/10.1037/a0017457.

58 **a boogeyman in George Soros:** J. Wilson and A. Flannagan, "The Racist 'Great Replacement' Conspiracy Theory Explained," Southern Poverty Law Center, May 17, 2022, https://www.splcenter.org/hatewatch/2022/05/17/racist-great-replacement-conspiracy-theory-explained.

58 **Second Amendment fanatics:** D. Arkin and B. Popken, "How the Internet's Conspiracy Theorists Turned Parkland Students into 'Crisis Actors,'" NBC News, February 21, 2018, https://www.nbcnews.com/news/us-news/how-internet-s-conspiracy-theorists-turned-parkland-students-crisis-actors-n849921.

58 **stemming from rational hypervigilance:** M. Bilewicz, "Conspiracy Beliefs as an Adaptation to Historical Trauma," *Current Opinion in Psychology* 47 (2022): 101359, https://doi.org/10.1016/j.copsyc.2022.101359.

58 **type of learned suspicion:** J. C. Nelson et al., "The Role of Historical Knowledge

in Perception of Race-Based Conspiracies," *Race and Social Problems* 2, no. 2 (2010): 69–80, https://doi.org/10.1007/s12552-010-9031-1.

58 **chronic social devaluation:** J-W. van Prooijen, J. Staman, and A. P. M. Krouwel, "Increased Conspiracy Beliefs Among Ethnic and Muslim Minorities," *Applied Cognitive Psychology* 32, no. 5 (2018): 661–67, https://doi.org/10.1002/acp .3442.

59 **conspiracy theories vilifying Jewish people:** D. Jolley, R. Meleady, and K. M. Douglas, "Exposure to Intergroup Conspiracy Theories Promotes Prejudice Which Spreads Across Groups," *British Journal of Psychology* 111, no. 1 (2020): 17–35, https://doi.org/10.1111/bjop.12385.

59 **mile-a-minute voice of Candace Owens:** C. Owens, *Blackout* (New York: Simon and Schuster, 2020), https://www.simonandschuster.com/books/Blackout/Candace -Owens/9781982133276.

59 **Owens's family sued the school board:** C. Owens, "An Open Letter from Candace Owens," *Stamford Advocate,* March 5, 2016, https://www.stamfordadvocate .com/local/article/An-open-letter-from-Candace-Owens-6872591.php.

60 **She launched a blog:** J. Bernstein, "The Newest Star of the Trump Movement Ran a Trump-Bashing Publication—Less Than Two Years Ago," BuzzFeed News, May 15, 2018, https://www.buzzfeednews.com/article/josephbernstein/ the-newest-star-of-the-trump-movement-ran-a-trump-bashing.

60 **"hit pieces" by "the Left":** "On Her Journey from Left to Right," *The Rubin Report,* September 28, 2017, https://www.youtube.com/watch?v=BSAoitd1BTQ.

60 **grossing more than $7 million:** Andrea Suozzo et al., "Blexit Foundation Inc, Full Filing," ProPublica, Nonprofit Explorer, accessed May 9, 2013, https://proj ects.propublica.org/nonprofits/organizations/833032236/202101209349301305/ full?fbclid=IwAR3e5ENhJx8qyaftkRIRoEEL1vutyWCyoTGnRoGVu8JtADU jOAWGIGsmsH4.

60 **debunked allegation that Bill Gates:** A. Dent, "Did Bill Gates Test Unapproved Vaccines on Children in Africa?," *The Dispatch,* April 22, 2020, https://thedispatch .com/article/did-bill-gates-test-unapproved-vaccines/.

60 **claim that Soros was paying Black people:** D. Alba, "Misinformation About George Floyd Protests Surges on Social Media," *New York Times,* June 1, 2020, sec. Technology, https://www.nytimes.com/2020/06/01/technology/george-floyd -misinformation-online.html.

60 **BLEXIT was paying travel and lodging costs:** R. Scott and W. Steaken, "Candace Owens' BLEXIT Group Pays for Some Attendees' Travel to Trump's White House Event," ABC News, October 10, 2020, https://abcnews.go.com/Politics/candace -owens-blexit-group-pays-attendees-travel-trumps/story?id=73531036.

61 **senate intelligence committee investigation:** *Report of the Select Committee on Intelligence, United States Senate, on Russian Active Measures Campaigns and Interference in the 2016 U.S. Election,* vol. 2, *Russia's Use of Social Media,* November 10, 2020, https://www.intelligence.senate.gov/sites/default/files/documents/Report _Volume2.pdf.

61 **Foreign agents disguised as Black Lives Matter activists:** R. DiResta et al., *The Tactics and Tropes of the Internet Research Agency* (Austin, TX: New Knowledge, 2019).

61 **partisan lies exploiting trauma:** S. Rodriguez and M. Caputo, " 'This Is F---ing Crazy': Florida Latinos Swamped by Wild Conspiracy Theories," *Politico,* September 14, 2020, https://www.politico.com/news/2020/09/14/florida-latinos -disinformation-413923.

61 **Campaigns to manipulate minorities:** *A Growing Threat: The Impact of Disinformation Targeted at Communities of Color (EventID=114642)*, April 28, 2022, https://www.youtube.com/watch?v=qXv_1TDyNY4.

CHAPTER 6

65 **Hayes was better known as "Praying Medic":** D. Hayes, "The 'Praying Medic' Was an Atheist Until God Spoke to Him in a Dream," Sidroth.org, November 20, 2016, https://sidroth.org/television/tv-archives/dave-hayes-praying-medic/.

67 **like "being in the special forces":** K. Mantyla, "Dave Hayes Says Being a QAnon Conspiracy Theorist Is 'Like Being in the Special Forces,'" Right Wing Watch, September 17, 2021, https://www.rightwingwatch.org/post/dave-hayes-says-being-a-qanon-conspiracy-theorist-is-like-being-in-the-special-forces/.

67 **"You are a digital soldier":** K. Mantyla, "Dave Hayes: MAGA World's 'Army of Digital Soldiers' Will Soon Replace the Mainstream Media," Right Wing Watch, June 5, 2019, https://www.rightwingwatch.org/post/dave-hayes-maga-worlds-army-of-digital-soldiers-will-soon-replace-the-mainstream-media/.

68 **only one in four American adults:** R. Kobau et al., "Well-Being Assessment: An Evaluation of Well-Being Scales for Public Health and Population Estimates of Well-Being Among US Adults," *Applied Psychology: Health and Well-Being* 2, no. 3 (2010): 272–97, https://doi.org/10.1111/j.1758-0854.2010.01035.x.

68 **identifying villains to unite against:** C. Schöpfer et al., "'Where There Are Villains, There Will Be Heroes': Belief in Conspiracy Theories as an Existential Tool to Fulfill Need for Meaning," *Personality and Individual Differences* 200 (2023): 111900, https://doi.org/10.1016/j.paid.2022.111900.

68 **journey to self-actualization:** J. Drury et al., "The Phenomenology of Empowerment in Collective Action," *British Journal of Social Psychology* 44, no. 3 (2005): 309–28, https://doi.org/10.1348/014466604X18523.

72 *National Geographic* **article:** M. Wei-Haas, "Strange Waves Rippled Around the World, and Nobody Knows Why," National Geographic, November 28, 2018, https://www.nationalgeographic.com/science/article/strange-earthquake-waves-rippled-around-world-earth-geology.

72 **Apophenia is a natural phenomenon:** Duke Today staff, "Brain Center Automatically Searches for Patterns, Real or Imagined," Duke Today, April 7, 2002, https://today.duke.edu/2002/04/huettel0402.html.

72 **bedrock of conspiracy theory thinking:** J.-W. van Prooijen, K. M. Douglas, and C. De Inocencio, "Connecting the Dots: Illusory Pattern Perception Predicts Belief in Conspiracies and the Supernatural," *European Journal of Social Psychology* 48, no. 3 (2017): 320–35, https://doi.org/10.1002/ejsp.2331.

72 **illusory patterns perceived in random noise:** R. Berkowitz, "QAnon Resembles the Games I Design. But for Believers, There Is No Winning," *Washington Post*, May 11, 2021, https://www.washingtonpost.com/outlook/qanon-game-plays-believers/2021/05/10/31d8ea46-928b-11eb-a74e-1f4cf89fd948_story.html.

75 **poured her energy into LuLaRoe:** B. Aho, "AG Ferguson Sues LuLaRoe over Pyramid Scheme," Attorney General's Office, Washington State, January 25, 2019, https://www.atg.wa.gov/news/news-releases/ag-ferguson-sues-lularoe-over-pyramid-scheme.

76 **majority of sellers never turned a profit:** M. DeLiema et al., "AARP Study of Multilevel Marketing," 2018, https://amazingprofitsonline.com/wp-content/uploads/2021/02/AARP-Foundation-MLM-Research-Study-Report-min.pdf.

CHAPTER 7

85 phenomenon known as the "validity effect": L. E. Boehm, "The Validity Effect: A Search for Mediating Variables," *Personality and Social Psychology Bulletin* 20, no. 3 (1994): 285–93, https://doi.org/10.1177/0146167294203006.

85 "tribal epistemology," a term coined by journalist David Roberts: D. Roberts, "Donald Trump and the Rise of Tribal Epistemology," Vox, May 19, 2017, https://www.vox.com/policy-and-politics/2017/3/22/14762030/donald-trump-tribal-epistemology.

85 Yet when researchers presented those images: B. F. Schaffner, "This Is What Trump Voters Said When Asked to Compare His Inauguration Crowd with Obama's," *Washington Post*, December 7, 2021, https://www.washingtonpost.com/news/monkey-cage/wp/2017/01/25/we-asked-people-which-inauguration-crowd-was-bigger-heres-what-they-said/.

86 And when people's firmly held beliefs are challenged: J. T. Kaplan, Sarah I. Gimbel, and Sam Harris, "Neural Correlates of Maintaining One's Political Beliefs in the Face of Counterevidence," *Scientific Reports* 6, no. 1 (2016): 39589, https://doi.org/10.1038/srep39589.

90 2018 analysis of the popular r/conspiracy subreddit: C. Klein, P. Clutton, and V. Polito, "Topic Modeling Reveals Distinct Interests Within an Online Conspiracy Forum," *Frontiers in Psychology* 9 (2018), https://doi.org/10.3389/fpsyg.2018.00189.

91 Brain-imaging studies have revealed: J. Kimmel and M. Rowe, "A Behavioral Addiction Model of Revenge, Violence, and Gun Abuse," *Journal of Law, Medicine and Ethics* 48, no. S4 (2021): 172–78, https://doi.org/10.1177/1073110520979419.

91 more prone to seeing illusory patterns: M. Shermer, "Michael Shermer: The Pattern Behind Self-Deception," TED Talk, February 15, 2010, https://www.ted.com/talks/michael_shermer_the_pattern_behind_self_deception/transcript.

CHAPTER 8

97–98 renowned psychologist Abraham Maslow: Wichita State University, Office of Instructional Resources, "Hierarchy of Needs," 2023, https://www.wichita.edu/services/mrc/OIR/Pedagogy/Theories/maslow.php.

98 a vulnerability exploited by cults: M. Rousselet et al., "Cult Membership: What Factors Contribute to Joining or Leaving?," *Psychiatry Research* 257 (2017): 27–33, https://doi.org/10.1016/j.psychres.2017.07.018.

98 extremist movements: R. Borum, *Psychology of Terrorism* (Tampa: University of South Florida, 2004), Office of Justice Programs, https://www.ojp.gov/pdffiles1/nij/grants/208552.pdf.

104 had shifted—not shed—her conformation bias: P. Krekó, " 'Conformation Bias': Political Tribalism as a Driver of Disinformation," *Power 3.0: Understanding Modern Authoritarian Influence* (blog), January 15, 2019, International Forum for Democratic Studies, https://www.power3point0.org/2019/01/15/conformation-bias-political-tribalism-as-a-driver-of-disinformation/.

CHAPTER 9

113 when only a minority of women were working: U.S. Dept. of Labor, *Women Workers in 1960: Geographical Differences,* Bulletin 284 (Washington, DC: Government Printing Office, 1962), Federal Reserve Bank of St. Louis, https://fraser.stlouisfed.org/files/docs/publications/women/b0284_dolwb_1962.pdf.

115   **One in every five Americans who agreed:** PRRI staff, "The Persistence of QAnon in the Post-Trump Era: An Analysis of Who Believes the Conspiracies," Public Religion Research Institute, February 24, 2022, https://www.prri.org/research/the-persistence-of-qanon-in-the-post-trump-era-an-analysis-of-who-believes-the-conspiracies/.

116   **diminishing sense of "mattering":** M. Stanley, "The Pernicious Decline in Purpose in Life with Old Age," *Psychology Today,* April 15, 2014, https://www.psychologytoday.com/us/blog/making-sense-chaos/201404/the-pernicious-decline-in-purpose-in-life-old-age.

116   **started to feel "invisible":** "Invisibility in Later Life Survey Results," Gransnet, Online Surveys and Product Tests, conducted 2016, accessed October 30, 2023, https://www.gransnet.com/online-surveys-product-tests/feeling-invisible-survey-data-results.

116   **the psychological toll of getting older:** E. van Wijngaarden, C. Leget, and A. Goossensen, "Ready to Give Up on Life: The Lived Experience of Elderly People Who Feel Life Is Completed and No Longer Worth Living," *Social Science and Medicine* 138 (2015): 257–64, https://doi.org/10.1016/j.socscimed.2015.05.015.

CHAPTER 10

127   **Most American children received their first smartphone:** Common Sense, *The Common Sense Census: Media Use by Tweens and Teens, 2019* (San Francisco: Common Sense Media, 2019), https://www.commonsensemedia.org/sites/default/files/research/report/2019-census-8-to-18-full-report-updated.pdf.

127   **The pandemic saw their social media use climb:** Common Sense, *The Common Sense Census: Media Use by Tweens and Teens, 2021* (San Francisco: Common Sense Media, 2022), https://www.commonsensemedia.org/research/the-common-sense-census-media-use-by-tweens-and-teens-2021.

127   **unable to recognize fake news:** S. Xu, A. Shtulman, and A. G. Young, "Can Children Detect Fake News?," *Proceedings of the Annual Meeting of the Cognitive Science Society* 44 (2022): 2988–93, https://escholarship.org/uc/item/9bh2z1q9#; E.-A. Dumitru, "Testing Children and Adolescents' Ability to Identify Fake News: A Combined Design of Quasi-experiment and Group Discussions," *Societies* 10, no. 3 (2020): 71, https://doi.org/10.3390/soc10030071.

127   **those from disadvantaged backgrounds:** P. N. Howard, L.-M. Neudert, and N. Prakash, "Digital Misinformation / Disinformation and Children," report, UNICEF Office of Global Insight and Policy, August 2021, https://www.unicef.org/globalinsight/media/2096/file/UNICEF-Global-Insight-Digital-Mis-Disinformation-and-Children-2021.pdf.

127   **The cognitive abilities required:** M. Anthony, "Cognitive Development in 6-7 Year Olds," Scholastic, accessed October 26, 2023, https://www.scholastic.com/parents/family-life/creativity-and-critical-thinking/development-milestones/cognitive-development-6-7-year-olds.html.

127   **After turning seven, they were more inclined:** S. Cottrell et al., "Older Children Verify Adult Claims Because They Are Skeptical of Those Claims," *Child Development* 94, no. 1 (2022): 172–86, https://doi.org/10.1111/cdev.13847.

129–130   **literally reshape the still rapidly developing brain:** M. T. Hoffman, "The Science of Early Childhood Development: Closing the Gap Between What We Know and What We Do," *Journal of Developmental and Behavioral Pediatrics* 29, no. 4 (2008): 261, https://doi.org/10.1097/DBP.0b013e3181833804.

130 **disproportionately affected by toxic stress:** L. Morsey and R. Rothstein, "Toxic Stress and Children's Outcomes," report, Economic Policy Institute, May 1, 2019, https://www.epi.org/publication/toxic-stress-and-childrens-outcomes-african -american-children-growing-up-poor-are-at-greater-risk-of-disrupted -physiological-functioning-and-depressed-academic-achievement/.

CHAPTER 11

137 **Religious belief was significantly positively correlated:** M. Frenken, M. Bilewicz, and R. Imhoff, "On the Relation Between Religiosity and the Endorsement of Conspiracy Theories: The Role of Political Orientation," *Political Psychology* 44, no. 1 (2022): 139–56, https://doi.org/10.1111/pops.12822.

138 **one in four white Evangelicals:** Public Religion Research Institute staff, "The Persistence of QAnon in the Post-Trump Era: An Analysis of Who Believes the Conspiracies," Public Religion Research Institute, February 24, 2022, https://www .prri.org/research/the-persistence-of-qanon-in-the-post-trump-era-an-analysis -of-who-believes-the-conspiracies/.

138 **supporters of Christian nationalism:** Public Religion Research Institute staff, "A Christian Nation? Understanding the Threat of Christian Nationalism to American Democracy and Culture," Public Religion Research Institute, February 8, 2023, https://www.prri.org/research/a-christian-nation-understanding-the -threat-of-christian-nationalism-to-american-democracy-and-culture/.

140 **"Praying Medic," the self-proclaimed faith healer:** K. Mantyla, "Dave Hayes Is a Prophetic Mailman, Delivering Messages from God to Q," Right Wing Watch, April 26, 2019, https://www.rightwingwatch.org/post/dave-hayes-is -a-prophetic-mailman-delivering-messages-from-god-to-q/.

141 **French polymath Gustave Le Bon:** "Gustave Le Bon: Social Scientist, Sociologist, Anthropologist," Britannica, September 4, 2023, https://www.britannica.com/ biography/Gustave-Le-Bon.

141 **freeing them "from the sense of their insignificance and powerlessness":** B. Ehrenreich, "The Ecstasy of War," chap. 1 of *Blood Rites: Origins and History of the Passions of War* (New York: Metropolitan Books, 1997), https://archive .nytimes.com/www.nytimes.com/books/first/e/ehrenreich-rites.html?_r=1.

146 **statements denouncing QAnon:** J. Cook, " 'It's Out of Control': How QAnon Undermines Legitimate Anti-trafficking Efforts," HuffPost, September 13, 2020, https://www.huffpost.com/entry/how-qanon-impedes-legitimate-anti -trafficking-groups_n_5f4eacb9c5b69eb5c03592d1.

CHAPTER 12

164 **The parallels between QAnon lore and *The Protocols*:** United States Holocaust Memorial Museum, "A Dangerous Lie: The Protocols of the Elders of Zion," accessed October 26, 2023, https://www.ushmm.org/information/exhibitions/ museum-exhibitions/a-dangerous-lie-the-protocols-of-the-elders-of-zion.

CHAPTER 13

177 **collapse of a condo in Miami:** E. Palmer, "DeAnna Lorraine Thinks Miami Condo Collapse Was 'Deep State Operation,' " *Newsweek,* June 30, 2021, https:// www.newsweek.com/deanna-lorraine-qanon-florida-condo-collapse-john -mcafee-conspiracy-1605519.

180 **a wave of calls to poison control centers:** J. N. Lind et al., "Increase in Out-patient Ivermectin Dispensing in the US During the COVID-19 Pandemic: A Cross-sectional Analysis," *Journal of General Internal Medicine* 36, no. 9 (2021): 2909–11, https://doi.org/10.1007/s11606-021-06948-6.

CHAPTER 14

191 **feelings that naturally eroded with age:** M. Stanley, "The Pernicious Decline in Purpose in Life with Old Age," Psychology Today, *Making Sense of Chaos* (blog), April 15, 2014, https://www.psychologytoday.com/us/blog/making-sense-chaos/201404/the-pernicious-decline-in-purpose-in-life-old-age.

191 **He'd read an article:** J. Cook, "A Vaccine or This Marriage: Conspiracy Theories Are Tearing Couples Apart," HuffPost, July 24, 2021, https://www.huffpost.com/entry/anti-vaccine-conspiracy-theories-divorce_n_60faf8b6e4b05ff8cfc8086b.

CHAPTER 15

202 *New York Times* **article:** G. Russonello, "QAnon Now as Popular in U.S. as Some Major Religions, Poll Suggests," *New York Times,* May 27, 2021, sec. U.S., https://www.nytimes.com/2021/05/27/us/politics/qanon-republicans-trump.html.

202 **BuzzFeed News survey:** S. Koul, "Tell Us The Wildest Conspiracy Theories You've Been Hearing at School," BuzzFeed News, October 13, 2020, https://www.buzzfeednews.com/article/scaachikoul/are-you-a-teacher-dealing-with-conspiracy-theories.

202 **The single best way to counter fake news:** S. van der Linden and J. Roozenbeek, "Psychological Inoculation Against Fake News," in *The Psychology of Fake News* (New York: Routledge, 2020), 9, 147–69.

202 **media literacy training:** A. Huguet et al., "Exploring Media Literacy Education as a Tool for Mitigating Truth Decay," report, RAND Corporation, July 11, 2019, https://www.rand.org/pubs/research_reports/RR3050.html.

CHAPTER 16

210 **"harmful medical treatments":** J. Rottenberg, "Meet the Ojai Dad Who Made the Most Notorious Piece of Coronavirus Disinformation Yet," *Los Angeles Times,* May 13, 2020, https://www.latimes.com/entertainment-arts/movies/story/2020-05-13/plandemic-coronavirus-documentary-director-mikki-willis-mikovits.

CHAPTER 17

212 **"heaven on earth":** K. Mantyla, "Dave Hayes," Right Wing Watch, June 3, 2019, https://www.rightwingwatch.org/post/dave-hayes-christians-must-rethink-their-understand-of-the-end-times-because-trump-is-creating-a-utopia/.

216 **Trump alone had amplified:** A. Kaplan, "Trump Has Repeatedly Amplified QAnon Twitter Accounts. The FBI Has Linked the Conspiracy Theory to Domestic Terror," Media Matters for America, August 1, 2019, https://www.mediamatters.org/twitter/fbi-calls-qanon-domestic-terror-threat-trump-has-amplified-qanon-supporters-twitter-more-20.

220 **DeSantis accusing the corporation:** T. Carlson, "Tucker: How Is a Parent Supposed to Respond to This?," Fox News, March 29, 2022, https://www.foxnews.com/transcript/tucker-how-is-a-parent-supposed-to-respond-to-this.

AFTERWORD

229 **"sweep away the elites in power"**: PRRI staff, "Understanding QAnon's Connection to American Politics, Religion, and Media Consumption," Public Religion Research Institute, May 27, 2021, https://www.prri.org/research/qanon-conspiracy-american-politics-report/.

230 **weaker ability to "bounce back"**: J. Miller, "Psychological, Political, and Situational Factors Combine to Boost COVID-19 Conspiracy Theory Beliefs," *Canadian Journal of Political Science*, Cambridge University, https://www.ncbi.nlm.nih.gov/pmc/articles/PMC7338396/.

230 **America, by that measure, is seriously unwell**: B. Hope, "Study Shows Greater Increase in Depression and Anxiety in Minorities During the Pandemic," UAB News, May 9, 2022, https://www.uab.edu/news/health/item/12841-study-shows-greater-increase-in-depression-and-anxiety-in-minorities-during-the-pandemic.

230–231 **significant declines in traits related to socializing**: A. R. Sutin et al., "Differential Personality Change Earlier and Later in the Coronavirus Pandemic in a Longitudinal Sample of Adults in the United States," PLOS ONE 17, no. 9 (2022): e0274542, https://doi.org/10.1371/journal.pone.0274542.

231 **after Covid protections and assistance came to an abrupt end**: M. Potts, "Rents Are Still Higher Than Before the Pandemic—and Assistance Programs Are Drying Up," *FiveThirtyEight* (blog), January 9, 2023, https://fivethirtyeight.com/features/rents-are-still-higher-than-before-the-pandemic-and-assistance-programs-are-drying-up/; M. Casey and R. J. Rico, "Eviction Filings Are 50% Higher Than They Were Pre-pandemic in Some Cities as Rents Rise," AP News, June 17, 2023, https://apnews.com/article/evictions-homelessness-affordable-housing-landlords-rental-assistance-dc4a03864011334538f82d2f404d2afb.

231 **surges in bankruptcies and homelessness**: K. Brooks, "Bankruptcies Climb as Pandemic Aid Vanishes," CBS News, February 17, 2023, https://www.cbsnews.com/news/bankruptcy-filings-2022-company-personal-epiq/; K. Ronayne, M. Casey, and G. Mulvihill, "Homelessness Surging in Many Cities amid End to COVID Assistance," PBS NewsHour, October 6, 2022, https://www.pbs.org/newshour/nation/homelessness-surging-in-many-cities-in-amid-end-to-covid-assistance.

231 **School shootings leapt**: Z. Schermele, "School Shootings Hit All-Time High for Second Year in a Row," USA Today, September 14, 2023, https://www.usatoday.com/story/news/education/2023/09/13/school-shootings-hit-record-2021-2022/70841718007/.

231 **Hate crimes in big cities**: W. Carless, "Hate Crimes in Big Cities Hit Record High for Second Year in a Row, New Data Shows," USA Today, August 30, 2023, https://www.usatoday.com/story/news/investigations/2023/08/29/hate-crime-report-center-study-hate-extremism/70673688007/.

231 **record of billion-dollar climate disasters**: G. Oladipo, "US Sets New Record for Billion-Dollar Climate Disasters in Single Year," *The Guardian*, September 11, 2023, sec. Environment, https://www.theguardian.com/environment/2023/sep/11/us-record-billion-dollar-climate-disasters.

231 **more seniors are living alone than ever before**: D. Goldstein and R. Gebeloff, "As Gen X and Boomers Age, They Confront Living Alone," *New York Times*, December 1, 2022, https://www.nytimes.com/2022/11/27/us/living-alone-aging.html.

231 **without retirement savings:** M. Hoffman, M. Klee, and B. Sullivan, "New Data Reveal Inequality in Retirement Account Ownership," Census.gov, August 31, 2022, https://www.census.gov/library/stories/2022/08/who-has-retirement-accounts.html.

231 **a "risk of extinction" on par with nuclear war:** Centre for AI Safety, "Statement on AI Risk," accessed September 28, 2023, https://www.safe.ai/statement-on-ai-risk.

231 **fostering emotional resilience in kids:** J. M. Miller, "Psychological, Political, and Situational Factors Combine to Boost COVID-19 Conspiracy Theory Beliefs," *Canadian Journal of Political Science/Revue Canadienne de Science Politique* 53, no. 2 (2020): 327–34, https://doi.org/10.1017/S000842392000058X.

231 **Dr. Shauna Bowes, a clinical psychologist:** S. M Bowes, T. H. Costello, and A. Tasimi, "The Conspiratorial Mind: A Meta-analytic Review of Motivational and Personological Correlates," *Psychological Bulletin* 149, nos. 5–6 (2023): 259–93, https://doi.org/10.1037/bul0000392.

232 **"Satan-worshipping pedophiles" controlled the government:** Public Religion Research Institute, "Threats to American Democracy Ahead of an Unprecedented Presidential Election," PRRI, press release, October 25, 2023, https://www.prri.org/research/threats-to-american-democracy-ahead-of-an-unprecedented-presidential-election/.

Acknowledgments

To the characters of *The Quiet Damage* who allowed me into their lives and brought me through their journeys as they unfolded: Thank you for taking this leap of faith with me. I've learned so much from each of you—far more than I could squeeze into a book. Thank you for answering my intensely personal, sensitive questions, and the countless seemingly trivial ones that allowed me to write your narratives in such intimate detail. (I'm sure none of you miss my *Sorry—one last thing!* follow-up calls to inquire about the exact shade of yellow of your childhood home, or what you might have eaten for breakfast on a specific day five years ago.) Thank you for your time, your generosity, your candor, your understanding, and your bravery. Thank you, above all, for trusting me with your stories. Any good that might come from this book is because of you.

Thank you to Kevin Doughten, my (endlessly) patient editor, for seeing the potential in this project from the start, and for shifting my focus back to the big picture every time I got lost in the weeds. Weaving together five storylines with so many moving parts was a daunting task; I'm so proud of what we've accomplished here. Thank you for caring so deeply—not just about the book, but about the characters, handling each of their narratives with such grace and sensitivity. You've shown me thoughtful direction and limitless compassion at every turn, you've rolled up your sleeves and helped me plow through the many roadblocks, and you've pushed me to become a much better writer—for that, I cannot thank you enough.

Thank you to Justin Brouckaert, my talented agent at Aevitas, who approached me with the idea for *The Quiet Damage* at a time when I had never considered writing a book, then worked with me to churn out a proposal in a matter of weeks, and found it a perfect home at Crown.

Thank you to the Penguin Random House/Crown Publishing team for believing in the book and bearing with me through the process. Thank you to Amy Li for guiding me from one step to the next, and to Matthew Martin for lending your excellent, tireless counsel and attention to detail to a very delicate project. Thank you to Elisabeth Magnus and Terry Deal for copyediting the manuscript with such great care.

Thank you to George Zornick, my former editor at HuffPost, who helped me find my footing in this beat and granted me the time off work to dive into the early reporting.

Thank you to Columbia Journalism School and the Nieman Foundation for Journalism at Harvard for recognizing the value of reporting on this crisis and for greatly supporting my ability to do so by honoring me with the J. Anthony Lukas Work-in-Progress Award.

Thank you to my mom, Cindy, who stepped in as a babysitter, an editor, a cheerleader, and many other roles whenever I needed her, even flying down for long stretches to be here with me. Thank you for your patience, your brilliant feedback, and the myriad big and little things you've done to help me along the way. Truly, I could not have done this without you. Thank you to my husband, Kyle, who listened to me read just about every single draft of every single chapter aloud without complaining (much), and who always kept me moving forward. It's been a long couple of years—three moves through three states in a pandemic, a twice-postponed wedding, an extremely premature baby, a first book. . . . Thank you for holding everything together when I couldn't. Thank you to my dad, Steve, and my brother, Ben, who were always there to encourage me (while knowing better than to ask, *How's the book coming?*). Thank you to Wyatt, light of my life, for bringing me so much joy in a challenging time. Thank you to Kate for helping me keep things in perspective when I felt overwhelmed. I love you guys.

ABOUT THE AUTHOR

Jesselyn Cook is an investigative journalist who has written extensively about online conspiracy theories and their offline harms. *The Quiet Damage* is her debut book. Prior to covering the tech beat at NBC News, she was a senior reporter on the national enterprise desk at HuffPost and an adjunct journalism professor at the University of La Verne. She holds a master's degree in international relations and journalism from New York University and was a recipient of the 2023 J. Anthony Lukas Work-in-Progress Award from Columbia Journalism School and Harvard's Nieman Foundation honoring "the best in American nonfiction writing." For her reporting on the destructive toll of QAnon and other conspiracy theories on American families, she has been featured on programs such as CNN's *The Whole Story* documentary series and *Anderson Cooper 360*.